SCIENCE   AND   SOCIETY

ECONOMICS
AND
ACTION

by

PIERRE MENDÈS-FRANCE
Former President of the French Government

and

GABRIEL ARDANT
General Commissioner for Productivity (France)

A UNESCO PUBLICATION
NEW YORK, COLUMBIA UNIVERSITY PRESS
1955

Printed in 1955 by G. Thone, Liège
for
The United Nations Educational, Scientific and Cultural Organization
19 avenue Kléber, Paris-16ᵉ
and
The Columbia University Press
2960 Broadway, New York 27, N.Y.

[Translated from the French]

Printed in Belgium
SS 54 X 1 A

In undertaking the publication of the Science and Society series, Unesco is concerned to show that research carried out in the various social science fields has already led to important practical results. The different works in the series will examine, in relation to various branches of science, to what extent these results can serve as a basis for rational action and indicate a logical line of conduct for individuals or communities.

The present work, the first of the series, describes the contribution of economics and the help that this science can provide, at the present time, for those who seek instruction from it. The book will be followed by a study devoted to social psychology, and subsequently by other studies which, in the light of scientific discoveries, will endeavour to show how the resources of knowledge can alter and correct the so-called fated course of history.

PREFACE TO THE ENGLISH EDITION

When a Frenchman writes on what is the subject of this book, with the purpose of explaining the usefulness of economics, it is with a considerable measure of embarrassment that he faces his Anglo-Saxon readers.

Even in France the very nature of such a book, which is designed to make the progress in economic analysis comprehensible to men who are not economic and financial experts, calls for a degree of 'popularization' technique, though it is not easy to determine the precise extent to which that technique should be employed. What are the kinds of data that are understandable by men who have received a good general education but no specific economic or financial training? We run a double risk—either of treating certain data over-summarily and thus making them appear, wrongly, as if they were obvious, or of dwelling at excessive length on arguments that are already well established and familiar.

The danger is all the greater when writing for an international public, since knowledge of economic processes varies from country to country. This inspires a certain fear that the present book may, on many points, seem too elementary and 'obvious' to our Anglo-Saxon readers. Those readers may also find that we have devoted over much space to a recital of facts and events with which they are already familiar, having themselves lived through them at home.

Great Britain is, indeed, one of the countries where economic theory has most clearly and most completely been translated into fact. This was true even in the earliest days of economics. The theories of Adam Smith, Ricardo and others are faithfully reflected in Victorian England. While we are alive to the factual circumstances which enabled nineteenth-century England to practise free trade in virtually its fullest sense, it remains true that thought and action harmonized more obviously in that country than elsewhere. Thus the Charter of the Bank of England, as established by Peel's Bank Charter Act, clearly illustrates Ricardo's theories on money.

This strict application of principles—so out of keeping with what is generally thought to be the nature of the Anglo-Saxons—is found at other junctures, nearer our own time. England's return to the gold standard, effected with scant regard for economic difficulties, is a typical example of a complete system of thought—that which had governed England for generations—being applied.

Such procedures have their advantage for the progress of theory itself; they reveal, in clearer outline, its shortcomings and errors. J. M. Keynes evolved the principles of his general theory largely because the effects of a policy inspired by the classical theory were visible to him and he was accordingly led to look for the errors contained in the assumptions on which that theory relied.

Similarly, by basing much of its post-1931 action against unemployment on a lowering of the rate of interest, England showed both that this procedure was effective and that its effectiveness was circumscribed. It is as if England had wished to perform for the world, once again, a vast laboratory experiment.

During World War II, Great Britain displayed an even greater attachment to the science of economics. Not only did she resort to the services of economists for the direction of her war effort and her action against inflation; but in the full tide of battle, on the eve of the Normandy landings, she did not hesitate to proclaim the principles of the policy of 'full employment', thus applying de facto *the conclusions of the most recent theoretical works.*

There could have been nothing more striking or more moving, for a man living in London at that time, than to read the relevant White Paper, which reflected the will to build a new world on rational foundations. We, for our part, have never forgotten this experience, and the memory of it has been with us when writing the present book.

But it is important, in a world which tends to be no longer mindful of what the 1929 crisis taught us, that this lesson should not be forgotten. Full employment has not been achieved in all states, and the problem of unemployment is acute in certain countries which are among the most populated, and the poorest, in the world. Simultaneously, critics are appearing in the field of theory, ideological attacks developing strongly at the very moment when circumstances dictate that the progress registered by science in recent decades should be turned to account for the solution of the underdeveloped countries' major problem.

Something more, no doubt, remains to be done before we can attain to a more accurate knowledge of economic processes and so devise and implement, with a smaller margin of error, a policy of full employment unaccompanied by inflation. We must nevertheless not forget the advances we have already made, or, more especially, lose sight of what must remain our permanent objective—to seek, through economic science (a science that is constantly concerned with action), for the technical and hence the effective means of realizing our ideal of progress.

This progress must be sought, not merely in security of employment —though that is a prime objective—but also in an improvement of living standards—which depends in part, but only in part, on better distribution. The world is at present faced with the problem of how to make better use of human resources—a problem which may be described as that of efficiency, output, or productivity. It is a field in which science has already provided certain pointers (these we can use to better effect than we at present do, especially in budgetary technique), but we are far from having studied every aspect of the problem. Much remains to be done in order to determine what courses governments should select and, as a consequence, the methods which should govern the regulation of private enterprise, planned investment, and the management of public undertakings. The scientific bases for the choice must be accurately identified and, at the same time, the results must be given practical effect through technique. We are confident that, in this vast field where the task to be accomplished is tremendous, the economists no less than the politicians of the Anglo-Saxon world will have new contributions to make.

CONTENTS

B. *Considered Mechanisms*

INTRODUCTION

Most people, and many indeed of their rulers, believe that economics are of no use in the conduct of public affairs. Yet, some economic conception will be found to underlie every technique or institution. Old and new policies alike bear the stamp of the theories they imply or develop.

The great number of these theories is no sufficient reason for denying their value or for not recognizing their applications. If they are many, it is because the economist, in the last analysis, is trying to influence realities and thus tends to stick closely to events. When his theory no longer allows him to explain phenomena, he sets about modifying it; hence doctrinal arguments and the variations that ensue from them.

In any case, every body of ideas has certain practical conclusions of its own. The interaction of economic theories and policies is seen all through modern history. The mercantile growth of Spain under Philip II, of France under Colbert and of England under Cromwell had already taught the rulers that fluctuations in a country's stock of money are an essential factor in its prosperity or stagnation. In the first modern States, ministers controlled the movement of metallic currency, tried to attract specie, and even restricted goldsmith's work and the wearing of metal embroidery. All of them organized export industries in order to bring in precious metals. Much later, theorists like the German Friedrich List, and the American Daniel Raymond, persuaded countries like Germany and the United States to adopt a similar policy.

In opposition to this system, the classical theory was characterized by a belief in the benefits of *laisser-faire* and private enterprise, both in order to improve production in each business and to ensure a generally balanced economy, reducing the duration and effects of shortages to a minimum, and making possible at all times the distribution of goods and the employment of all those who wanted to work. From the start, liberalism had both its practical and its theoretical aspects. Thus, in France, it took root in what was called *la secte,* some of whose members were responsible rather for the scientific side, others for propaganda in philosophic circles, others for the implementation of foreign experiments. Turgot, for instance, exactly symbolizes this combination of theory and practice. As we read the notes, memorials and letters he wrote while he was intendant of Limoges or comptroller-general, we are struck by his constant preoccupation with the practical problems that faced him: to reduce famines, improve the basis of taxation, develop manufacturing, meet the needs of the State in terms of a logical system, a science of economics, and even a political science. In the Revolution surviving members of the group saw an occasion to put their theories into practice. The event in fact was to show the superiority of those who have a reasoned system over those who are content with a vague feeling that reforms are needed, that abuses must be checked, without having any clear idea of what is to take the place of the system discarded. Du Pont de Nemours has pointed out that public opinion was not favourable to the physiocratic theories, whose schematic character and unfamiliar conclusions were disturbing. However, the physiocrats often carried the day, simply because they offered a coherent system with a conviction born of slow incubation. No doubt many things would have come about in a similar way without their action and without the help of any scientific theory—for example, the abolition of a great many indirect taxes, assessed at excessive rates and collected by harassing methods; the revolutionary outbreaks themselves, of course, brought pressure upon the Assembly. Yet, had it not been for the theory of the *produit net,* which put the whole burden of taxation upon the landed proprietor, the fiscal system might not have undergone that extreme simplification which reduced it to direct taxation alone— or almost alone—and made the property tax the country's main fiscal contribution.

The application of liberal theory met with its greatest success in England; over a long period, Adam Smith, Ricardo and less famous economists evolved and upheld the policy of the country—the policies of Cobden, Gladstone and even Disraeli.

In point of fact, the juridical system of the nineteenth century, its economic régime and, with qualifications, its institutions and financial techniques, were dominated by liberal theories, systematically revised and pruned. A system which made competition between enterprises and non-intervention by the State the condition of economic progress, a system by which production and consumption had automatically to balance, led necessarily to the minimum of State intervention. One aspect of this system was a balanced budget: the government had to spend what it collected by taxation, no more and no less, so as to disturb individual economic activity as little as possible. The role of the State being restricted to certain functions of a very general character, to the exclusion of all industrial and commercial operations, budgetary control began and ended with specifying these expenditures, setting them out in a single document, and ensuring that the maxima fixed by the political powers were strictly observed. The issue of currency was made as independent as possible of State action, thanks to its metallic base and to the rules that governed currency issue, if not the relative autonomy of the issuing houses. Taxation was not to modify either the structure of society or the distribution of wealth.

This does not mean that the capitalist system was altogether faithful to the theoretical blue-prints from which it was transferred. Its inconsistency in the field of foreign trade has often been remarked on. Nor was the principle of the balanced budget always respected. As regards currency issue, States have never stuck to the negative attitude recommended by certain economists—to say nothing of the inflation of the last two wars. Thus, in several respects practice was not in keeping with theory. Nevertheless, the general principles remained. Their influence was to become strikingly apparent after the first world war. If some countries were determined to revert to pre-war parity, it was because classical theory had taught them that they had nothing to fear from its lasting effects on the economy. The adoption of a policy likely to counteract the 1929 crisis was delayed in all countries, and particularly in some of them, for the same kind of reasons.

These events led in turn to a parallel series of theoretical research and new techniques. The classical system had already been criticized by the Socialists, above all by Karl Marx. The practical conclusions drawn by Lenin, who combined the study of economic phenomena with the preparation and carrying out of a revolution, are well known. A work like *The State and Revolution* gives as a basis for collectivism an analysis of the 'contradictions' of capitalist society, the tendency towards monopolies, the fall in the rate of profits, slumps and the threat of slumps.

Generally speaking, the depressions—the 1929 crisis in particular— were the occasion for self-examination on the part of economists and politicians, who had to admit that, if liberal theory had not provided them with a satisfactory solution, neither had empirical improvisation brought any real remedy. Seldom had the need for a scientific theory been so apparent. Some countries then took inspiration from the

writings of Hobson, Wicksell and, later, Keynes. These economists
—particularly Keynes—supplementing earlier studies by a thorough
examination of currency mechanisms, showed how a capitalist economy,
when left to itself, tends towards unemployment. A whole number
of practical solutions stemmed from this theoretical system. A new
significance and function were given to financial institutions, budgets,
credits, currency, taxation. Scientific theory thus gave birth either
to a different use of old techniques, or to the use of new ones. This
was the case notably in the Germany of Dr. Schacht, in post-1931
Britain, and in the United States of the New Deal.

The influence of scientific theory on actual policies, obvious in
some cases, is in others less easy to discover. Very often rulers seem
to act on the simple idea of continuing to do what has always been
done. As a matter of fact beneath this empiricism there is some
general conception of economic realities—the very development of
economic history gives abundant proof of this; there is the idea that
at certain times there should be no intervention, while other times and
other places call for maximum controls. But confused ideas may be
fallacious—there is every likelihood that they will be. If one thing
stands out clearly among the events of the past as in recent happenings,
it is the gravity of the consequences of policies based on ignorance
of economics, or on its fallacies. Anticipating what will be said later,
we shall mention only the admission by many able thinkers that
Weimar Germany would not have known the six million unemployed
who made Hitler's success if it had not been for the error of an
economic policy based exclusively on classical theory. It is no paradox
therefore to argue that the second world war and all its consequences
resulted from an economic fallacy.

Since economic facts are considered to be common knowledge, and
statesmen and their electors do not have in this sphere the blind faith
in the expert that they have in the sphere of physics or chemistry,
the public needs to be convinced. It is not enough to enlighten a
few people; the people at large must be made acquainted with these
problems, if not in detail at least in essence, and made aware of the
importance of a logical policy.

That, precisely, is the purpose of this work: to show the importance
of economics by concrete examples taken from the history of the last
thirty years. To do this, it has been necessary to pick out both the
consequences of hasty, empirical policies—or policies based on error—
and the effects of policies inspired by more exact examination, and
particularly by advances made in economics during this period. The
difficulties of this demonstration should not be underestimated. In

the first place it is not possible to talk about experiments without recalling the scientific facts on which they are based. Thus a number of essential facts have to be condensed in language generally understood. This could only be done—or rather attempted—at the price of simplifications which are sure to shock the specialist at the same time as they demand an effort on the part of the general reader. Further, some characteristic examples must be given of the application of economics to human behaviour. When we consider the complexity of the events that shape concrete history, we see how difficult it is to isolate one of these facts—a series of particular economic measures— and to seek its effects. In many cases we shall have to be content with probabilities. For the same reason we have had to be satisfied with a few examples, taking specially into account the availability of different sources of information. No doubt profounder knowledge would have furnished us with better examples.

The obligations imposed by the nature and scope of this work restricted us to certain aspects of economics. It seemed that two problems were of particular importance, both in theory and in practice: the problem of equilibrium and the problem of choice.

The problem of choice can be put as follows. The central preoccupation of classical economics was to determine how man, individually and collectively, can make the most of limited resources; it tended to neglect the problem of a global balance—how to avoid shortages and over-production—or at least to believe that it was non-existent. For the last thirty years this problem has been in the forefront: facts have forced it upon us. We are now realizing that the problem of choice has been unduly neglected. So far as certain régimes have resolved the problem of the overall plan, they have to apply themselves more to the problem of optimum employment. In this domain too we have to point out not only what must be done by the statesman if he is to profit from existing analyses, but also the need for the economist to perfect these analyses, many of which are very incomplete.

PART I

THE PROBLEM
OF
EQUILIBRIUM

CHAPTER I

THE BEGINNINGS OF ECONOMICS
AND ECONOMIC POLICY

The problem of a balance between supply and demand, production and consumption, is one of the earliest that administrators and theorists alike tried to solve. It may be said to have first arisen when the 'closed' economy gave way to the economy of exchange.

Within the closed economy, in which each family tends to produce all it needs, its food, tools, furniture, the question of adapting supply to demand does not arise—or rather the problem solves itself. A peasant property of the later Middle Age, or the farms of certain districts in our own time, give an approximate picture of the closed economy. The members of the family—or the group of workers on the estate—obtained almost everything they needed by their own labour. If new tools or furniture were required, they went and cut the wood and carved out their plough-handles, beds or chests. If they needed more food, they cleared an area of forest. The women spun wool and wove garments as required. Demand preceding supply, everything that was produced was of course used up.

But as soon as exchanges began multiplying, the problem of a balance was bound to arise. As soon as man produces not to consume but to sell, as soon as he procures most of his food, clothing, tools, by purchase, the following questions present themselves: Will consumers be able to find what they need? Will producers be able to sell all they reap and manufacture? The adaptation of production to consumption not being immediate. how will it be brought about? Is there not a danger of shortages of essential goods or of over-production? This twofold threat of shortage and famine on the one hand, and of over-production on the other, has been a constant preoccupation since the renaissance of trade—that is, in Western Europe, since the twelfth or thirteenth century.

THE DREAD OF FAMINE AND THE POLICING OF GRAIN

But for our experience of the war years, we could hardly imagine that for hundreds of years—let us say until the end of the eighteenth century—men lived in almost constant fear of famine. [1] Since the second world war we are more ready to understand their anxieties and behaviour.

Man's first reaction to the beginnings of the exchange economy was to realize that equilibrium will not be achieved automatically. The city or the State must see to it. The first care of the authorities is to ensure that the essential crops are produced, be it wheat or barley in countries like France under the *ancien régime* and nineteenth century Russia, or rice in the China of the Tsing dynasty. At the same time consumption is controlled so as to avoid wastage of vital foodstuffs. The authorities make sure that wheat or certain other foodstuffs are not sent beyond the borders of the State or province, or even some smaller district, unless there is a surplus. Finally they keep a close control over hoarding, which is a source of speculation. Producers' and traders' prospects of profit must not be allowed to deprive the population of necessary foodstuffs. Granaries were carefully watched, traders obliged to sell, and producers, to bring their crops to the market.

Measures of this kind were adopted mainly in time of famine, under pressure from the consumers, who, if necessary, themselves opposed movements of flour and inspected traders' granaries. Administrators —sovereigns, their ministers and representatives—considered it their duty to see that these measures were applied. A whole system, of which the policing of grain formed an essential part, resulted from the conception men had of the problem of consumption.

THE PROBLEM OF OVER-PRODUCTION, THE GUILD SYSTEM AND MERCANTILISM

The problem of over-production worried them no less. When production tends to increase, man's first reaction is to ask how he will dispose of the surplus product. Will there be sufficient buyers? Are heads

---

1. It was not that famines were unknown within a closed economy. But they were obviously due to natural phenomena, or to the laziness and improvidence of the producers.

of businesses in danger of having to sell at a loss, and are workers in danger of unemployment? These fears are not new. Along with the growth of trade and the considerable advances made around the sixteenth century went the existence of a great many people with no occupation, called idlers, vagabonds or beggars, and whom we today would call the unemployed.

To deal with this problem—how to avoid a production that finds no market—the first means that came to mind was to limit production by submitting heads of businesses—the masters—to a control which restricted their number and determined how many workmen, journeymen and apprentices they might train and employ. This was one of the aims of the *régime corporatif* (guild system), which was more or less developed according to the region and the town, but which aimed everywhere at organizing industry and commerce.

This system had other purposes. The monarchies saw in it a means of controlling the activity of populations which were often turbulent and of facilitating the collection of taxes. Nevertheless, the guild system with its limitation of output was considered a means of preventing supply from outrunning demand. When sovereigns thought it advisable to permit the setting up of larger establishments—the first factories—they considered that they should only do so when the new establishments had a chance of finding markets.

But it soon became apparent that the guild system was not sufficient to ensure the employment of all available labour. An early solution was to sell abroad what could not be disposed of on the home market. To export more than was imported seemed the standard way of 'giving work' to the largest number. But the same conclusion was very soon reached by more complex reasoning. If the manufacturers cannot sell their products, it is perhaps because exchange is badly organized. Now the medium of exchange is money. Could not the blocking of the markets be due to a lack of money? If potential buyers had more money, they could buy more—and the sellers in their turn could use the money thus earned for further purchases. In times of depression the public always has the idea that money is short.

Hence the concern of the authorities with increasing the quantity of money. One of the first measures that came to mind was to prohibit the export of currency—to organize what we should call exchange control; this was, roughly speaking, the system of Western Europe from the Middle Ages up to the nineteenth century. But the economist of that day detected the flaw in this policy, at least when applied too rigidly. To prohibit the export of metallic currency was to deny oneself the opportunity of buying abroad products that could be sold again at a higher price. The best way of obtaining a surplus of currency was to sell abroad more than one bought. The title of Laffemas's work, published in 1602, is significant: *Comme l'on doibt permettre la liberté du transport de l'or et de l'argent hors du royaume et par tel moyen conserver le nostre, et attirer celuy des estrangers* (How to permit the movement of gold and silver beyond the kingdom and thus conserve our own supply and attract that of foreigners). [1]

From this emerged the theory of a surplus trade balance. This objective led to limiting the importation of manufactured goods by the imposition of customs duties, but encouraging the importation of raw materials and stimulating exports by tax remissions or subsidies, and setting up new industries which would enable the country to become self-sufficient and have goods to export, etc.

From this time on, it also became apparent that the problem of equilibrium considered from the monetary point of view had another aspect. Lack of currency meant a relatively high rate of interest. Now it was obvious that too high a rate of interest discouraged new enterprises and investments, which cannot be considered worthwhile unless they bring in more than the current rate of interest. So sovereigns tried to reduce the interest rate—directly, by prohibiting rates above a certain figure and, indirectly, by encouraging the growth of monetary stocks.

Thus there came into being what is generally known as the mercantile system. It was based on the idea that production is likely to lack markets unless action is taken by the State. From the causes of this threat of over-production—particularly the money cause—an economic policy was deduced. By and large, this policy was followed by the principal financial rulers of Western Europe in the sixteenth century, and above all in the seventeenth. The credit for it has often been given to one of the most famous of these leaders, Colbert, but Colbert only followed the example of some of his predecessors— notably Laffemas and Richelieu—and we could as well quote many other mercantilist statesmen, such as Burghley in England and Philip V in Spain.

---

1. This new trend in economic thought is also seen in the well-known work of an English author, Thomas Mun, published in 1621, under the significant title: *A Discourse of Trade from England unto the East Indies answering to Diverse Objections which are usually made against the same.* Mun shows that buying goods abroad that can be resold at a profit is a means of increasing the treasure, that is to say increasing the currency circulation, and is more effective than restricting the export of specie. Similar observations may be found in Richelieu's *Testament.*

CHAPTER II

THE CLASSICAL THEORY
OF EQUILIBRIUM

What may be called the classical system [1] grew up in opposition to
the mercantile system—that is, it was opposed to the theories that
justified the older system as well as to their applications. At the time
when the classical system came into being—towards the second half
of the eighteenth century—it rested on the rise of a class of traders
and industrialists and a class of landed proprietors who resented the
restrictions that the control system placed in the way of their initiative.
It is thus easy to show the influence of the interests of the middle class,
which was on the way to acquiring economic and political power, on
ideas that could be favourable to it.

But blunders militated against the success of economic intervention
by the State at this time—as at all others. The first of the classical
economists had no difficulty in pointing out how the acts of the authorities often had a contrary effect to that intended. They it was who
showed the existence of natural mechanisms—laws similar to those
that the science of physics was beginning to discover—which tended
to restore equilibrium and to ensure the adaptation of supply to
demand, of production to consumption.

THE MECHANISM OF PRICES
AND THE ACHIEVEMENT OF EQUILIBRIUM

The essential mechanism was the mechanism of prices. Economists
showed how by its action alone shortages could be avoided: when pro-

---

1. The classical theory is not old and has not always been accepted as self-evident. It was current
during a relatively short period in the history of economic thought. However, the importance
of its contribution to the progress of economics must not be underestimated.

ASSUMPTION UNIVERSITY LIBRARY

duction is inadequate, prices automatically go up. As a result, a selection is made between consumers; local producers dispose locally of foodstuffs that cost more there than elsewhere; producers from less affected districts send their products where they will fetch the best price; holders of stocks are tempted to sell in the hope of making a substantial profit. Above all, farmers are encouraged to increase their production.

All State intervention has the effect of hindering these reactions. To prosecute speculators means to prevent the building up of stocks, which are so useful for the distribution of production over a certain time. To prohibit the export of wheat means to discourage the extension of production. Why increase cultivation if there is no certainty of being able to sell at a good price, either within the province or on other markets?

The same kind of reasoning applied to the problem of over-production. If production increases, prices fall: consumption will be stimulated and production will be slowed down. The tendency will be towards an equilibrium.

THE LAW OF MARKETS

Classical economy even managed to establish the logical impossibility of general over-production, with the famous law of markets propounded by J.-B. Say. According to this theory, goods are exchanged for other goods; and, on the national or world scale, the entirety of goods for the entirety of other goods. Fundamentally, the baker buys his meat not with money, but with bread. [1] Thus exchange is completely subordinated to production, and new goods are new media of exchange. The existence of a partial disequilibrium, the necessity for labour to be redirected and for certain factories to be transformed, etc., are understandable. But general over-production is impossible, even inconceivable. So, too, is the existence of involuntary unemployment—and for the same reason. If labour cannot be employed at a certain level of remuneration it is because wages are too high

---

1. In the same way, when a car is manufactured, wages, profits and payments for various services, totalling altogether a sum equal to the price of the car, are put into circulation. Thus the manufacture of a car is concomitant with the creation of an equal amount of purchasing power; the volume of goods has increased, but there is no unbalance between aggregate supply and aggregate demand.

in relation to the possible selling price of the goods that it could manufacture. Once a lower wage is accepted, sales and, consequently, production and employment, again become possible.

DISAPPEARANCE OF THE MONETARY PROBLEM

According to this theory, the monetary problem lost the importance the first economists and governments had accorded it. Money was nothing but a commodity for exchange. Its abundance or scarcity mattered little. In fact, these concepts meant nothing. Here the classical economists took their stand on a theory generally known as the quantity theory of money, which can be put in the following way. The level of prices is proportionate to the quantity of money, the quantity of money governing the level of prices. Therefore there is no sense in increasing the quantity of money in order to stimulate activity. Prices will go up and everything will remain unchanged except that the figures on the price tickets will be a little longer. For the same reason, a shortage of money should give no occasion for worry. Selling at half the price does not matter if one buys at half the price as well and if the cost of labour and of raw materials is also established at a different level. Only the calculations will be modified.

Under these conditions the famous problem of the balance of trade which had haunted the mercantilists lost all significance. Economists were quick to emphasize the contradiction in wanting always to sell and never to buy. If all peoples wanted to do likewise, the result would be economic conflicts culminating in wars, of which a typical example in the past was the war waged by Louis XIV in the Netherlands with the approval of Colbert.

Again, why bother to obtain an export surplus and hence an inflow of currency, if this has no effect on the prosperity of the country? Here again, natural mechanisms come in to restore an equilibrium. If a country imports more than it exports, it will pay the difference with metallic currency. As a consequence, its monetary stock will diminish. Under the quantitative theory, prices will drop: they will fall below the level of foreign prices, which, with the inflow of currency, will go up. This disparity will stimulate export and discourage import. In this way equilibrium will be restored automatically, without state intervention.

THE POSITIVE CONTRIBUTION OF THE CLASSICAL THEORY

In this search for natural harmonies, the classical economists advanced the knowledge of economic phenomena. They revealed the existence of certain reactions which, on a free market, tend towards the adjustment of production and consumption by the mechanism of prices.

In this way they exposed certain fallacies in the economic policy of previous centuries—errors no different from those into which men fall today when they heedlessly adopt what appear to be remedies for one unbalance or another. Recent facts provide proof of this.

In cases of over-production, governments have tended to act in the following way. Either they have been content to set ceilings on prices without trying to influence production—a method calculated to encourage farmers to hang on to their crops in the hope of seeing prices rise later—or else they have bought a part of the harvest through some public body in order to maintain prices, not realizing that these steps, intended to avert over-production, are on the contrary a cause of it. The maintaining by 'artificial' means of a price too high to balance supply and demand had as a result the continuance of over-production; whereas a fall in prices would have led a certain number of producers to give up unprofitable production, and this would have ensured a balance. Between the two world wars, governments repeatedly adopted policies that flouted essential economic laws. The only result was the persistence of the very disequilibria they were trying to avert.

Another reaction to over-production is to restrict output. The classical economists were right in showing how this solution was contrary to the interests of consumers as a whole, and in emphasizing that it was aimed mainly at saving producers the effort of adapting themselves to new circumstances, of improving their methods and working conditions.

Economists also pointed out that it was a paradox in a time of shortage to be content with ordering the maintenance of prices, which might lead traders and producers to desert the official markets and to stock, thus increasing the very shortages the order was intended to remedy. This does not mean that the state should remain indifferent to the phenomena of shortages, but that by acting on one element of the natural mechanisms without touching the others it may injure the very interests it is trying to defend. If the state wants to maintain prices, it must control consumption, and control it effectively. France during the occupation and just after the liberation gave an example of badly organized controls, because they were illogical and ignored economic laws discovered by the classical economists when criticizing the steps taken by the governments of Louis XV or Louis XVI against famines.

It is important to acknowledge what was valid in classical thought when it showed the existence of natural laws that an earlier age tended to ignore or underestimate. In this way it helped to free man from a number of restrictions that hindered progress and prevented the setting up of new industries and new processes. It also encouraged the development of free exchanges, the abolition of excise duties, the relaxation of import prohibitions. In that transformation of the juridical and administrative sphere—the very condition of technical progress—known as the industrial revolution, the thinking of the liberal economists, Gournay, Adam Smith, Turgot, Ricardo, played a considerable part. In this period, as in others, it is difficult to say how much was due to intellectual progress and how much to changes in the conditions of production. However, when it is considered that an eminent economist like Turgot, as Minister, abolished guilds and statute labour, while giving freedom to the grain trade, one cannot deny the influence of economic thought on the economic policy of the late eighteenth century.

The classical economists recommended complete freedom of foreign trade. On this point they were little heeded, except in the England of 1846, [1] for too many interests were threatened. Similarly, contrary to the theorists, who attached no importance to currency, the governments encouraged the setting up of issuing houses, which were given certain facilities for adjusting the issue of currency to economic crises.

On the whole, however, the economic policy of the nineteenth century signified the practical application of classical theory. It is characterized by non-intervention on the part of the State and its refusal to consider that there could be any problem of global equilibrium with which the State should be concerned.

But, very soon, the facts were destined to reveal what was incomplete, and consequently fallacious, in classical thinking.

---

1. Date of the Repeal of the Corn Laws.

CHAPTER III

SHORTCOMINGS
OF THE CLASSICAL THEORY

During the nineteenth century and at the beginning of the twentieth, it would seem, according to the conclusions of classical economics, that one of the problems of equilibrium—shortages—ceased to exist. Famines were disappearing from the countries of Western Europe. Each country was able to meet temporary deficits in production by appealing to other countries, this owing to improved transport facilities brought about by scientific progress, and to the freer exchanges permitted by a comparatively liberal régime. It seemed, therefore, that governments had wisely given up the policing of grain which had preoccupied the ministers of the *ancien régime*.

ECONOMIC CRISES

The other disequilibrium, over-production, still remained, manifested periodically in the phenomenon known as an economic crisis. This usually began with resounding bankruptcies, a collapse of prices and the suspension of new businesses. The crisis proper was followed by a period of depression, during which sales dwindled, stocks piled up and factories paid off part of their staff. The depression would last two or three years, after which business revived, production went ahead, prices rose, and new businesses were opened, until the next crisis would impend. The crisis thus appeared as a phase in a cycle whose total course would be about seven years.

Take for example the crisis of 1847. This was preceded by economic expansion, the development of railway construction, the formation of new companies, and prosperity in the textile, metallurgical and mining industries. Prices rose and credit expanded. The crisis came in 1847 with the fall in railway shares; it spread to the mining and metallurgical industry, thence to other industries. In England as in France, banks failed; unemployment became widespread. In England, during the winter of 1847-48, 100,000 more workers fell on the rates. In France, 780,000 workers became unemployed when work stopped on railway construction. In Paris, 100,000 workers were unemployed. At the same time crime increased. In England the number of delinquents per 100,000 inhabitants rose from 169 in 1846 to 187 in 1847, and to 205 in 1848. The same thing happened in France. The political repercussions of the crisis are well known: riots and looting in England, the 1848 revolution in France.

Superimposed on business cycles were movements of longer duration —periods of lower or higher prices. During the latter, activity was fairly well sustained and crises less acute. During periods of lower prices, on the other hand, business was slack, the periods of prosperity were fewer, the crises more pronounced and the depressions more acute. Roughly, the world experienced a period of falling prices from the end of the wars of the First Empire in France until about 1850, and a period of rising prices from 1850 to 1873, a period of falls from 1873 to about 1895, a period of rises from 1895 until the first world war.

THE CLASSICAL THEORY'S LACK OF AN EXPLANATION

Classical theory gave no account or gave but an imperfect account of all these phenomena, crises and depressions. It did not of course deny the necessity for certain adjustments following the errors of entrepreneurs, producers or middlemen. Nor did it exclude the bankruptcy of entrepreneurs less cautious than others and the need for some workers to change their employment. But it did not explain that all-embracing disequilibrium known as a crisis, which affected some industries more than others, but affected them all in some way. Above all, it did not explain the length of the depression period of cycles. The necessity for lowering too high prices could be understood, but why could this fall not be brought about more quickly, and why, once it had taken place, did production not continue, ensuring employment for all who wanted to work? Why, for decades, was business slack, as it was in the first half and at the end of the nineteenth century?

Classical analysis furnished no explanation, the less so as governments had followed more closely the teachings of the liberal school. The contradictions between facts and theoretical conclusions, and notably the scandal of periodical unemployment, felt the more hardly in an age when the workers' conditions were more wretched, could not but evoke many attempts at explanation. It would be idle to review all the theories about crises. The most important are the main series of explanations that seem to have contributed most to economic knowledge. Two kinds of criticisms of the classical theory should be stressed. One of these tends to attribute the disequilibrium to the structure of society; the other consists in analysing monetary mechanisms and their repercussions on investment.

DISEQUILIBRIUM AND THE STRUCTURE
OF CAPITALIST SOCIETY

The first series of criticisms was made very early—at the time of the depression that followed the wars of the Empire—by Sismondi and Malthus in particular. These were taken up by various authors usually classified as Socialists—and by Marx and his disciples. They may be summed up as follows.

Since the worker receives only part of the selling price of what he makes, the working class as a whole cannot buy back the totality of the goods that have been produced. The difference, that is, what the worker does not receive, goes to the capitalist class in the form of interest, profits, rents and dividends. If the capitalist class spent all its income, there would be no problem of equilibrium. There would of course be problems of equity. It could be asked whether the distribution of income was the fairest possible; luxury and poverty would still be seen side by side. But the total product would be absorbed; there would be neither over-production nor unemployment. But this is not what happens. Those whose incomes increase save a part of this increase, thus diminishing the outlets for production. The inequality of wealth, which is a feature of capitalist society, is thus reflected in a strong tendency to save, which means a deficient consumption and a restricted market.

No doubt this theory does not explain all the aspects of disequilibrium, in particular the rhythm of economic cycles, the alternation of periods of rising prices and falling prices; but it does explain—or it

32

seems to—the possibility, and even the likelihood of an all-embracing economic disequilibrium.

THE CLASSICAL OBJECTION

But here the theories of under-consumption come up against an objection, which classical theory may be said to have anticipated, for it is to be found in Adam Smith, J.-B. Say and Ricardo. According to them, saving takes the form of investment. The person who saves forgoes the purchase of consumer goods in order to buy producer goods. The employer who does not spend all his income enlarges his factory, buys machinery; if he does not give work to the producer of consumer goods, he gives work to the builder or the toolmaker. Since the aggregate income is thus spent, there seems no possibility of an all-embracing disequilibrium.

THE MARXIST REPLY

There was an easy reply to this, and Marx quickly supplied it. One cannot go on investing, that is, adding to the means of producing more consumer goods, without increasing consumption itself. When the factories are built, the machines installed, and when goods pour forth in larger and larger quantities, who will consume them? Investment postpones disequilibrium, it does not abolish it.

It is with the purpose of deferring this moment that capitalist society is always looking for new markets, new opportunities for investment. This quest is of great importance. Since Marx, a number of writers, Hobson, Rosa Luxembourg, Lenin, have observed that capitalist states, in order to prevent profits from disappearing through over-investment, were led to try to export more than they imported: hence conflicts over the capture of markets, the struggles for supremacy in countries as yet untouched by western technique and open to new investment; hence imperialism in all its forms; hence war itself.

THE WEAKNESS IN THE MARXIST REPLY

However, from the beginning, this reply did not seem altogether satisfactory. If capitalists can no longer invest in their own country, it is not only because the profits from investment tend to diminish, but because this decrease is greater than the rate of interest. If the rate could be lowered, investment would again be possible.

An answer to the classical theory thus required a further analysis of monetary phenomena and their influence on investment. It was by comparing and perfecting earlier research and combining this analysis with the theory of under-consumption that Keynes, just before the second world war, evolved his general theory of employment.

CHAPTER IV

THE GENERAL THEORY
OF EMPLOYMENT

The years following the first world war were years of such confusion that the classical theory was inevitably called in question. The 1921 crisis was short lived, but in one country, Great Britain, the re-establishment of the currency was followed by chronic unemployment. It was the 1929 crisis which, above all, led the economists to examine their postulates. The extent of the crisis, the duration of the depression, its grave social consequences and the utter dismay with which millions of men who saw themselves deprived indefinitely of all hope of living except by relief and charity, shattered all belief in the natural harmonies of the classical system. The whole economic system of countries in which technical progress had been earliest and quickest was challenged.

It is easy to understand the stir caused by the publication of an overall theory offering to explain phenomena to which no one could remain indifferent, and at the same time suggesting specific remedies. The explanation offered by Keynes in his *General Theory of Employment, Interest and Money* (published in 1937) resulted from his simultaneous use of the under-consumption theories of Malthus, Sismondi and the Socialists, and of economic analyses for which Wicksell's research had prepared the way. The general theory was a synthesis of economic, psychological, sociological and monetary studies.

Keynes re-examined the observations of his predecessors on consumption and saving. The man whose income is increasing does not increase his expenditure in the same proportion. The rich man spends only a part of his income. Inequality of wealth thus increases the propensity to save. But—and this is no doubt his most important contribution—Keynes had an answer to the classical reply that savings are reflected in investment, that is to say in another kind of expenditure. The man who saves may invest, he may lend to those who invest; but he may also be content to increase the quantity of money in his possession; he may hoard. What happens in this case? A man spends less than his income and does not make up for this reduction in his purchase of consumer goods by purchases of producer goods. The outlets for producers as a whole are reduced. This loss of outlets means, of course, a loss of income, and therefore of purchasing power.

MOTIVES FOR HOARDING CURRENCY

An obvious objection will be raised. Why should anyone hoard unproductive money when he can earn interest on it by lending it or profits by investing it? The objection can only be answered by analysing the motives that impel people to hoard or not to hoard money. The holding of cash, of course, meets the wish to have the minimum funds required to make current payments. But it also satisfies the desire for prudence. There are circumstances—the threat of war or of internal disturbances, for example—in which the holding of metallic currency is preferred to the holding of securities that one is not sure of being able to liquidate quickly enough in case of need. The holding of cash has another advantage. If a private person can foresee a rise in the rate of interest, he profits by not lending now what he can lend at a better rate in a few months' time. Generally speaking, the more the rate of interest drops, the more one can expect it to rise in the future. The interest rate thus appears to be subject to two factors: the quantity of existing money and the strength of the desire to hold cash, a desire which Keynes called 'liquidity preference'.

POSSIBLE UNDER-INVESTMENT

It is thus understandable that investment may not be able to make good the diminution in consumption resulting from saving. In a 'capitalist' society, investment depends on private businessmen, whose actions are governed by the desire for profit. What decides them to invest is the prospect of profits—the net profit they are likely to make. If it means that they must borrow, the net profit is equal to the difference between the gross profit of the investment and the interest on the sums they have borrowed. If they use their own capital, it is just the same, for they are depriving themselves of the possibility of lending at the current rate of interest. What matters, moreover, is not the real profit from the investment but what the entrepreneur hopes to make. Here Keynes used an idea, that of anticipation, which Swedish economists, Mr. Myrdal in particular, had already hit upon.

The anticipated yield of investments [1] depends on many factors, but particularly on market prospects. Reduced consumption may cause fear lest the possibilities of sale will diminish and prices fall—and consequently it may normally reduce the anticipated yield of the investment. If this diminution in anticipated gross profit were accompanied by a still greater drop in interest, the net profit from the investment would increase and reduced consumption could be compensated by an increased investment. But, as we have seen, the rate of interest depends on monetary factors not directly bound up with variations in savings. It is thus possible that a part of the means of production remains unused. This is obviously the case when the anticipated yield of investment in a minus quantity—which is possible in a period of falling prices. If it is thought that in a few years' time prices may be 10 per cent lower than they are now, for example, an investment looks as though it may cost more than it would bring in. But the rate of interest cannot be minus, for the holder of money can always keep it.

COMPARISON BETWEEN KEYNESIAN REASONING AND CLASSICAL REASONING

To get a clear idea of Keynesian reasoning on this essential point, we may compare it with classical reasoning.

Both are almost in agreement on the effect of the interest rate on investment. The classical economists had reverted to an economic law discovered centuries before, according to which people only invest if they can expect a profit higher than the rate of interest. When the interest rate rises, a number of investments which had until then been possible cease to be so; a fall, on the other hand, reveals new possibilities. This is why Turgot, using a frequently quoted image, compared the rate of interest to the level of the sea, which, when it falls, makes possible the cultivation of more land and when it rises, reduces the cultivable area.

---

1. What Keynes called the 'marginal efficiency of capital'.

But here again the classical economists believed in the virtue of natural mechanisms—and it is at that point that the two arguments part company. For the classical economist the rate of interest is the price that ensures equality between the supply of capital and the demand for it. The supply corresponds to savings, the demand to investments. Should savings increase, the supply, which coincides with savings, increases also and the rate of interest will begin to fall; and this fall will ensure the absorption of all the capital, enabling the propensity to save to be satisfied and to be converted into a larger volume of investment. Should the desire for investment increase, following some new discovery—as at the advent of the railways—or owing to the colonization of new territories, the demand for capital increases and the rate of interest rises. This rise plays a dual role: in the first place, it permits a selection between possible investments, only the most profitable being chosen; in the second place, it stimulates saving, which is attracted by higher remuneration. By this dual effect, comparable to that which enables the price mechanism to ensure the balance of supply and demand, the interest rate ensures that the propensity to save and the propensity to invest correspond and, consequently, ensures full employment, for every diminution in consumption automatically results in a compensatory increase in investment.

This reasoning is not so simple and watertight as it appears. The word 'capital' is ambiguous and has no precise meaning. If the material means of production are meant, such as factories and machines, it cannot be said that their supply and demand directly influence the interest rate: variations in the supply and demand of machinery influence the price of machines. Interest is not the price of machinery, it is the price of the money lent. It certainly results from supply and demand, but from the supply and demand of money. Supply depends on different factors, the discovery of new mineral deposits, the policy of banks of issue. Demand depends on the different factors that govern the desire for money, the need of money for business transactions, the desire for security or speculation. It may happen that some unexpected event influences the desire for money, and consequently the interest rate, without influencing the propensity to save, for example, the threat of war or of internal strife. In such circumstances there is a monetary tension and a rise in the rate of interest due to the fact that everyone is trying to increase the quantity of cash in hand. This rise in interest may suffice to reduce the prospects of investment and, consequently, bring about under-employment. This is only one example to show the imprecision of the classical picture. Nevertheless, saving and investment have an influence on the interest rate, but the influence is indirect, being limited to the degree to which they modify the liquidity preference, that is to say the need or the desire for money. The increase in saving tends to bring down the price of products, thus reducing one element in liquidity preference, the need of money for current transactions. Conversely the development of investment has the effect of raising prices, which increases the need for money. But, once again, saving and investment are not the only factors in the desire for money. and this is why the desire to save and the desire to invest do not necessarily correspond. This being the case, it is understandable that there may be relatively long periods of under-employment, which may alternate with states of full employment.

Should entrepreneurs, for one reason or another, have the impression that they can make fruitful investments—on the occasion of a new invention, railways for example—investment will tend to develop. The laying of railways, the purchase of metallurgical products, will in their turn lead to the building of factories, the fuller working of coal and iron mines, etc. Investment will easily absorb all the resources made available by saving. All those who want to work will find employment. But when the most profitable lines have been opened up and there remain only secondary lines, and when the results of these prove less favourable than was anticipated, prices will tend to fall; the interest rate, even if it drops, will be too high for the starting of new enterprises to be possible; workers will be dismissed and will be unable to find other employment.

The phenomenon is more complex in that investment reacts on consumption, and vice versa. If workers are unemployed, consumer expenditure diminishes. This reduction in markets affects the profits and the prospects of profits in industries making consumer goods. In this sector too, investment falls off, causing a further reduction in consumption, and so on. By a series of chain reactions, the disequilibrium is accentuated. Conversely, every advance in investment brings about an increase in consumption, which sets off another increase in investment, etc.

Finally, the whole of this analysis makes it apparent that economic disequilibrium, general over-production, unemployment, under-employment—so many different aspects of the same thing—are neither illogical nor inconceivable, because there is a propensity to save, which may, in certain circumstances, be particularly strong and because, owing to the existence of money, saving need not take the form of investment.

THE CONSEQUENCE OF UNDER-EMPLOYMENT:
REVISION OF ECONOMIC LAWS

The possibility of states of under-employment modifies a whole series of economic laws or precepts whose application was bound up with the existence of full employment—although the classical economists never noticed this implied postulate. A number of laws believed to be valid under all circumstances are only valid in a state of full employment. In times of under-employment, an increased demand brought about by the issue of paper money will result not in a rise in prices, but in increased aggregate production, made possible by the reabsorption of the unemployed labour. An increase in savings—the condition of the development of investment in times of full employment—will cause a reduction of investment in times of under-employment.

By this change of perspective, which necessitated a reappraisal of economic thinking, Keynesian theory represented an intellectual revolution comparable to the discovery of non-Euclidian geometry and its use by contemporary physics. Just as the world in which Euclidian geometry applies appears as a particular case, so the economy of full employment to which the 'classical' laws apply appears as a particular case in a general economic theory.

THE IMPORTANCE OF MONEY

Keynesian reasoning contradicts classical reasoning also in the important place it gives to money, which Keynes' predecessors dismissed as insignificant. In this it resembles the arguments of the mercantilists, which although poorly expounded were based on a correct intuition. Viewed in this light, Keynes' analysis has something disconcerting about it, and no doubt this makes the 'general theory' harder to understand, especially by those who might draw practical conclusions from it. There was something attractive about the classical theory that money was simply a medium of exchange, so that economic life was reduced essentially to the exchange of goods for other goods. But if we think of what money is, we realize that its intervention in trade is charged with consequences. Money is a commodity which enables one to obtain every other kind of commodity. This faculty of choice represents a considerable advantage, but it is not without its drawbacks.

It is conceivable that the person who holds purchasing power and suspends his decision may prevent producers from working. Moreover, money, or at least metallic currency, has a characteristic that distinguishes it from other economic goods: its production is not elastic. The demand for money and a drop in prices cause a certain increase in the mining of gold; but this reaction is not as strong with regard to precious metals, whose production depends in part on the chance discovery of new veins, as it is with regard to other goods, whose supply reacts more quickly and amply to the demand. The conservation of metallic currency is therefore, under some circumstances at least, more advantageous than that of commodities which cost more to conserve and which are more easily devalued by the development of production. These advantages which money has for its holder explain why the saver may prefer holding his money to investing it.

The theory of employment may be understood if we look at it from another angle. It is obvious that for a community there is something contradictory in wishing to invest indefinitely without increasing consumption in an equal proportion. The aim of investment is to increase the means of production, which are intended to put more consumer goods at man's disposal. When there is a prospect of great technical advances, it is advantageous to stimulate investment, to set up a heavy industry, then a transforming industry, which will permanently raise the standard of living. This is what American and European states did in the nineteenth and early twentieth centuries and what the Union of Soviet Socialist Republics did after 1917. Railways, electricity, motor car factories meant so many openings for the world's labour force. But one cannot go on investing without increasing consumption.

To refuse indefinitely to increase consumption—when earlier savings have made it possible to increase investment and expand production—leads to an impasse. This situation, which the Marxists are fond of depicting, can only be resolved by a series of crises.

EXPLANATORY VALUE OF THE GENERAL THEORY

The explanatory value of the Keynesian construction was striking. It appeared that humanity had been dominated for centuries by the threat of under-employment. The political reactions of governments inspired by mercantilist theories, their monetary preoccupations and their policy of a trade balance, were now explained. At the same time it was easier to understand the importance for the economic development of the world of the great discoveries of precious metals, Alexander putting into circulation the treasures of the kings of Persia, the discovery of America, the opening up of the Potosi mines, and later those of California, Australia and South Africa. It was understandable too that states continually threatened with over-production had a tendency to export their unemployed, that is, to export more than they imported, an attitude seemingly absurd, in order to ensure the full employment of their labour force. It was understandable too that this policy of looking for markets had led to conflicts and to wars.

On this point the Keynesian analysis was in agreement with that of his countryman Hobson, whose book, *Imperialism* (published in 1902), showed how the shortcomings of an economic policy that ignored the necessity of developing home consumption led to imperialism and war. It was also in agreement with Rosa Luxembourg, who treated a similar theme in her book, *The Accumulation of Capital* (1913), and with Lenin's *Imperialism, the Highest Stage of Capitalism.*

All in all, the 'general theory of employment' made it possible to understand how the worker had been weighed down, and still was, not only by the low level of his wages, but also by the constant threat of being deprived of all possibility of work. But Keynes offered more than an explanation; he suggested remedies. Their applications can be put under the general heading of the 'policy of full employment'.

THE POLICY
OF FULL EMPLOYMENT

The measures that should be taken to ensure full employment may readily be deduced from the analysis itself. Under-employment results from under-consumption, combined with under-investment, due to too high a rate of interest. Theoretically, it is possible to influence both these factors.

INFLUENCING CONSUMPTION

Under-consumption is due in large measure to the fact that many consumers are limited in the satisfaction of their needs by too small an income, while a minority do not consume the whole of their incomes. In a way, the inequality of wealth, which is the cause of hoarding, explains under-consumption.

In theory, there are several ways of equalizing incomes.

We may transform the structure of society, for example by expropriating large estates and redistributing them amongst landless cultivators. We may also restrict profits by price control and the limitation of profit margins. Or wages can be raised by government decree. We can, by the same means, reduce private debts, on the assumption that creditors, being richer than debtors, consume proportionally less.

But there is another way of equalizing incomes without tampering with the economic structure: taxation. The political and social development of the nineteenth century revealed the possibility of correcting the inequality of wealth by means of taxation. Systems of graduated income taxes and estate duties, if not capital levies, were drawn up with this end in view. From the middle or the end of the nineteenth century, therefore, taxation appeared not only as a means of obtaining resources for the treasury, but as a weapon of social reform. The Keynesian analysis leads to the recommendation of an equalizing tax not so much in order to distribute wealth more equitably, as to ensure economic equilibrium by developing consumption.

In similar fashion, indebtedness can be reduced without modifying contracts in a formal way, simply by raising prices. Any policy of raising prices implies some transfer of income from creditors to debtors, and consequently tends to increase consumption.

INFLUENCING PRIVATE INVESTMENT

The influence upon private investment is limited. If graduated taxation goes beyond a point, it is likely to discourage enterprise and, consequently, investment. Moreover, in a society in which wealth was fairly equally distributed and the standard of living relatively high, the propensity to invest might not balance the propensity to save.

Investment can be influenced by the state in different ways. Private investment depends on the relation between the prospects of profit and the rate of interest. The state must first see that the prospects of profit are not diminished by a prolonged fall in selling prices. The tendency to a continuous fall in prices will encourage entrepreneurs to avoid any expense that might lead them to produce more, for selling prices might be lower than cost prices and not enable them to pay the interest and depreciation on capital borrowed. If the likelihood of a fall in prices is great, any reduction in the interest rate may be insufficient to offset the effects.

For this reason the 'theory of employment' advises against any policy of steadily and progressively lowering prices—at least during a depression. It is not the lowering of prices as such that is harmful, that is the immediate lowering, but the prospect of future drops. If Keynes criticizes the policy of lowering prices in order to overcome a depression, it is because this fall, whatever the intentions of governments, is always likely to be interpreted as the harbinger of further falls. For the same reason he advises against the lowering of nominal wages, which normally results in the lowering of prices, which in turn brings about a further drop in wages, etc., thus causing the restriction of investment.

It may almost be said that Keynes considers a moderate rise in prices to be a means of combating under-employment. We must also know how to bring about this rise in prices, which itself depends on increased consumption and investment. [1]

The reduction of the rate of interest is another means by which the state can encourage investment. To borrow Turgot's image again, its action in such a case resembles that of countries which, by an operation equivalent to lowering the sea-level, have managed to bring new land into cultivation and give work to more people. Since it depends on the quantity of money, it is possible to reduce interest by increasing the issue of currency. This raises certain problems, of course, because the amount of metallic currency may be inadequate. There have been times when, thanks to the discovery of new mineral reserves, an addition to the stock of precious metals has been enough to provide an expanding economy with the currency it needed. This was the case in 1850: the discovery of ores in California enabled the French economy to issue from the relative depression that had followed the wars of the Empire. In the same way, the long period of falling prices and difficulties that began in about 1873 came to a close towards the end of the century with the possibilities opened up by recent discoveries and inventions—electricity and motor cars in particular—but also thanks to the contribution of the Transvaal gold mines. However, the economy may not enjoy the benefits of these contingencies. To maintain the convertibility of money at the existing rate may deprive one of the possibility of reducing the rate of interest far enough.

The Keynesian analysis thus aimed at a radical change in the conduct of monetary policy. According to classical economics, the state should content itself with guaranteeing the weight and fineness of the currency and with supervising the use of weights and measures to ensure honesty in business transactions. Taken in a rather wider sense, this role led the state to restrict to one bank, more or less under its control, the issue of notes, which are more convenient to carry than metallic currency and which, by slightly exceeding metallic reserves, was able to give more flexibility to exchanges.

But the note was only a substitute for metal; it had to be readily convertible, and the whole policy of the bank of issue, the technique of variations in the rate of interest, had as their principal object the preservation of the monetary stock. Should gold go out of the country, following a deficit in the trade balance, the bank of issue had to

---

1. The very fact of changing the gold equivalence of the monetary unit can, by creating expectations of a rise in prices, bring the rise about. Generally speaking, any policy that consists in increasing investment—or consumption—by one of the methods indicated here can, by creating an expectation of a rise in prices, bring the rise about. Yet the rise in prices must not be such as to offset other measures—by reducing the purchasing power of wage-earners, for example.

intervene and raise the discount rate in order to attract foreign capital, and to reduce the home demand by exerting pressure on prices. The bank of issue could thus reduce imports, increase exports and re-establish the balance of trade, while safeguarding the convertibility of the currency.

The 'theory of employment' was intrumental in giving the interest policy of the bank of issue another aim, for it was designed to achieve full employment by reducing the discount rate in times of unemployment. But it is obvious that this policy might not be consistent with the maintenance of convertibility—at least at the existing rate. In such a case, according to Keynesian reasoning, it was the parity or convertibility of the currency that had to be sacrificed.

But when the bank of issue contents itself with loans of a few months, it only influences short-term interest rates. Investment pre-supposes longer-term loans. Therefore, if we are to favour full employment, we must exert an influence on the long-term rate of interest. The solution is to use the issue of currency for purchasing long-term securities, government bonds for example, in order to bring up their quotations on the market, which means that the rate of interest is lower. The custom of purchasing securities on the open market by the bank of issue had long existed in Britain, and since 1913 in the United States, but with a different purpose from that assigned to it by Keynes. In most other countries the statutes of the banks of issue did not authorize this practice, which was to constitute an important feature of the policy of full employment.

One condition of a drop in the interest rate, therefore, is an increase in the quantity of money. Now the issue of currency depends on the banks—the banks of issue and the deposit banks. It is perhaps worth pointing out here that there are two sorts of currency: fiduciary currency, usually known as bank notes, and deposit accounts that can be used by cheque and transfer, 'representative money'. [1]

Now this representative money can vary considerably if the owners of accounts are not confident of being able to withdraw their deposits at any moment. This is just what happens as a rule at the beginning of crises, and this reduction of representative money is one of the causes of the economic depression.

Accordingly, in order to avoid a reduction in that part of the currency which consists of bank deposits, it would appear that the public must be made confident in the management of the banks. Apart from other considerations, the state may be led to intervene in the

---

1. On the concept of representative money, see Chapter VIII, Part I.

management of the deposit banks, prohibit certain of their operations and control their activity, in order to keep the rate of interest sufficiently low. In addition, the desire to pursue a monetary policy that will ensure the fall of the interest rate and full employment presupposes state action on banks, both on the bank of issue and the deposit banks. In this sense the strengthening of the powers of the state over credit institutions can be considered one of the practical conclusions of the 'theory of employment'.

PUBLIC INVESTMENT

But, under some circumstances, lowering the rate of interest may not be enough to offset the diminution in the profit expected from investment. The state is then left with the possibility of itself making the investment necessary to ensure full employment. In the 'general theory', the policy of big public works takes on a significance rather different from that usually given it. When the states makes an investment, it not only gives work to the unemployed, it increases aggregate demand, both directly and indirectly. The increased income resulting from this increased demand is in part spent; this expenditure increases aggregate income by a further amount, itself partly spent, and so on. Thus, in a period of under-employment, an investment of x brings about an increase in demand of a volume that may exceed x. This is what is called the multiplier principle, which had been discovered by an English economist, Mr. Kahn, and included by Keynes in his system.

However, public investment can only have this effect if it is financed otherwise than by taxation, that is by loan or by currency issue. Any taxation which reduces individual incomes reduces personal expenditure, and consequently the demand for consumer goods. This means that the unbalanced budget, which classical theory considered as always wrong, ceases to be so in a period of under-employment. This is what perhaps struck public opinion the most: that what it had believed to be the wisest and most virtuous policy, the balancing of the budget, might in certain circumstances be inadvisable.

The 'general theory' thus led to budgetary policy, like monetary policy, being regarded as one factor in an overall economic policy. The idea of the balanced budget still prevailed, but in a different form. In periods of prosperity the balanced budget is again necessary, and even an 'over-balanced' budget can contribute towards restricting undue

47

consumption and rash speculation. It is thus conceivable that this sequence of 'over-balanced' and 'under-balanced' budgets may cancel out. Hence the idea of the cyclical budget: over a period of *x* years, budget surpluses and deficits will balance. Thus it is possible, when the state of the cycle demands it, to pursue a policy of a budgetary deficit for the purpose of ensuring full employment.

THE MEANING OF THE FULL EMPLOYMENT POLICY

In order that the meaning of full employment may be better understood, it may help to define its field of application and at the same time to contrast it with other conclusions that have been or might be drawn from the analyses on which it is based.

The field of application of the employment policy can be defined in space and in time. In time: it is not unnecessary to say that the measures recommended are only valid in periods of under-employment. When demand is large, that is when a war has destroyed consumer and producer goods, or when new discoveries have opened up fields for investment, or when a country that was economically backward has perceived the possibilities of applying methods used elsewhere, the problem is usually not one of stimulating expenditure but of providing consumer and producer goods. This explains why we cannot quote applications of the theory of employment during the period that began with the second world war. Here the problem consisted essentially in resisting the excessive aggregate demand that breeds inflation.

THE PROBLEMS OF UNDERDEVELOPED COUNTRIES

The same remarks are valid for what are usually called the underdeveloped countries. It is not that the problem of employment is non-existent in these regions, but that unemployment there has a special aspect. Lacking a certain minimum of producer goods, a part of the population is obliged to work for a very inadequate output. Peasants continue to cultivate the land unproductively, whereas if equipped with a minimum of tools they could work in industry. Hence it is sometimes said that these countries suffer from disguised unemployment. There is therefore an employment problem in these countries, but it exists in terms which require a special analysis and special remedies that may partly differ from those included under the concept of employment policy. The latter is only applicable as such to countries that are relatively industrialized, relatively advanced, relatively rich. Thus when, in 1948, the United Nations carried out an inquiry into the problem of full employment, the underdeveloped countries replied that it did not concern them—at least not in the form in which the questions were put. Let us make it clear from the beginning that we do not underestimate the importance of the problem of employment in under-developed countries, but its study alone would take us beyond the dimensions of the present work. Moreover, it is a field in which scientific analysis has not yet been able to make sufficient progress —to our knowledge—for applications of it to be made.

As things are, the main conclusion that the policy of employment can offer in this field is the necessity of encouraging the richer countries to obtain for the underdeveloped countries a surplus of wealth, and especially of producer goods, which will facilitate the full employment of the resources of the richer countries and an improvement in the standard of living of the underdeveloped countries.

COLLECTIVIST ECONOMY

Nor does the policy of employment, in the form in which it is presented, apply directly to countries under a collectivist régime. Since the state fixes the volume of investment, it can do so according to the quantity of available resources—manpower and means of production— and to the volume of goods that it considers should be put at the disposal of consumers. It has no reason to leave idle a part of its personnel or a part of its machinery. Nothing that Keynes has to say about the attitude of the entrepreneur guided by prospects of profit from investment, applies to a régime in which the state owns the means of production. It is thus understandable that the Soviet economy, for example, for all its difficulties of every kind, has been spared the crises of the capitalist economy.

DEEPER MEANING OF THE POLICY OF EMPLOYMENT: PRIVATE INITIATIVE

Nevertheless the author of the 'general theory' did not conclude from his researches that it is impossible to achieve full employment without completely changing the structure of society. If this is so, it is because his analysis led him to attach great importance to the monetary factor. It follows from the 'general theory' that under-employment does not derive solely from the structure of society, but from the combination of a certain structure with monetary institutions which prevent the necessary conversion of savings into investments. This is why he considered that an appropriate monetary policy should largely help to reduce unemployment. [1]

But there is another reason, which must be stressed. A main characteristic of the policy of full employment, as outlined by Keynes, is that it assumes some positive action on the part of the state in regard to the economy—in other words it rejects *laisser-faire*; in this respect it contrasts with the policy of non-intervention which stemmed from the classical theory. But the policy of full employment is also characterized by the fact that it does not require that the state shall be responsible for the management of enterprises.

Keynes thought it advisable to leave in private hands the maximum of economic freedom compatible with full employment. Private persons, as consumers, must choose on what they shall spend their money and, as producers, must choose their method of production and their investments. In particular, he thought that the entrepreneur is able to choose the most efficiency machinery and the most profitable investments. The role of the state, in the policy of employment, is to create an economic climate, market conditions within which private persons may act in the way most favourable to the general interest. The measures that he recommends are aimed, for example, at allowing entrepreneurs to make bigger profits, but the state reserves the right to take away from them by taxation a large enough portion of these

---

1. This observation might suggest conclusions very different from those of the 'general theory'. If metallic currency is a cause of under-employment, it is because its production is relatively inelastic; hence the advantage of saving by hoarding currency rather than by making investments. But let us suppose that one could define money as a group of different products—copper, iron, wheat, etc. In this case, any increase in the desire for money would take the form of a money increase—to take the argument further, any saving in money would at the same time be an investment in goods. To save, it would be necessary to produce.

This formula would have various advantages to which we shall return later. Is it practicable? Without its having been applied, it is hard to say, Speculation upon the possibilities and advantages of this solution would take us beyond the scope and nature of this study, but it was necessary to mention it.

profits to correct an undue inequality of wealth. In the same way, the entrepreneur must himself decide which is the most profitable investment. But the state, by its influence on the rate of interest, can make profitable certain investments which otherwise would not be so or would not appear so. Again, the investments made directly by the state have the primary purpose of increasing, by their indirect effects, the number of markets available to the country, and therefore the volume of private investment; it rests with the entrepreneur to make the most of this modification of the market.

To borrow Turgot's metaphor once again, the authorities act in the same way as a state which, by a system of dykes and canals, lowers the sea-level in a whole region, but leaves it to the farmers to make the most of the new land, to decide whether they will plant wheat, oats or potatoes, whether they will turn it into pasture, whether they will cultivate it with oxen, horses or tractors, etc. Therefore it is a policy which retains great faith in private initiative, in the field where it can be effective. [1]

Although the state has not to take over the functions of the entrepreneur, there is one function that can be entrusted largely to the state: investment policy. From the analyses of Keynes it appears that the unstable element in an economy is investment. It is unstable because it is subject to fluctuations in the opinions of entrepreneurs. Keynes repeatedly insists—and he was not the first—that investment and, consequently, full employment, depend on the opinion the investor has of his probable profit. Let us suppose that certain investments are highly profitable, paying more than the current rate of interest; if investors do not see them in this light, if they underestimate their capacity to yield a profit and overestimate the risks, the investments will not be made. The converse can also happen. It may, therefore, be asked whether the state should not take over the responsibility for allocating investments generally. This conclusion goes beyond the function with which Keynes wished to entrust the state. It is one thing to carry out public works intended to give rise to an increase in aggregate demand distinctly greater than their volume; it is quite another to draw up a general plan of investment, that is to decide how a total volume of investment shall be distributed among different branches of the economy, and to endeavour by various measures to get this policy implemented.

---

1. Whether or not the individual always chooses for the best is another question, which will be examined in the second part of this work.

THE EMPLOYMENT POLICY AND PEACE

The employment policy can finally be opposed to certain conclusions that may have been or may yet be drawn from it as regards commercial policy. If an increase in aggregate demand can bring about an increase in employment, we can see the valid element in the policy of the trade balance. To create an export surplus may be one way of ensuring full employment, or of approaching it. This can be arrived at by the manipulation of customs duties, or by the newer technique of quotas, by subsidies for exports, or finally by devaluation of the currency. To decide that the national currency is worth less than foreign currencies is tantamount to increasing exports—a means of ensuring full employment—provided that a rise in prices on the home market does not neutralize the difference.

Keynes was aware that his analysis afforded an explanation of this policy and that it rehabilitated the logics of the old mercantilists. At the same time he thought that this conclusion was not in agreement with the spirit of his analysis. [1] To use this process is to adopt a policy which solves the problem in one country only by aggravating it in another; it is, moreover, and above all, a policy that leads to commercial antagonisms, and even to war. On this point Keynes' conclusions are in agreement with those of Hobson, Rosa Luxembourg and Lenin.

If it is admitted that under-employment is due to a shortage of home markets—at least in some countries, for others suffer the re-percussions—it is best to solve the problem by enlarging the market through an increase in the purchasing power of the least privileged and through increased investment.

Summing up, it would appear from what has gone before that, although the policy of full employment derives from the 'theory of employment', the two cannot be put on the same footing. It is theoretically possible that, although Keynes' analysis is roughly correct, the conclusions he drew from it may be incomplete and that, while admitting his point of departure, one may arrive at different conclusions. All that can be said at present is that the study of its applications should enable us to judge whether they have given better results

---

1. This does not mean that a country cannot gain by devaluing in order to restore its trade balance—a measure that cannot be considered contrary to the spirit of the policy of employment. It is one thing for a country not to allow a depression to be foisted upon it by other countries; but quite another to transfer to them the unemployment it is experiencing, for lack of an appropriate economic policy.

than the classical analysis. The preceding considerations suffice to explain why these applications should be sought in countries that are relatively developed, relatively industrialized, and in which the institution of private property still retains a large measure of vitality. [1]

---

1. This does not mean that the analyses of the 'theory of employment' cannot be applied in collectivist economics. We shall have something to say about this later.

4

CHAPTER VI

THE CLASSICAL THEORY
AND ITS APPLICATIONS IN PERIODS
OF DEPRESSION AND UNEMPLOYMENT

The period between the two world wars is of exceptional importance —to the theorist, to the statesman, and to the ordinary man anxious about his future. To counter the depressions which immediately followed the first world war and later the 1929 crisis, two kinds of policy were pursued: those inspired by classical theory more or less brought up to date; and those based, if not upon the general theory of employment, at least upon partial analyses, which were gradually co-ordinated in a more general system.

Seldom have the effects of combining incomplete theories with analyses that kept close to realities been seen so clearly. Both policies can be judged by their effects upon the volume of production and on the number of unemployed. Of course, it can always be argued that such and such a policy—which was not adopted—would have been more effective than another. However, the experiments made in various countries provide sufficient material from which to draw certain positive conclusions.

Among the policies inspired by the classical analysis the following examples may be singled out: (a) Britain's return to the gold standard after the first world war; (b) the policy of the gold-bloc countries after the 1929 crisis; (c) the Bruning policy of 1932; (d) the Laval policy of 1935.

BRITAIN'S RETURN TO THE GOLD STANDARD
AFTER THE FIRST WORLD WAR

The 1914-18 war, the methods used by the belligerents to raise the necessary funds, i.e. inflation in some form or other, had as their consequence a rise in prices, which varied from country to country, but was

54

everywhere considerable. The burden of reconstructing the devastated areas and, in many cases, a refusal to embark upon financial reform led to the continuance, for several years after the peace, of methods which precipitated ruin and, in several countries, involved the total disappearance of the currency.

It was obvious, with the cessation of hostilities, that economic life could not be resumed satisfactorily while monetary instability persisted. It was also evident that the choice lay between two policies. One was to stabilize currency in the neighbourhood of the level it had in fact reached. The other was to revalue it gradually and to lower prices almost to the 1913 level so that gold convertibility could be restored. This really meant giving back to the monetary unit its pre-war purchasing power.

In some countries this solution was manifestly impossible and therefore was not attempted. This was the case in the defeated countries or those that succeeded them. The only possibility was to arrest the accelerated flight of the currency. In other countries the impossibility was less obvious and the governments of France and Italy for a long time cherished the illusion of being able to revalue their currencies. However their financial mistakes were such that by the time it became possible to arrest the rise of prices, these had soared so high that a return to pre-war parity was seen by all sensible men to be an idle dream. Accordingly, in 1926, France stabilized its currency at a rate that sanctioned a four-fifths depreciation. But in Britain the situation was visibly different. Steps taken to check the fall of the pound, the financing of the war by measures in which taxation had played a relatively large part, a courageous budget policy which had led to the rapid wiping out of the deficit, an economic situation unaffected by material devastation, and the need to reconstitute industry and rebuild houses—all these factors had limited the depreciation of British currency so that a return to pre-war parity did not seem, as in other countries, an impossibility or flagrantly absurd. The objective then was a practicable one. But was it to be desired?

There were two opinions about this, of which much the more influential was that held by the liberal school of thought. Since a return to pre-war parity was possible, this school argued, it must be made. There were strong arguments in its favour: respect for contractual engagements, the prestige of the pound sterling, the stimulus to saving, etc. But the difficulties were equally obvious. There was the necessity of readjusting the whole scale of prices and wages, unless all possibility of export was to be lost. But here the economic training of British administrators, experts and bankers made itself felt, and the liberal theory led to a minimizing of the difficulties. There was held to be no reason why wages and prices should not adapt themselves naturally, and fairly easily, to the new parity of the currency. All the necessary adjustments would be effected by the liberal mechanisms. In any case nobody believed in the possibility of an unbalanced economy, a general over-production and a chronic unemployment which neither Ricardo nor J.-B. Say had found at the end of their equations. But for this fundamental belief in natural economic harmonies, British policy would certainly have been different.

Only one discordant voice was raised, that of a young economist, J. M. Keynes, who, although he had not then fully evolved a new economic theory, had already observed a number of weaknesses in the liberal system. By the end of 1923 he had warned his country, and others, against the policy of revaluation and deflation, in a short book entitled *Monetary Reform*. But his views were considered heretical and went unheeded. [1] Thanks to a policy of an 'overbalanced' budget (see Table 1) and to a rise in the rate of interest, [2] Britain managed to make the pound convertible again on the pre-war basis; the return to the gold standard was achieved in 1925.

TABLE 1. Budget of the United Kingdom (in millions of pounds).

Year	Revenue	Expenditure	Revenue surplus
1920	1 229.6	1 665.8	−326.2
1921	1 426.0	1 195.4	+230.6
1922	1 124.9	1 079.2	+ 45.7
1923	914.0	812.5	+101.5
1924	837.2	788.9	+ 48.3
1925	799.4	795.8	+ 3.6

Wholesale prices between 1920 and 1928 dropped as follows: 1920, 338; 1921, 217; 1922, 179; 1923, 177; 1924, 191; 1925, 185; 1926, 173; 1927, 167; 1928, 164.

But British prices were still high compared with world prices, and costs of production, especially wages, did not fall in the same proportion as selling prices. The result was a loss of exports and production

---

1. So did his later warnings, particularly in 1925, when he explained all the difficulties that the British economy would encounter and forecast conflicts which duly materialized. Some of Keynes' articles of this time will be found collected in a small volume entitled *Essays in Persuasion*.
2. Average discount rate of the Bank of England: 1923, 3.50; 1924, 4.00; 1925, 4.60; 1926, 5.00.

and the appearance of more or less chronic unemployment (see Table 2).

TABLE 2.

Year	Exports	Number of insured unemployed
1913	634.8	—
1920	1 557.2	—
1921	810.3	2 038 000
1922	823.2	1 464 000
1923	885.8	1 229 000
1924	940,9	1 263 000
1925	927.5	1 243 000
1926	778.5	1 432 000
1927	832.0	1 194 000
1928	843.9	1 334 000

THE 'CLASSICAL' EXPLANATION OF BRITISH UNEMPLOYMENT

Liberal theory was thus faced with another problem—the contradiction between the facts and its own analysis—with the aggravating circumstance that unemployment was disturbingly widespread, looked as though it would persist indefinitely, and was afflicting the very country which had remained faithful to the teachings of the school. Instead of revising its postulates, classical theory sought an explanation in the imperfections of the modern world. If the natural mechanisms did not function—and obviously they did not—it was because the blindness of man had upset them. Such was the case put forward in 1925, and again in 1931, by Mr. Rueff. [1]

If unemployment persisted, it was because wages were kept too high. The index of wages was higher than that of wholesale prices: hence the fall in production, for business heads could not manufacture products which sold at less than their cost price. The relative inflexibility of wages was the basic cause of unemployment.

In addition, further statistical examination showed a close correla-

---

1. In an article entitled, 'Les Variations du Chômage en Angleterre' (Fluctuations in Unemployment in England), in the *Revue Politique et Parlementaire* of 10 December 1925; in a communication from the same writer and on the same subject to the *Société d'Economie Politique*, on 5 December 1925; and in an article (signed XXX) published in the *Revue d'Economie Politique* in 1931, under the title 'L'Assurance Chômage cause du Chômage Permanent' (Unemployment Relief a cause of Permanent Unemployment).

tion between the variations in this difference, expressed by the ratio of the wage index to the price index, and fluctuations in unemployment. Table 3 is taken from one of the previously mentioned studies by Mr. Rueff:

TABLE 3.   Average quarterly values of the indexes used. [1]

1st quarters	Wages [2]	Wholesale prices [3]	Ratio between (2) and (3)	Unemployed Percentage of total trade union membership
(1)	(2)	(3)	(4)	(5)
1919	207	249	0.831	2.7
1920	231	309	0.747	1.9
1921	276	227	1.215	8.5
1922	215	162	1.327	16.5
1923	177	158	1.120	13.0
1924	174	166	1.048	8.3
1925	181	169	1.071	9.1
1926	180	147	1.22	10.4
1927	181	143	1.265	13.0
1928	180	141	1.279	10.2
1929	99.5	83.6	1.190	11.5
1930	98.7	76.9	1.283	13.2

1. The figures in columns 2, 3 and 5 are taken from the monthly bulletin of the London and Cambridge Economic Service.
2. Professor Bowley's index base: 100 in 1913.
3. Board of Trade index base: 100 in 1913.

The explanation of this relative rigidity of wages lay in the existence of unemployment relief, which by enabling the worker to live without working had abolished a part of the classical mechanism—the pressure exerted by unemployment on the worker, who was obliged to accept any wage, no matter how reduced, in a period of falling prices.   This explained the title of one of Mr. Rueff's articles: 'L'assurance Chômage cause du Chômage Permanent' (Unemployment Relief a cause of Permanent Unemployment).   Basically, this liberal economist waived aside the phenomenon of unemployment: unemployment in Britain was not involuntary unemployment—something impossible to explain—it was a voluntary unemployment.   Thus the fact so embarrassing for the theory, the existence of a million unemployed, was simply dismissed. There was no involuntary unemployment.

Analysis of the facts alone revealed a flaw in this reasoning.   Let us suppose that the workers had accepted bigger wage reductions.

These reductions would normally have resulted in a restriction of home markets, and therefore in a bigger drop in prices. The prospect of falling prices in itself could only have encouraged entrepreneurs to wait, to reject or postpone any plans for investing—and consequently to prolong unemployment: of what use would it be to re-employ a worker at a wage 10 per cent lower than the previous wage if the prices of the extra goods that would be produced were likely to drop by 10 per cent, and goods already in hand could not be disposed of?

CONSEQUENCES OF THE 'CLASSICAL' ANALYSIS

From the scientific point of view, the reasoning was incomplete, and therefore incorrect. Nevertheless it weighed heavily on the course of events. Classical economy had found a satisfactory explanation of disharmony and unbalance in the rigidity of the real world, whose state intervention upset the natural mechanisms, the free play of prices, wages and production. To obtain economic equilibrium one had only to combat this rigidity, to force the economy if necessary to make the adjustment of prices upon which progress and prosperity depended. The lesson thus learnt was not lost. Bruning applied it in 1932, Laval in 1935.

THE POLICY OF THE GOLD-BLOC COUNTRIES

Faced with the 1929 crisis and the intensified depression of the ensuing years, most countries first reacted by maintaining an economic and financial policy in keeping with the conclusions of classical theory—a policy sooner or later to be rejected.

Prices were too high, the consequence of wild speculation, and a drop retrieved the situation. A number of speculators were ruined, inefficient businesses disappeared and workers had to change their jobs, remedial measures temporarily disagreeable for some people but excellent in themselves. Of course, wages and prices as a whole would have to be adjusted to the new situation. This was a matter of a few months—a year perhaps. It was useless to try to avoid the necessary process of liquidation and to hinder the free play of natural economic laws by monetary or other artifices. The duty of the state was to preserve the instrument of exchange intact, to maintain the gold stand-ard and the convertibility and parity of the currency.

In this context, we may quote a statement made by the governor of the Banque de France to the shareholders on 28 January 1932:

'The gradual liquidation of the artificial systems we have tried to introduce since the war is, in our opinion, a decisive step towards economic recovery. We have always refused to accept those short-sighted solutions, whose dangers we foresaw. We consider that it is more than ever our duty to give the franc the metallic guarantee which is the only stable basis for a currency. We regard gold convertibility not as an obsolete obligation, but as a necessary discipline. We see in it the only effective safeguard for the security of contracts and commercial morality.'

The currency was threatened in different ways, notably by the budgetary disequilibrium resulting from the diminution in fiscal revenue more or less linked to the volume of business. The first task of the authorities was to restore the balance of the budget, to make the cuts required to adjust the volume of expenditure to the size of the revenue. This idea rested once again on the implicit or explicit belief in the spontaneous recovery of the economy, in the impossibility of general over-production and under-employment.

Accordingly, the gold-bloc countries, Belgium, France, Italy, the Netherlands, Poland and Switzerland, maintained the convertibility and the parity of their currency for several years. [1] Czechoslovakia pursued the same policy until 1934.

They did not, of course, apply the conclusions of the liberal school altogether strictly. They felt it impossible to dispense with unemployment relief, they carried out public works, they did not always achieve a balanced budget, some at least of them subsidized their farmers. Nevertheless, such measures as these were looked upon as unavoidable concessions, palliatives contrary to their general policy, which rested fundamentally on belief in the virtue of liberal mechanisms. [2] The result was a slowing down or a standstill in business.

---

1. On 3 July 1933, the governments of these countries issued the following statement:
   'The undersigned governments,
   'Convinced that the maintenance of their currency is essential for the economic and financial recovery of the world, for the resumption of credit and for the safeguarding of the social progress achieved in their countries;
   'Confirm their express desire to maintain the free functioning of the gold standard in their respective countries at present gold parities and within the framework of the existing currency laws;
   'Ask their central banks to remain in close contact in order to give the present statement its fullest possible effect.'
2. In the following tables the figures in italics correspond to the year in which each country changed its monetary policy: France in 1936, Belgium in March 1935, Italy in 1934, Switzerland in 1936, Czechoslovakia in February 1934.

EXPORTS

This policy had as its first consequence a reduction in exports.

TABLE 4. Exports (in millions of currency units).

Countries	Year							
	1929	*1930*	*1931*	*1932*	*1933*	*1934*	*1935*	*1936*
Belgium	31 783	26 067	23 069	14 813	14 032	13 540	*15 786*	19 524
France	50 139	42 835	30 436	19 705	18 474	17 850	15 496	*15 442*
Italy	14 888	12 115	10 037	6 811	5 991	*5 224*	5 238	5 458
Nether-lands	1 989	1 718	1 312	846	726	712	675	*746*
Switzer-land	2 076	1 746	1 335	768	818	822	792	*881*

PRICES

A second consequence was the gradual fall in prices, insufficient to offset the price fall in countries that had devalued their currency, but enough to reduce the propensity to produce and invest.

TABLE 5. Wholesale prices.

Countries	Year							
	1929	*1930*	*1931*	*1932*	*1933*	*1934*	*1935*	*1936*
Belgium	100	87.4	73.6	62.5	58.9	55.6	*63.1*	69.1
Czechoslovakia	100	88.8	80.6	74.5	72.2	*74.0*	77.2	77.4
France	100	88.4	80.0	68.2	63.6	60.0	54.0	*65.5*
Italy	100	89.5	78.1	73.0	66.5	65.0	*71.5*	80.1
Netherlands	100	89.9	76.5	64.8	63.1	63.2	61.7	*64.0*
Poland	100	88.8	77.5	68.0	61.4	57.9	*55.1*	56.1
Switzerland	100	89.6	77.7	68.0	64.5	63.6	63.6	*67.7*

THE RATE OF INTEREST

Such a policy required the maintenance of a relatively high interest rate. This was the means of bringing down prices, in order to achieve the necessary adjustment of home prices to prices abroad. It was a consequence of the desire to protect the currency. As people expected devaluation, these countries repeatedly suffered large exports of capital and substantial exports of gold. To arrest this, the classical step was to raise the discount rate. In any case, currency expansion had to be guarded against, for it might have lowered the long-term interest rate, as shown in the yield of government stock.

Table 6 indicates the movements in the yield of government stock.

TABLE 6. Interest rate: yield of government stock.

Countries	Year							
	1929	1930	1931	1932	1933	1934	1935	1936
Belgium	4.52	3.94	3.98	4.51	4.54	4.08	3.90	3.72
Czechoslovakia	5.76	5.68	5.73	6.50	6.06	5.84	5.21	4.45
France	3.98	3.44	3.48	3.84	4.38	4.14	3.88	4.32
Italy	5.14	5.21	4.90	4.77	4.35	4.09	4.75	4.68
Netherlands [1]	3.94	3.81	3.86	3.89	3.68	3.35	3.43	3.32
Poland [2]	12.80	11.44	12.60	15.20	14.28	11.36	10.75	10.10
Switzerland	4.38	4.07	3.78	3.62	3.84	4.05	4.52	4.27

1. Perpetual stock.
2. Mortgage debentures.

INVESTMENT

The effect of this relatively high rate of interest, combined with the fall in prices, was to reduce investment. A significant picture may be obtained by comparing the indexes of building activity in a number of countries. The drop in France, Switzerland and Czechoslovakia is unmistakable and contrasts with the situation in other countries. The only exception is the Netherlands, where building activity remained relatively high. And of all the gold-bloc countries Holland was the one in which, for reasons too involved to enter into here, the rate of interest was lowest.

TABLE 7. Indexes of building activity.[1]

Country	Unit	1929	1932	1933	1934	1935
Argentina	In thousands of square metres	—	1 195	1 144	1 484	932
Australia	Value in millions of Australian pounds	4.2	5.7	8.6	14.0	20.4
Canada	Value in millions of Canadian dollars	235	39.5	21.6	26.8	46.3
Czechoslovakia	In millions of cubic metres	—	6.5	3.3	2.7	1.9
France	Index	100	81	74	67	56
Germany	In thousands of rooms	548	196	276	424	251
Japan	In thousands of square metres	491	1 197	1 722	1 641	1 786
Netherlands	In thousands of housing units	47.3	41.3	44.4	52.6	42.2
Sweden	In thousands of rooms	29.3	34.9	23.3	27.1	43.6
Switzerland	In thousands of dwellings	2.9	2.7	2.5	2.7	1.7
	In thousands of flats	9.3	13.2	9.9	11.0	6.7
Union of South Africa	Value in millions of South African pounds	—	2.0	2.1	4.2	6.9
United Kingdom	In thousands of houses	71	91	119	137	157
United States of America	In millions of square feet	388	74	73	64	137

1. League of Nations. *Revue de la Situation Economique Mondiale*, fifth year, 1935-36, p. 140.

PRODUCTION AND UNEMPLOYMENT

The ultimate consequence was a reduction or a standstill in industrial output which—particularly after a certain date—contrasted with the movement in other countries, and the continuance or increase of unemployment. In a country like France, unemployment was limited by the economic structure of the country; but it was none the less persistent.

TABLE 8.   Index of industrial production.

Countries	Year							
	1929	1930	1931	1932	1933	1934	1935	1936
Belgium	100	89	81	69	72	73	82	87
Czechoslovakia	100	89	81	64	60	67	70	80
France	100	100	89	69	77	71	67	70
Italy	100	94	87	77	84	97	111	128
Netherlands	100	91	79	62	69	70	66	72
Poland	100	82	70	54	56	63	67	72
World [1]	100	86	75	63	71	77	85	96

1. Not including the Union of Soviet Socialist Republics. If the Union of Soviet Socialist Republics were included, the world figures would be substantially higher.

TABLE 9.   Number of unemployed. [1]

Countries	Year								
	1929	1930	1931	1932	1933	1934	1935	1936	1937
Belgium	12	36	110	210	210	234	211	154	126
Czechoslovakia	23	51	102	184	247	245	235	208	151
France	—	2	56	273	276	345	426	431	350
Italy	300	426	734	1 006	1 018	963	?	?	?
Netherlands	24	37	82	153	163	160	173	169	137
Poland	129	226	299	255	249	342	381	367	375
Switzerland (%)	1.8	3.4	5.9	9.1	10.8	9.8	11.8	13.2	10

1. The figures are taken from the *Revue Internationale du Travail,* in which the meaning and origin of each one of them may be found.   They are in thousands except for Switzerland, which is a percentage.

The League of Nations, in its report on the world economic situation in 1936, contrasted the evolution of the gold-bloc countries with that of the other countries in the following terms:

'Apart from the altogether exceptional expansion of industrial production in the Union of Soviet Socialist Republics, the most striking
feature of the table is the divergence revealed, after the middle
of 1935, between the curve of industrial activity in the gold-bloc
countries and that of other countries. At the end of 1934 the
deflationary policy pursued in the gold-bloc countries had reduced
industrial activity to a level almost one-third below the average level
in 1929 and only just above the lowest point recorded during the
summer of 1932, before general recovery set in. At the same time
the situation was rapidly improving in the paper-currency countries,
as well as in Germany and Italy; in the last two countries the steps
taken by the state to stimulate activity and thus secure work for the
unemployed had played a decisive part. The combined index of
industrial output in the paper-currency countries had regained the 1929
level at the end of the first quarter of 1934 and continued its upward
movement during that year and in 1935; by the end of the first quarter
of 1936 it was 15-20 per cent above the 1929 level. On the other
hand, in the gold-bloc countries, industrial activity fell towards the
end of 1934. It tended to improve in the autumn of 1935 and the
early part of 1936, but this recovery appears modest when compared
not only with the uninterrupted expansion of the paper-currency
countries, but also with the marked improvement to be noted at the same
time in countries which reduced the legal parity of their currency and
later established a fixed ratio between that parity and gold.'[1]

THE BRUNING POLICY AND THE LAVAL POLICY

But the protagonists of liberalism when they viewed the situation in
Britain were concerned, as we have seen, about the contradictions in
which the facts seemed to involve them. They thought that they had
found an explanation for this lack of harmony in the inflexibility of
an economy which, owing to the intervention of the state or of professional bodies, lacked the elasticity necessary to the interplay of
economic laws. Rueff had emphasized the effects of a policy of unemployment relief, which hindered the readjustment of wages. Other
economists observed that the intervention of producers' associations

---

1. League of Nations, *Revue de la Situation Economique Mondiale,* fifth year, 1935-36, p. 35.
   (French text.)

prevented the prices of monopoly products from falling as much as those in sectors open to competition. Finally, it had to be admitted that the existence of long-term contracts maintained certain prices, rents or debentures at a higher level than selling prices.

This analysis was not incorrect. The rigidity of the economy is a fact and it was worth mentioning and, to a certain extent and under certain circumstances, correcting it. The mistake was to make it the sole and exclusive cause of the depression and of unemployment. This was to ignore the other factors in the economic disequilibrium. Another mistake was to belittle the effects of policies intended to force adjustments which did not come about by themselves, or did so too slowly, failing to perceive the further repercussions of these policies.

This was shown by two typical examples of this application of classical principles, the Bruning experiment in Germany and the Laval experiment in France.

THE BRUNING EXPERIMENT

For reasons that do not interest us here, Germany was one of the countries in which the crisis was most acute. The number of unemployed, already large in 1927 and 1928 (about 1,350,000), rapidly rose to 1,892,000 in 1929, to 3,076,000 in 1930, and to 4,520,000 in 1931. When Chancellor Bruning took office on 30 March 1930, there were 3,041,000 unemployed. On the basis of 100 in 1929, industrial production had fallen to 85.9 in 1930, and to 67.6 in 1931. To meet this situation, the Chancellor tried to reduce the budget deficit by cutting expenditure and to facilitate the resumption of business by lowering the various elements in cost price. Budget cuts were made by a series of decrees, of which the most important was that of 8 December 1931. We may quote as an example a provision according to which administrations were not allowed to begin any new building before 31 November 1934 without the authorization of the Reich Government or the Government of the Länder, while civil servants' salaries were cut by 20 per cent, old age pensions reduced, etc. Taxes were increased on incomes, beer, tobacco, business turnover (rate raised from 0.85 to 2 per cent). In private enterprise all relatively rigid 'prices' had to be lowered: rents by 10 per cent, cartel goods by 10 per cent, with similar measures for branded products at fixed prices, interest on private debts, etc. Wages were to be lowered by 20 per cent. A price commissioner was appointed to bring down the prices of products on the free markets.

The aim was to facilitate the adjustments of the liberal mechanism by overcoming certain 'rigidities'. In the same way, in conformity with the liberal theories on unemployment relief, the distribution of relief was subjected to restrictions: certain classes of workers were excluded, the terms of compensation were made stricter, the period and scale of payment being reduced.

Table 10 shows the reduction in the number, and especially in the percentage, of paid unemployed.

TABLE 10.

Periods	Average number		Percentage receiving relief
	of unemployed	receiving relief	
April 1930 - March 1931	3 483 000	1 843 000	52.9
April 1931 - March 1932	4 819 000	1 539 000	31.8
April 1932 - March 1933	5 577 000	860 000	15.4

Thus a large number of the unemployed became the responsibility of emergency relief organizations and of the general relief administered by commissioners. Naturally, this policy made comparatively little provision for public works designed to combat unemployment: 350 million Reichsmark for the railways, 200 millions for the postal services, 200 millions for housing, 100 millions for roads, 250 millions for 'emergency work' already organized by the office for unemployment relief. The results of this policy of restricting demand were as follows: the index of industrial output fell from 85.9 in 1930 to 53.3 in 1932; the number of unemployed rose from 3,075,000 in 1930 to 4,519,000 in 1931, and to 5,575,000 in 1932 (6,034,000 in March 1932).

It has often been remarked—but it is worth repeating—that these 6 million unemployed, and the fears of those who were still at work and of heads of businesses, were among the important causes of Hitler's rise to power. Seldom has the application of a mistaken scientific system had such far-reaching and disastrous consequences!

THE FRENCH EXPERIMENT IN 1935

The French policy of 1935 is almost a replica of the Bruning programme. It was based on the same principle: to set the state on its feet again by natural mechanisms which, for some reason or another, were not functioning by themselves, and to break down the rigidities preventing equilibrium.

The situation in France was a follows: wholesale prices had fallen from 706 in 1929 to 389 in June 1935, the index of industrial output, on the basis of 100 in 1928, was only 73 in June 1935. The efforts of preceding governments had been concentrated, unsuccessfully, on doing away with the budget deficit. It was becoming evident that French prices were too high in comparison with foreign prices that had been readjusted by devaluations: hence those exports of gold which, in the summer of 1935, led to the formation of a government granted full powers, with Pierre Laval at its head. The new government passed a series of decree laws enacting reductions of 10 per cent in civil servants' salaries, in interest on the public debt and in rents, and various reductions in the prices of monopoly goods and services—gas and electricity tariffs for instance.

What were the results? No doubt, in this matter as in others, the upholders of a policy can argue that it was interrupted just at the time when it was beginning to bear fruit. Nevertheless the figures for industrial production and unemployment during the months following deflation showed a continuance of the slump in French economy.

TABLE 11.

Periods	Index of industrial production [1]	Number of unemployed
1933: Monthly average	84	276 000
1934: Monthly average	78	345 000
1935: July	73	380 000
August	73	380 000
September	74	373 000
October	75	385 000
November	75	409 000
December	75	439 000
1936: January	77	477 000
February	78	487 000
March	79	465 000
April	80	443 000
May	80	422 000

1. Basis 100 in 1938.

The analysis of the theory of employment explained these results without any difficulty. The reductions that had been made were not taken as an adjustment after which wages and prices would tend to rise, but as the prelude to further reductions. It would seem that some heads of businesses made the reduction in civil servants' salaries a pretext for trying to lower wages. This expectation of further reductions could not favour the expansion of production or investment, especially as the rate of interest was relatively high, the state not having adopted a monetary policy that might have brought it down. Ignoring the factors that govern the rate of interest, the authorities evidently believed that its fall—that is a rise in stocks—would inevitably follow from an economy budget and the 'defence of the currency'. They failed to appreciate the influence of the quantity of money upon the rate of interest. In any case, even a considerable drop would not have been enough to offset the reduction in the prospective yield from investments. A large-scale policy of state investment might have had this effect, but this was excluded by the consensus of opinion that first place must be given to the defence of monetary parity and the balancing of the budget. The failure of the 1935 experiment was a surprise only to those who could not free themselves from the arguments of classical economy.

CHAPTER VII

SOME APPLICATIONS OF
THE THEORY OF EMPLOYMENT
BETWEEN 1931 AND 1936

It may seem paradoxical to talk about applications in 1931, 1933 or 1935 of a theory that was only formulated in 1937.   But in his *Treatise on Money* (published 1930), as in his criticisms of English monetary policy made from 1925 to 1931, Keynes had already outlined an analysis and, therefrom, an economic policy opposed to the classical analysis and policy and which may well have influenced politicians and experts.   Moreover, Keynes took inspiration from earlier studies, Marx's as well as Wicksell's, Knapp's and Fischer's.   He was the exceptional interpreter of a body of ideas which, even before the appearance of the theory of employment, may have influenced statesmen, if only implicitly.   These showed by their actions from day to day that they did not rely exclusively on the spontaneous play of classical economy.

To what extent was this so?   It is hard to say of politicians who did not see fit to state the grounds for their policy or of others whose speeches were limited to more or less summary considerations.   It is even possible that some measures were adopted more or less empirically. There was no need to know the multiplier theory in order to open up workshops for the unemployed, though such a policy, if carried out on a large scale, would imply disbelief in the effectiveness of the liberal mechanisms.   It cannot be denied that the extent and persistence of the 1929 crisis led some politicians to seek other remedies than those traditionally suggested.   The expression, 'brains trust', which came into being at this time to describe the experts surrounding the head of a state, is significant of the need that was felt to have recourse to economics as a guide to action.   The measures taken were incomplete in the same way as were the analyses underlying them.   If some of the policies adopted had only a partial success, it was no doubt because they rested on partial analyses.

One last word.   The belief that the natural mechanisms—even helped

70

along by the state—could not suffice to restore prosperity and to abolish unemployment found expression in widely differing measures, which have nothing in common except their opposition to the liberal attitude. Some consisted in restricting the volume of production in order to adapt it to shrinking markets. The applications of this idea were numerous: plans for restricting the output of raw materials, reduction of crops, limitation of the right to set up new businesses, the destruction of stocks of food, coffee, wheat or cotton. These were all spontaneous reactions similar to those of former times. It is not surprising that 'corporatist' ideas reappeared. These measures or ideas have been interpreted as the application of a deliberate desire to control the economy. To avert over-production, the state fixed the volume of production in accordance with needs. These were reactions based on an erroneous interpretation of the economic position in that they tried to adapt production to markets, whereas it would have been better to ask whether the markets were not insufficient, whether there were not some unsatisfied needs, and whether an effort should not be made to satisfy them.

Other measures were aimed at abolishing unemployment by working upon the trade balance. To restrict imports, the quota system was used to supplement the old method of customs duties—which were also increased. Monetary devaluations, which had the effect of reducing the prices of local goods as compared with foreign goods, were employed as a means of limiting imports and increasing exports. This was not their sole purpose, but it was one of them.

In one way the Keynesian analysis explained this policy: to export more than one imported was a means of increasing aggregate demand, and therefore production and employment. But, in another way, this return to the mercantilist policy of the balance of trade was not an application of the 'theory of employment'. Its author—or his followers—drew attention to the inconsistency of desiring to export more than one imported in order to ensure full employment. Basically, this meant trying to transfer one's unemployment elsewhere, to the importing country. It was obvious that this kind of race between countries could not restore the international economy and might accentuate the threat of war.

The only measures that can really be considered applications of the 'theory of employment' are those aimed at increasing home consumption and investment.

Four policies may be selected as examples: British policy from 1931 to 1938; German policy—generally connected with the programme of Dr. Schacht; President Roosevelt's 'New Deal' policy; Swedish policy.

BRITISH POLICY FROM 1931 TO 1938

The British policy of 1931-38 contrasts with that which preceded it. It is hard to say what part economics played in the actions of the responsible authorities, but it can scarcely be doubted that Keynes' criticisms and analyses, and the fact that his predictions concerning the results of the return to the gold standard and pre-war parity had been proved right, counted for something in the planning and pursuit of policy. This said, it must be admitted that the abandonment of the convertibility of the pound in 1931 was unavoidable in any case. One event that stood out at the time was the drop in world prices; moreover the persistent deficit in the balance of accounts and the export of capital, due to the fact that Great Britain had large short-term credits in Austria and Germany not likely to be immediately recoverable, led to very large withdrawals of funds from London during the summer of 1931. The exports of gold reached such proportions that, on 21 September, the government had to suspend the convertibility of the pound.

If this decision was imposed upon Britain by material necessities, in several other countries—the Dominions, [1] the Scandinavian countries and Portugal—which quickly copied London, the decision was a considered one. In any case, the abandonment of the gold standard was part of an overall policy characterized by its efforts to overcome unemployment by financial mechanisms, that is by modifying the price level and lowering the rate of interest. For this to work, the devaluation must not be accompanied by a rise in home prices, which might have cancelled its effects. Consequently, it was desirable to avoid an excessive increase in the aggregate home demand and not to encourage speculation. Such is the basis of the policy of the balanced budget which British governments followed during the whole of this period. The British budgets for 1931, 1932 and 1933 had only a slight surplus of expenditure. In 1934, 1935 and 1936 there was a small surplus of revenue.

What were the effects of this policy?

---

1. Except South Africa, which did not adopt the English monetary policy until 1932. Canada had depreciated its currency before the depreciation of the pound.

THE EVOLUTION OF FOREIGN TRADE

The gold standard having been abandoned, the exchange value of the pound fell. By means of a stabilization fund, which bought and sold pounds and foreign currencies, the government limited fluctuations. As home prices did not go up, the devaluation of the pound created a margin between home and world prices which encouraged exports and discouraged imports, and consequently stimulated home production. Exports did in fact increase, though slowly and moderately —from £390 million in 1931 they rose to £425 million in 1935— whereas imports dropped from 797.5 to 700.7, partly on account of a higher protective tariff. In this way the deficit in the trade balance was reduced from £407 million in 1931 to £276 million in 1935.

But devaluation had another effect. Entrepreneurs no longer had any reason to expect a fall in home prices. Thus the extension of production, the reconstitution of stocks, and investment, became profitable once more. The more so as the other factor on which the prospective yield of an investment depends, the rate of interest, was reduced by deliberate monetary policy.

THE DROP IN THE INTEREST RATE
AND THE PROGRESS OF INVESTMENTS

The economic analyses that most influenced British policy [1] seem to have been those that stressed the effects of the rate of interest and the possibility of stimulating the economy by lowering it. This policy of lowering the interest rate was only made possible by devaluation of the pound. Devaluation had removed the incentive to export capital, so it was no longer necessary to attract or retain capital by a very high rate of interest. On the contrary, devaluation induced certain foreigners to buy a currency whose parity was no longer in danger of being modified. In 1932 the Bank of England progressively reduced its discount rate from 6 per cent to 2 per cent, giving the signal for a drop in every country over the whole of that year. The discount rate of the Bank of England remained fixed at this figure until 1938.

---

1. cf. the joint declaration made in 1933 by the governments of Great Britain, Canada, India, Australia, New Zealand and the Union of South Africa, in reply to the gold-bloc declaration, confirming their adhesion to the monetary principles previously adopted at Ottawa and setting forth their position once more. The following passage may be quoted: 'In the monetary sphere the first step towards a rise in prices was stated to be the creation and maintenance within the limits of sound finance of such conditions as would assist in the revival of industry and trade, including low rates of interest and an abundance of short-term money.'

Other factors came into play, especially the inflow of capital from countries which feared a depreciation of their currency. Money was so abundant that in 1935 the banks had to make an agreement to prevent the auction rate of Treasury bonds from falling below $\frac{1}{2}$ per cent. The drop in the discount rate could not fail to influence the long- and average-term rate of interest. But the authorities also tried to influence the rate directly, for—and here it is worth while recalling the analyses of the economists—it determines the volume of investment more than does the discount rate.[1] The open market policy, that is, the purchase of government bonds on the market by the Bank of England (the Bank of England's portfolio of government stock rose from £45.3 million on 27 January 1932 to £90.6 million on 25 January 1933), as well as purchases by other banks, brought about a rise in the quotations of the stock, that is to say, a fall in the rate of interest. The yield of $2\frac{1}{2}$ per cent Consols dropped from 4.53 to 3.46 between January and July 1932. In January 1935. it was 2.7 per cent. Thus in June 1932 a large part of the British debt was converted with an interest rate reduced from 5 per cent to $3\frac{1}{2}$ per cent. This policy was also pursued by some of the Dominions. In Australia, for example, from October 1932 to February 1934, there were seven conversions of public loans involving a total capital of £110 million, with a rate of interest reduced from 4 or 6 per cent to $3\frac{1}{2}$ or 4 per cent.

Table 12 shows the movement of the long-term and short-term rate of interest in the United Kingdom.

TABLE 12.[1]

| Year | Interest (annual averages) | |
	$2\frac{1}{2}$ % Consols	London : bills of exchange at 90 days
1929	4.60	5.26
1930	4.48	2.57
1931	4.39	3.61
1932	3.76	1.87
1933	3.38	0.69
1934	3.08	0.82
1935	2.91	0.58

1. League of Nations. *World Production and Prices*, 1935-36.

1. cf. the previously quoted declaration by the governments of Great Britain and the Dominions. The following passage is worth notice: 'Among the factors working for the economic recovery of the countries of the Commonwealth, special importance attaches to the decline in the rate of interest on long-term loans.'

The effects of the fall in the interest rate may be seen in the increase in issues: the (net) new issues for the United Kingdom increased regularly between 1931 (£40 million) and 1935 (£207 million).

THE TREND OF PRODUCTION AND UNEMPLOYMENT

The increase in industrial output was mainly the effect of increased investment, and of the greater number of houses built. This may be observed in Table 13.

TABLE 13.   Industrial production (Board of Trade index).

Year	Index		Houses built
	general	building	
1929	100	100	71 000
1930	92.3	105.7	—
1931	83.8	91.5	—
1932	83.5	105.9	91 000
1933	88.2	140.8	119 000
1934	98.8	157.2	137 000
1935	105.7	177.2	157 000

In 1936, the League of Nations Economic Intelligence Service wrote in its *Monetary Review,* as follows:

'The building boom, based on cheap money, was a very important element in the British recovery.... The indirect repercussions of the building boom on other industries are difficult to trace in detail, but there can be no doubt that the rise in the monetary demand for goods all along the line represented in large measure the spending of funds which had been originally put into circulation through the building industry.' [1]

This clearly confirmed the conclusions of the policy of employment as regards the possibility of a monetary effect on the rate of interest and the influence of the rate of interest on investment.

----

1. op. cit., p. 13.

If the results obtained are judged by the degree of unemployment, a considerable improvement will be noticed as shown in Table 14.

TABLE 14.

Year	Unemployed	
	Number	Percentage of union members
1929	994 091	8.2
1930	1 464 347	11.8
1931	2 129 359	16.7
1932	2 254 857	17.6
1933	2 110 090	16.4
1934	1 801 913	13.9
1935	1 714 844	13.1
1936	1 497 587	11.2
1937	1 277 928	9.4

In 1935 or 1936, however, there was still a fairly large number of unemployed. In this respect, British economic policy had not been completely successful. But it must be remembered that only a part of the conclusions of a theory of employment had been applied. Great Britain had not thought fit to increase public investment as well as acting on money: we have seen that the budget was still balanced. The British Government's concern to avoid a rise in home prices, which would have compromised exports—a vital necessity for the country—is understandable, as is its desire to preserve the value of British currency as far as possible. Nevertheless, the fact remains that British policy between 1931 and 1938, in both its successful and its less successful aspects, is a typical case of what can be done by the deliberate application of the achievements of economic thought.

GERMAN POLICY FROM 1932 TO 1938

In March 1932 the number of unemployed reached 6 millions. The resultant discontent was one factor in the rise to power of the Nazi party, whose leader had stressed the importance to the workers of more stable employment. [1]   It was natural that when he was appointed Chancellor in January 1933 he should try by all means to absorb the mass of unemployed in Germany.   Bruning's failure was in a way the failure of classical economy.   Other considerations apart, the Hitler government was obliged to think of alternative methods.

THE MEANS

As in other countries, the measures adopted in Germany were of different kinds.   Some were aimed at thinning out the labour market by discouraging the paid employment of women. [2]   A labour service was set up with a similar purpose—the problem being to obtain work for the labour thus recruited.   The reintroduction of military service naturally served the same end.

Other measures were aimed at reducing imports. Dictated in a sense by Germany's lack of foreign exchange, they also helped to provide more outlets on the home market.   Autarchy, which was at this time or later introduced with the object of preparing for economic warfare, that is the manufacture of goods that a blockaded Germany would not be able to obtain on the world market, also increased the number of jobs.

Another objective was to raise the price of agricultural produce, and consequently increase the purchasing power of the farmers.

The rate of interest was acted upon by the Reichsbank buying bonds. This open market policy, authorized by the law of 27 October 1933, had the effect of bringing up the quotations of government stock, which could then be converted, reducing the rate of interest from 6 to 4.5 per cent. [3]   But the measure which enabled the Hitler government to absorb the largest proportion of all the unemployment created by the crisis was the policy of public works: the building of roads, drain-

---

1. In the second chapter of *Mein Kampf*, Hitler described instability of employment as one of the workers' worst scourges:
     'The insecurity of one's daily bread soon grew to be in my eyes one of the darkest aspects of the new life . . . rapid alternation of work and unemployment and the consequent perpetual seesawing of income and expenditure eventually destroyed many people's sense of thrift and intelligent planning.'
     It was perhaps because Hitler worked in the building industry—the industry most affected by alternations of prosperity and slump—that he adopted Dr. Schacht's financial technique.
     Another influence should be noted, that of Gottfried Reder, whose views on 'enslavement through interest' were in line with, or at least prepared one to understand the monetary conditions of full employment.
2. Women were encouraged to mind the home and to take up domestic service.
3. The index of fixed interest securities (6 per cent) rose from: 61.4 on 4 April 1932, to 86.2 on 13 April 1933, 89.6 in June 1934, 94.0 in December 1934, 96.0 in January 1935.

ing swamps, clearing land, and electrification. Later, other expenditures took precedence over these works and were the main factor in maintaining full employment: the policy of intensive rearmament in 1936 and 1937, the policy of economy autarchy in 1936 and 1939, with all the investment this implied. Although military preoccupations counted for something in the policy of public works carried out from 1933 onwards, these differed from those that came later in that their main purpose was the absorption of the unemployed. Viewed in that aspect they are a special application of a certain economic school of thought. Economically speaking, these works were financed by the issue of currency. Actually the issue was partly camouflaged by the following procedure. The Reich, or the provincial or local body which placed orders, paid the contractors or entrepreneurs by handing them over bonds known as 'work bills'. [1] These bills bore interest, were discountable by the banks, and rediscountable by the bank of issue, the Reichsbank. The contractors could hold on to the bills; in this case work was financed by a loan; if they had the bills discounted by the banks, and if the banks kept them in stocks and shares, the operation took the form of an increase in deposit accounts, that is an issue of representative money: the contractor could use his bank credit to pay by cheque; if the bank had the bill rediscounted by the bank of issue there was—or there could be—an issue of paper money. Fundamentally, these operations were the same. Even when the holder kept the bill, he did so because he knew that it could easily be discounted. It had for him therefore the value of real money. But this mechanism reduced, or staggered, the issue of money in its most visible form, paper money, which the public is most ready to consider as inflation.

Other provisions, too, were framed with the object of preventing a fear of inflation from causing speculative reactions which might have undermined public confidence in the currency. Exchange control prohibited a fall—an official fall at any rate—in the mark in terms of foreign currencies; price control stood in the way of speculative rises. The blocking of wages had the same effect. In addition, Treasury bonds and, later, funded loans of these bonds, reduced the increase in the quantity of money.

The policy pursued may therefore be summed up as follows: public works financed not by taxation but by loan or the issue of currency, hence an increase in aggregate demand, which, in an economy part

---

1. More exactly, a special fund opened a credit in favour of the local community. Within the limits of this credit, it met the bills that the entrepreneur or contractor drew on the community.

of whose labour force was unused. would take the form of an increase in production and not a rise in prices. [1]

It will be observed that this machinery was an imitation of that already set up by the two chancellors who succeeded Bruning in 1932, von Papen and von Schleicher.

The Papen plan included supplementary orders—up to 302 millions—and a bonus of 400 Rm. to private entrepreneurs for every additional workman taken on, and tax abatements up to the sum of 1,500 millions. Orders placed with industry were paid by means of bills rediscountable by the Reichsbank. The tax certificate could be used to pay certain taxes between 1 April 1934 and 31 March 1939.

The Schleicher plan, or *Sofort-Programm*, set aside 500 million Rm. for the immediate engagement of unemployed workers upon supplementary public works. They were paid with bills similar to those of the Papen plan. Thus the machinery already existed—Hitler's contribution was to use it on a much larger scale. [2]

A few figures will give an idea of the scale of this public works policy. The 1932 programmes (567 million Rm.) were followed by two programmes in 1933, one for 500 millions, the other for 1,000 millions, as well as 1,400 millions for the building of motor roads. In 1936 the programme of public works carried out since 1932 was valued at 7.5 milliards of Rm. The programme was close upon completion, when wholesale rearmament became the main factor in the expansion of production.

As regards the means of financing, the following indications will suffice: between 1932 and 1936 the internal debt—not including work bills—increased by about 5,000 million Rm.: it rose from 8,922 millions to 14,026 millions.

The circulation of Reichsbank notes rose from 3,560 million Rm. in 1932 to 4,980 million in 1936, to 8,225 million in 1938. In 1938 the Bank of Issue held about 5 or 6 thousand millions in work bills.

---

1. This was not exactly the theoretical construction that served to justify these operations. The theory used was that of 'pre-financing' (*Vorfinanzierung*): the state counts on the increase in business resulting from public works to swell the revenue from taxation in years to come. The bonds issued—of which some took the significant form of taxation bonds—may then be repaid, or used and cancelled. We may remark, however, that the indirect effects of public works had been pointed out by German writers. In an article on 'Fighting Unemployment by Big Public Works', Dr. Hans Syrup wrote: 'It is needless to emphasize that the indirect effect of public works does not stop at the industries supplying material; by increasing the purchasing power of the workers it employs, it also stimulates industries supplying consumer goods. The carrying out of public works means an increase in the total income of workers and entrepreneurs, by reason of the increase both in the number of wage earners and in individual incomes. But the wages of labour constitute by far the largest part of the national income.' (*Revue d'Economie Politique*, 1934, p. 1457.)
2. Incidentally the tax certificates had little effect; entrepreneurs, who had no confidence in the future, made almost no use of them.

THE RESULTS

What were the results of this policy?   According to the classical theory, it should have set prices rising, since there was an uncompensated increase in demand and an increased quantity of money in circulation.   Actually prices did not rise as much as this theory would lead one to predict.

The index of wholesale prices (basis 1913-14 = 100) was: 1932, 96; 1933, 93; 1934, 98; 1935, 102; 1936, 104; 1937, 106; 1938, 106.

This relative stability of prices cannot be explained solely by the controls, though these were not without effect.   In the last analysis, it was the expansion of production that prevented violent rises.   The increase in demand meant work for the unemployed, an increase in output, and an increase in revenue from taxation made possible by this revival of business (see Table 15).

TABLE 15.

Year	Number of unemployed	Index of industrial production	Revenue from taxation (in millions of Rm.)
1932	5 575 000	53.3	(1931-32) 6 812
1933	4 804 000	60.7	(1932-33) 5 821
1934	2 718 000	79.8	(1933-34) 5 932
1935	2 151 000	94.0	(1934-35) 6 766
1936	1 592 000	106.3	
1937	1 233 000	117.2	
1938	673 000	126.0	

1. Basis 1929 = 100.

It may therefore be said that the German experiment associated with the name of Dr. Schacht was an application of the analysis underlying the theory of employment and that it confirmed the potential efficacy of one of the remedies proposed, the recourse to public investment.

THE NEW DEAL

It was in the United States that the world crisis broke out, with the Wall Street crash on 24 October 1929 and it was in the United States too that the crisis was most severe. Industrial production was halved: the index dropped from 100 in 1929 to 81 in 1930, to 68 in 1931, to 54 in 1932. The index of wholesale prices dropped from 100 in 1929 to 90.7 in 1930, to 76.6 in 1931, to 68 in 1932. Unemployment on a vast scale made its appearance: 3,809,000 unemployed in 1930, 8,113,000 in 1931, 12,478,000 in 1932, [1] that is 25 per cent of the working population. The generality of the phenomenon is not surprising. It bears out the theory according to which communities that are the richest and in which wealth is most concentrated are more liable than others to experience unemployment and idle plant.

THE HOOVER POLICY

The attitude of the government in power, President Hoover's, in this situation was in accordance with the teachings of classical theory. The crisis would be of short duration, it had only to be denied, as J.-B. Say had denied the very possibility of over-production, and the return of prosperity proclaimed. [2] There was no reason for the state to deviate from its policy of non-intervention; the natural mechanisms would restore activity. For the same reasons, it should refrain from paying doles to the unemployed. For a long time President Hoover maintained that the federal government should refuse to contribute to this expense. In his message of 8 December 1931 he upheld that the true American tradition was to help the unemployed by appeals to public generosity and by the action of local communities. This was the lesson of liberalism, reinforced by neo-liberalism. At most, the government might mitigate certain effects of the depression, in order to minimize price fluctuations and avert unnecessary insolvencies. It was no use descending to the trough of the curve, since prices would rise of themselves. Hence the following measures: a policy of easy credit, at a low rate of interest: the prospect of falls in prices was such that, even on these terms, businessmen did not consider it paid them to borrow. To limit the collapse of farm prices, the Farm Board made loans to co-operatives to enable farmers to stock part of their crops and only sell under more favourable conditions. As prices continued to fall, the Farm Board eventually became the owner of huge stocks which it had in the end to sell at a loss or give away.

---

1. The figures quoted here and further on are taken from the Conference Economic Board of 20 May 1940.
2. 'Prosperity is round the corner' was the familiar slogan.

At last to counteract the panic that seized depositors, the government set up a Reconstruction Finance Corporation, which advanced $1,800 million in a year to banks and railway companies. Here again the failure was manifest. Limited to relief on a small scale, included under a general policy of non-intervention, President Hoover's few measures did not prevent the crisis from worsening. The publication, at the end of 1932, of the names of banks that had received loans from the RFC sowed fresh distrust in depositors, and caused a number of bank insolvencies. In several states, a moratorium was proclaimed. In February and March 1933 the movement spread. When Roosevelt came into power, on 4 March 1933, the banks were closed in 32 states, and one of his first acts was, on 6 March, to suspend bank operations throughout the country and put an embargo on gold. The number of unemployed at that time had risen to 14 millions.

SCIENTIFIC BASIS OF THE NEW DEAL

Roosevelt had of course to find a different theoretical basis from the classical one, whose results, or what appeared as such, were only too obvious. There were several currents of thought in the air. Some economists, following Irving Fisher, were stressing the disadvantages of price instability, and particularly the low level of prices, which have the effect of increasing individual and business indebtedness. [1] Several of them—Moley, Tugwell, Berle and Warren—met in the new President's 'brains trust'.

Others had recognized the importance of the different forms of under-consumption, discovered back in the nineteenth century and developed later in the 'theory of employment'. This attitude was partly in keeping with the American concept of high wages put forward by Ford, according to which a business must not consider wage rises purely from the point of view of cost price, but also as a means of expanding markets. Others again had been struck by the considerable increase in the means of production, in the output of each worker. They drew the conclusion that enough could be produced with shorter working hours.

On the same observation—the huge increase in equipment—was based another idea that investment was excessive because it had been made without consideration for possible markets and without any

---

1. But these writers do not seem to have stressed the effect of a drop in prices on the propensity to invest as much as the 'general theory of employment' does.

overall plan.   There were two ideas here: the desirability of a managed economy which would eliminate duplication and wastage; and the necessity for reducing excessive production and plant in general. Some of these ideas had been adopted or ventilated by a group of men who had joined forces in about 1920 under the name of the Technical Alliance and dispersed some years later.   In 1931 they came together again and called themselves 'technocrats'. [1]

THE DUAL TENDENCY OF THE NEW DEAL

If one looks for the guiding principle behind these ideas, traces of which are to be found in Roosevelt's speeches before he came to power, two main tendencies may be discerned.   The first was concerned with over-production and consequently aimed at reducing, restricting and controlling output.   The second emphasized the inadequacy of the demand. due to under-consumption, and also, it would appear, under-investment in certain directions.   The measures adopted by President Roosevelt, which together constitute what is known as the New Deal, can also be divided into two main classes: measures aimed at restricting production, and those aimed at increasing consumption and investment. [2]   The former were mainly a matter of economic and social regulation, the latter of financial technique.

MEASURES TO RESTRICT PRODUCTION

Restrictive measures may be looked on as a means of adjusting production to a reduced consumption.   In this sense, they may be said to contradict every economic analysis according to which a surplus aggregate production really means a deficiency in consumption, which could be greater if all normal needs were met.   Not that certain re-

---

1. The originator of these views was Veblen, an economist who died in 1929. It was Howard Scott who rallied Veblen's followers and called their common fund of ideas 'technocracy'.   For this trend in American economic thought, see G. Pirou, *Les Nouveaux Courants de la Pensée Économique aux États-Unis.*
2. In January 1936 the President recalled the main items of his 1933 programme: 'The national policy which we then adopted sought to stop the downward economic spiral by taking simultaneous action along a dozen fronts.   The chief objectives were: to make bank deposits secure, to save farms and homes from foreclosure, to start public works on a large scale, to encourage home building, to increase farm crop values, to give useful work instead of a dole to the needv unemployed, to reduce all interest rates, to increase foreign trade in both exports and imports, to extend government credit to railroads and other privately owned activities, to reduce unsound and generally disastrous speculation, to eliminate starvation wages, to seek a higher level of values and then to maintain those values.'

strictions—and especially shorter working hours for wage earners—cannot be regarded as legitimate progress, as the natural application of the considerable technical advances made so rapidly in the years preceding the crisis. But these come under a policy of permanent reform, conceivable both in times of prosperity and in times of depression. It is one thing to reduce working hours because it is thought that scientific advances will allow this to be done without compromising the standard of living of the community, and because this in itself is a sign of social progress; it is quite another to do so because there is unemployment, and no other remedy for it can be found. In the latter case, it could not prima facie be said that this limitation, like any measure of restricting production, was an application of the analyses of the 'theory of employment'.

But the question is not so simple as that. The limitation of production may be regarded as a means of increasing aggregate demand, on the following grounds. A diminished output naturally results in a rise in prices, which more than compensates the loss in takings due to the diminution in sales. This is well known to monopolists, who tend to restrict production in order to increase profits. The restriction of production can therefore be consonant with an increase in the relevant producers' income. Now, it is possible that these producers are less wealthy than their customers. In this case, the operation has the effect of transferring income from one class to another, that is, increasing the purchasing power of a social class whose desire to consume is strongest. The limitation of production thus entails a sort of levelling down of incomes, which brings about increased consumption.

This was one of the purposes of the agricultural policy. Even before 1929, the improvement in agricultural techniques, achieved after the first world war, together with the recovery of agriculture in the devastated countries, had resulted in a relative fall in agricultural prices. They collapsed altogether after 1929: in 1931 the index of wholesale prices in general in the United States had fallen to 61.5, while agricultural prices had fallen to 45.7. This meant a considerable loss in the purchasing power of farmers. It was calculated that in February 1953 farmers could only buy 50 per cent of what they bought in 1914. The Agricultural Adjustment Act tried to remedy this situation by levying taxes on certain important agricultural commodities—wheat, cotton, maize, etc. These taxes, which were intended to be borne by the consumer, made it possible to grant subsidies to farmers who agreed to limit their output. Any farmer wishing to receive this subsidy had to give an undertaking to the state that he would leave a certain part of his land uncultivated and not increase the fertilizers used on his cultivated land. The effect of these measures was a reduction of the area under cultivation and, on account of several years of drought, which added their effects to that of the government policy, a considerable drop in production (see Table 16).

TABLE 16. Evolution of production (in millions of quintals).

	1931-32	*1932-33*	*1933-34*	*1934-35*	*1935-36*
Wheat	273 000	202 000	143 000	135 000	164 000
Cotton	37 000	28 000	28 000	20 000	23 000
Maize	657 000	738 000	597 000	349 000	559 000

Between 1933 and 1935 agricultural prices almost doubled, going from 51.4 to 80.9, whereas other prices only rose moderately, from 71.2 to 79.6. Hence a considerable boost was given to agricultural incomes. According to Mr. Wallace, they had dropped by $6.5 milliards between 1929 and 1932, and increased by 5 milliards between 1932 and 1937. [1]

We may observe from the start that this revaluation of agricultural incomes was attended by an expansion of industrial markets. It was just when agricultural price indexes had almost reached the indexes of other goods, in 1935, that industrial production began definitely to increase. This may be a coincidence, but it is worth noting.

As regards industry, the National Industry Recovery Act (NIRA) of 15 June 1933 prescribed the establishment for each industry of a code regulating the conditions of competition, the methods of fixing prices, and the organization of work. The codes were to be drawn up by the industries themselves, under government control. In their absence, the President could lay down certain rules. In all some 546 codes were drawn up. [2] In this field the aim was twofold. Industry was to be allowed to make profits again by encouraging what had been prohibited by the anti-trust law, that is, agreements intended to limit competition. On the other hand, wages were to be raised and working hours reduced. [3] In this way profits were to serve to increase the purchasing power of the working class, the consuming class par

---

1. Other economists have given different figures. There was in any event a considerable increase.
2. They were preceded by a provisional code submitted to the parties concerned for approval. The latter undertook to limit working hours (40 hours or 35 hours according to the branch), to accept a minimum wage, and not to increase their selling prices more than was necessitated by increased costs of production. Those who had signed were authorized to use the Blue Eagle brand mark.
3. Employers had also to recognize the workers' right to form unions.

excellence. In this sense, the policy of codes could be regarded as a policy aimed at increasing purchasing power. Incidentally, in 1935 and 1936 the main provisions of the NIRA were declared contrary to the Constitution by the Supreme Court of the United States of America.

MEASURES TO INCREASE DEMAND

The other measures were aimed more directly at increasing demand, consumption and investment. Those intended to influence consumption included, as we have seen, the 'egalitarian' tax. In this connexion, we should mention the act of 30 August 1935, which increased the scale of income tax—up to 75 per cent for income in excess of $5 million—and of death duties, for which the rate was increased to 70 per cent above $50 million. The opposition called this programme a 'share the wealth program'. The revenue act of 28 June 1936 employed another method to increase consumption: this was to levy a supplementary tax on undistributed company profits. Such profits are really a form of collective saving; if a company accumulates profits that it could distribute as dividends, it restricts the incomes, and therefore the expenditure, of its shareholders. This tax is an example of the application of the conclusions of economic analysis regarding underconsumption and its causes.

Other measures—those directed towards raising prices—may be regarded as having as one of their objects to influence consumption by reducing the burden of those who consume the greatest part of their resources, debtors. But they were also directed at increasing production and investment.

INFLUENCING INVESTMENT

The New Deal, like the 'theory of employment', attached much importance to encouraging private investment by monetary action. The Roosevelt policy tried to influence two factors that govern the decisions of entrepreneurs: prospective prices, on the one hand, and the rate of interest and credit facilities generally, on the other.

INFLUENCE ON PRICES

The abandonment of the gold standard and the devaluation of the dollar differ from suspending convertibility of the pound in that these steps were not taken under the direct and immediate pressure of exports of gold or capital. When, on 5 March 1933, the President declared an embargo on gold, the dollar weakened and then automatically caught up to par again. When, therefore, on 19 April, he declared officially that the United States of America was abandoning the gold standard, it was a considered decision. Following this announcement, the dollar began to fall, to 18, 17, then 16 francs, due to an export of capital—which, unlike that in other countries, was welcomed by the government, because it was calculated to bring about the drop in the dollar that was desired. But when the dollar reached 16 French francs, capital began to flow back again. To avert or limit this movement, the President then resolved to announce each day the rate at which gold would be bought by the government. Finally, in January 1934, the government decided to stabilize the dollar provisionally at 59 cents, which corresponded to a devaluation of about 40 per cent. [1] This was certainly and typically a calculated decision. The motives were mixed. The desire to increase exports was obviously one of them—and here the devaluation of the dollar was in a way a reaction to the devaluation of the pound. But it would appear that the determining cause was the desire to raise home prices. To increase prices, or rather to create an expectancy of a rise in prices, was to eliminate the anticipation of a fall, which was the cause of the halt in investment, and to influence the prospective yield of investment.

The rise in prices was also intended to reduce indebtedness by diminishing the purchasing power of debts. This objective seems to have been particularly sought after. The author of the amendment to the Farm Relief Currency and Inflation Act, which made possible the depreciation of the dollar, called it the 'most important financial measure in the history of the world; it transferred $200 thousand million from the creditor class to the debtor class'; apart from the social advantages that might accrue, the diminution of creditors' incomes in favour of debtors' could be regarded as a kind of transfer of wealth from the rich to the poor—that is, to those who consumed proportionally more. In this sense, the reduction of indebtedness was a means of stimulating consumption.

What was this method worth as a means of setting off a rise in prices? It has been said that the level of home prices is not directly affected by the gold parity of the currency. But, apart from its action on import prices with repercussions on home prices, apart from the

---

1. By the Farm Relief Currency and Inflation Act of 12 May 1933, the President had been authorized to reduce to one-half the quantity of gold corresponding to a dollar.

purchases of gold it made possible, devaluation signified a determination to raise prices, which in itself was an inducement to entrepreneurs to speculate in the same direction.

In fact wholesale prices went up considerably: 1932, 68; 1933, 69; 1934, 79; 1935, 84; 1936, 85.

INFLUENCE ON THE RATE OF INTEREST

But it was necessary to influence the other term of the ratio that can induce the businessman to invest, the rate of interest. The policy of credit expansion implied an increase in the quantity of money in circulation. The first condition was to restore depositors' confidence in the banks. A bill adopted in the early days of the new presidency enabled the government to classify banks in three categories: those which would reopen their doors immediately; those which would do so only after some form of reorganization, including an increase in capital subscribed by the Reconstruction Finance Corporation; those which would go into liquidation. Later laws enacted a general reform of bank organization (minimum capital, veto on taking certain shares, increased controlling power of the Federal Reserve Banks, etc.).

Within this framework, the increase in money circulation resulted in part from the purchases of government bonds on the free market by the Federal Reserve Banks and ordinary banks. These purchases were a continuation of those that had been made between 1929 and 1932; they were, moreover, in accordance with American practice, where the open market had been known for years. [1] The largest purchases, those by the Reserve Banks, had been made between 1929 and 1932 ($1,800 million). [2] Later on, and up to 1937, these purchases were relatively small. Other banks, however, made relatively large purchases of government bonds.

If Federal bank purchases stopped in 1934, it was because of the gold imports, [3] a consequence of the devaluation of the dollar, which had lead people in countries whose currency had not been brought

---

1. The 1913 law, which set up the Federal Reserve Banks entrusted with the issue of fiduciary money authorized them to buy and sell government bonds. As from 1932, these operations were used systematically to regulate and control credit.
2. However, at certain times these purchases were not as large as they would have needed to be to halt deflation and the spread of the depression. On the other hand, a law of 27 February 1932, the Glass-Steagall law, added to the possibilities of purchase on the free market.
3. From 30 June 1933 to 31 December 1935 the stock of gold currency in the affiliated banks increased by $6,094 million.

into line [1] and in which depreciation was a probability to look to the dollar as a currency of refuge. This import of gold served as a backing for the monetary expansion of the reserve banks.

The effects of this policy may be seen in Table 17, which shows the movement of the different kinds of interest rate.

TABLE 17. [1]

Year	Discount rate of the FRB New York	Treasury bonds	Treasury debentures	Bank advances in 27 cities in the south and west
	%	%	%	%
1929	5.16	3.25	3.60	6.14
1930	3.04	2.49	3.28	5.72
1931	2.12	1.49	3.31	5.39
1932	2.81	0.90	3.66	5.62
1933	2.56	0.52	3.31	5.56
1934	1.55	0.30	3.10	5.17
1935	1.50	0.15	2.70	4.69
1936	1.50	0.15	2.47	4.35
1937	1.33	—	—	—

1. League of Nations, *Monetary Review*, 1936-37 (p. 157 of French text).

PUBLIC INVESTMENT AND THE BUDGET DEFICIT

Along with monetary action directed at private investment, the Roosevelt policy gave a very large place to public investment financed by loan, and consequently entailing a budget deficit. A preliminary remark should be made here. It has often been said that, on the contrary, the President's budget policy began with economies, with budgetary deflation. It is possible that his ideas evolved during 1933 and that the opinions of some of his advisers obtained precedence over those of others. Nevertheless, it is hard to be sure, not is there necessarily such incompatibility between the policy pursued at the beginning and that pursued later.

One of the results of the crisis had been to create a deficit; the 1930-31 budget closed with a deficit of $462 million, the 1931-32 budget with a deficit of $2,472 million. This deficit was one of the causes of the panic that developed at the end of 1932 and the beginning of

1. Of the $1,739 million worth of gold imported in 1935, more than two-thirds came directly from France and the Netherlands, which had retained the monetary parity they had before the crisis.

1933. Americans viewed it as a symptom of disorder, of the collapse of institutions. Paradoxically perhaps, the budget deficit contributed to a tightening up of activity. The expression of a determination to set public finances in order can be a way of restoring public confidence.

In addition, the very idea of influencing aggregate demand by public investment leads to a distinction between the ordinary budget—the budget of current state expenses, which gains by being balanced—since otherwise when normal activity was resumed one would be faced with a deficit that would be hard to make up—and the extraordinary budget. Expenditure on public works is easy to restrict or cut out fairly quickly once the situation has come back to normal and inflation had to be averted.

Moreover, in so far as the government, to carry out these works, relied on loans—perhaps because it had not realized the similarity between loans and currency issues, or because it feared that the public would not understand[1]—it felt bound to give some proof of its financial wisdom by effecting certain economies. However this may be, under the Economy Act of 20 March 1933, the President reduced civil servants' salaries, ex-servicemen's pensions and various subsidies. Later on, most of these measures were revoked. In any case, from the first half of 1933, exceptional expenditure for the purpose of combating the crisis was provided for: the National Recovery Act of 16 June 1933 opened a credit of $3,300 million for the carrying out of public works.

Table 18 giving the total of revenue and expenditure for the years 1933 to 1938 shows the size of the budget deficit.[2]

TABLE 18.

Year	Total expenditure	Revenue	Deficit
1933	4 681	2 079	2 601
1934	6 745	3 115	3 630
1935	6 802	3 800	3 002
1936	8 476	4 116	4 360
1937	8 001	5 294	2 707
1938	7 324 [1]	6 906	418

1. Anticipated expenditure.

1. On this point, cf. Chapter VIII, Part I.
2. cf. F.-L. Closon, *La Politique Financière du Président Roosevelt,* Paris, 1937. The ways in which crisis expenditure was distributed, and the works carried out were diverse, and changed as time went on. A detailed analysis did not seem indispensable to this study.

The government obtained the necessary resources by loans, made possible by monetary expansion based on purchases of government bonds by the banks of issue and the deposit banks or on gold imports (see above).

RESULTS OF THE NEW DEAL

Table 19 shows the results of the New Deal in two columns: the movement of industrial output and the unemployment figure.

TABLE 19.

Year	Index of industrial production	Number of unemployed [1]
1929	100	429 000
1930	81	3 809 000
1931	68	8 113 000
1932	54	12 478 000
1933	64	12 744 000
1934	66	10 400 000
1935	76	9 522 000
1936	88	7 599 000
1937	92	6 372 000
1938	—	10 099 000

1. Conference Economic Board, 20 May 1940.

Going into more detail, several phases must be distinguished. Recovery was fairly rapid between April and July 1933. The index rose from 54 in March to 81 in June. But it fell back in the second half of the year, and towards the end of the year was down to 67-68. Production remained stationary in 1934. It picked up between the middle of 1935 and the beginning of 1937 (December 1935, 93; December 1936, 109; May 1937, 107), only to cede once more at the end of 1937 and in 1938.

Several questions, therefore, suggest themselves:

What was the cause of the indubitable recovery of industrial production between 1933 and 1937? It is hard to say what part restriction of production played in this. We have noticed that the application of the NIRA—enacted in June 1933—coincided with a recession; and that the periods of wage rises—nominal or real—did not correspond with increase in output as will be seen in Table 20. [1] Conservely, the increase in agricultural incomes, due in very large part to the drought, coincided with industrial recovery. It would take us beyond the limits of this study to discuss these matters in detail.

TABLE 20.

Year	Wages per hour [1]		Index of industrial production
	Nominal	*Real*	
1932	84	108	58
1933	83	111	70
1934	99	124	72
1935	102	123	81
1936	105	123	95
1937 (March)	112	127	—

1. Basis 1929 = 100.

Undoubtedly, two kinds of measures exerted an influence on economic recovery: on the one hand, devaluation, which replaced expectation of a continual fall in prices by the expectation of a rise; on the other hand, the policy of public works financed without recourse to taxation, which substantially increased demand.

But a second question arises. Why was recovery not more rapid and more complete? In 1935 the index of industrial production was only 76, while the number of unemployed still stood at 9.5 million. In this context we may note the slow progress of private investment, which did not keep pace with public investment. This is evidenced in the small volume of company issues compared with federal, local government and Treasury issues (see Table 21).

In 1936 a report by the Economic Intelligence Service of the League of Nations pointed out the relative inadequacy of the results obtained and explained it as follows:

'The indirect effects of the bringing of this new money into circulation were limited by two facts. First, a considerable part—it is impossible to say how much—of the money was used by its recipients to repay debts to the banks, loans on insurance policies, etc. . . . Second, since budget deficits and certain other parts of the government's economic programme had shaken the confidence of business

---

1. The increase in wages was particularly marked from 1933 to 1934, whereas production was at a standstill—almost the converse of the situation obtaining from 1934 to 1936.

TABLE 21. Issues of companies, federal and local government, and Treasury (in millions of dollars).

Year	Net issues		Treasury issues [1]
	Companies	Federal and local governments	
1929	8 002	1 417	—
1930	4 483	1 520	—
1931	1 550	1 309	—
1932	325	839	3 074
1933	160	547	3 022
1934	178	1 208	4 759
1935	403	1 005	3 484
1936	1 193	767.9	3 452

1. Figures as from 1932.

circles. there was a tendency for industrialists and traders not to reinvest at once the fresh money coming into their hands as the result of loans and government expenditure, but to use it for the repayment of bank advances or to increase their bank deposits. Loans to their customers by the affiliated banks fell steadily between the middle of 1933 and the middle of 1935—from 11,337 to 10,369 million dollars.' (Translated by Unesco from the original French.)

We may therefore wonder whether, in view of the potential wealth of America and its economic structure, state investment, large as it was, should not have been larger still.

Finally, we might seek the causes of the recession at the end of 1937 and 1938. We shall leave this problem aside, observing only that in 1937 the fear of a speculative rise led to deflationary countermeasures which caused a depression. But this was of short duration because of the war.

SWEDEN

Swedish policy resembles British in that the improvement in the economic situation was largely due to devaluation and its influence on exports, to monetary expansion and the drop in the rate of interest —combined with a slight rise in prices—after 1933. It differs from it in that monetary circulation increased mainly because the bank of issue and the deposit banks bought gold and foreign exchange owing to the improvement in Sweden's balance of payments. [1]

Sweden had been forced to abandon the gold standard in 1931; until 1933 its policy was on the whole one of deflation: reduction in public expenditure, reduction in wages. Nevertheless, devaluation was reflected in an increase in exports, especially after 1933.

TABLE 22.

Year	Exports [1]	Imports [1]	Credit + or deficit — balance [1]
1929	1 812	1 782	+ 30
1930	1 550	1 662	− 112
1931	1 122	1 428	− 306
1932	947	1 155	− 208
1933	1 079	1 096	− 17
1934	1 302	1 305	− 3
1935	1 297	1 476	− 179
1936	1 514	1 633	− 119
1937	1 994	2 111	− 117

1. In millions of crowns.

As soon as the Swedish krone was devalued, the Swedish government set about to maintain the stability of prices. Its first endeavour was to assure the public that there would be no considerable or rapid rise in prices. But when, in the spring of 1932, world prices continued to fall and a similar tendency became apparent in Sweden's home prices, monetary policy was deliberately diverted towards securing a certain rise in wholesale prices. Actually wholesale prices moved as follows (basis 100 in 1913-14): 1929, 140; 1930, 122; 1931, 111; 1932, 109; 1933, 107; 1934, 114; 1935, 116; 1936, 120; 1937, 137.

1. Movement of the balance of payments: 1931, — 127; 1932, + 89; 1933, +212; 1934, + 206.

These results were obtained by the purchase of foreign currencies, which prevented the exchange from rising and Swedish currency from appreciating, that is, avoided a fall in the prices of imported goods. These entries of gold and foreign exchange were reflected in an increase in monetary circulation:

TABLE 23.   Monetary circulation (in millions of crowns).

Year	Notes in circulation	Current accounts and short notice deposits at commercial banks
1931	583	610
1935	786	766
1936	893	892

The abundance of money had the effect of lowering the long-term and short-term rates of interest.

TABLE 24.

Year	Discount rate of the Central bank	Yield of the 7 government annuities
1929	4.74	4.56
1930	3.72	4.18
1931	4.09	4.22
1932	4.39	4.32
1933	3.17	4.02
1934	3.50	3.47
1935	2.50	3.19
1936	2.50	3.12

Unlike Great Britain, Sweden supplemented this action on currency and interest by a policy of public works financed by loan.   Until 1933, public works were essentially designed to provide direct relief to a certain number of unemployed.   After July 1933, the policy of public works was aimed less at this direct effect than at the indirect effect of developing consumption and investment in all sectors of the economy. In 1934 public works were considerably extended.   They were still on a large scale in 1935.   They were financed by loans, raised more easily on account of monetary expansion and the low rate of interest.

On this occasion, the Swedish government pronounced clearly in favour of the cyclical budget.

The results are expressed in the following few figures:

TABLE 25.

Year	Index of industrial production	Building industry	Number of unemployed	Percentage
1929	100	100	32 621	10.7
1930	102	128	42 016	12.2
1931	96	130	64 815	17.2
1932	89	119	90 677	22.8
1933	91	96	97 316	23.7
1934	110	120	84 685	18.9
1935	123	180	81 385	16.1
1936	135	208	71 884	13.6
1937	149		67 351	11.6

By 1936, Sweden's economic situation had definitely improved—although the number of unemployed was still relatively high. In preparation for the eventuality of another depression, the government set up a commission to examine the question of public works. The commission recommended a five-year plan, distinguishing between work that should be carried out immediately and work that might be undertaken when the employment situation demanded it. This second instalment was made ready so that it could be put into operation straight away if a slump came.

The Swedish government, therefore, tried to give practical effect to the conclusions of economic analysis, both by its idea of the cyclical budget and by this 'reserve' of public works.

CHAPTER VIII

SCIENTIFIC ADVANCES
AND THE
FIGHT AGAINST INFLATION

Inflation is a form of disequilibrium: it shows itself in a rise in prices, not the rise that might result from a change in the relation of supply and demand in regard to a particular product, but a general, continuous rise which there is no hope of stopping, sometimes a rise so rapid that it may lead to the disappearance of the currency. This is a typical form of disequilibrium and is the opposite of the continuous fall in prices that attends depression and under-employment. The effects of inflation are so familiar that they are often underestimated. All who depend on fixed incomes are ruined, whereas people who hold real values see their incomes increase. The fate of the wage earner worsens, stocking and speculation are encouraged, and saving made difficult. If inflation continues, normal trading becomes impossible because nobody is prepared to part with 'stable' values, even for a short time, in return for a currency which is rapidly depreciating. This is the well-known phenomenon of 'flight from currency'.

The political and social consequences of inflation, though less familiar, are equally serious. The destruction or impoverishment of the soundest elements in the population plays into the hands of would-be dictators. Inflation has very often been followed by phenomena of this kind: Napoleon took advantage of the demoralization that followed the collapse of the assignats; most of the countries of Central Europe were the scene of similar movements after the monetary disorders that accompanied and followed the first world war; the only one that escaped, Czechoslovakia, was the country that fought inflation most effectively. Hitler made recruits amongst the victims of inflation as well as amongst those of deflation.

At certain times and with certain peoples, therefore, inflation appears as a particularly dangerous disorder. Yet the nature of the phenomenon and its causes have remained relatively little known, and remedial action has suffered greatly from this failure of diagnosis. The question has been further obscured by a whole group of pseudo-scientific theories on the nature of money and the relation between money and prices. These ideas were current at the time of the first world war and it needed much advance in knowledge to discredit them. The first stage was reached with a truer perception of the nature and, one might say, the definition of money; further knowledge clarified the nature and causes of inflationary pressure by linking it first with variations in income, then with variations in demand. This intellectual progress was accompanied by corresponding advances in the technique of combating inflation.

NATURE AND DEFINITION OF MONEY

For a long time economists were inclined to believe that there was only one kind of money, metallic currency—gold or silver. Later they came to admit that banknotes were also money—paper money or fiduciary money. Further investigation brought them to recognize yet another form of money, bank deposits. Every deposit may be used for the payment of purchases, for settling debts, either by cheque or by transfer, that is by written transactions, such deposits being given the name of 'representative' money. It is not enough to see in these a form of money; it has to be admitted that the deposit bank can create money, just as much as the bank of issue. There is a tendency not to recognize this, for it may seem that a deposit, by definition, is only the counterpart of sums deposited and that to add representative money to fiduciary money is a duplication. This is a mistaken idea. When a bank grants a loan to a private person, it opens an account which he uses by drawing cheques in favour of his suppliers. The suppliers' accounts are augmented—money is created. Hence the Anglo-Saxon saying: credits make deposits. To make this phenomenon clearer, let us take the case where the deposit precedes the loan. The bank lends B money deposited by A, and the sum is paid in cash. Money is thus created, since one and the same sum can be used by B—to whom it has been paid—and by A, who can draw cheques on his account. One of the first economists to describe these phenomena was an Englishman, Hartley Withers, who wrote a small book entitled *The Meaning of Money* (published 1909). Today this idea is generally accepted and it has great practical importance. In the first place it should enable us to avoid the errors of certain countries, which think they are reducing inflation simply by reducing the issue of fiduciary money without any regard for representative money. Among the most typical errors of this kind is one that France repeatedly made after the first world war. The French went so far as to look upon every procedure facilitating the use of representative money, and, consequently, avoiding an increase in fiduciary money, as a means of limiting inflationary pressure. [1] Experience proved that it was nothing of the kind: France did not escape a rise in prices. This mistake was all the more disastrous because it was allied with another of which more will be said later.

A second series of applications of a better knowledge of money is seen in the reform of banking systems carried out in most countries during the last 20 years. If the deposit bank creates money, there is no reason why it should escape the controls imposed on the banks of issue proper. This is a matter of public service, and the state, as guardian of the exchange system, even under a liberal régime, cannot stand aside. Just as the state was responsible for the minting of coins so as to guarantee their weight and fineness, and just as it supervises the issue of banknotes, it should also control the issue of representative money, that is, the functioning of deposit banks. This control can take various forms: the requirement of a minimum of liquidity, prohibition of certain uses of money deposited, capital, etc. Provisions of this kind were often taken after the 1929 crisis and the bank failures, or again to facilitate state control of credit. Nevertheless they rest basically on this identity of fiduciary money and representative money, an identity which has been generally recognized by economics for the last 30 or 40 years.

It is possible that this idea will come to be applied more widely and that banks of issue and deposit banks will be almost completely assimilated. Some countries, notably Argentina in 1946, have drawn this conclusion. The deposits, guaranteed by the state, cannot be used by the banks that receive them. The banks can only use the money they obtain by rediscounting their securities, that is, the capital put at their disposal by the Central Bank, which thus controls the total issue of money and can direct monetary policy. Provisions of this kind are the direct offspring of the principle, 'loans make deposits'.

---

1. One of the most significant examples is the series of measures passed by the French Government in 1924-25 to limit the number of notes in circulation and, as it thought, avoid inflation. These were: the setting up of a bank of issue in Madagascar, the withdrawal of French notes from the Saar, a campaign in favour of the extension of payments by cheque, the remanufacture of notes with a view to withdrawing from the balance those that had been lost or destroyed since 1885. None of these measures affected income or demand, except by a psychological repercussion founded on public ignorance. But there are few more characteristic examples of the influence of economic theory—in this case wrong—on economic practice.

However, mistakes made in the definition of money become really important only when they are accompanied by a mistake in regard to the relation between money and prices.

THE QUANTITY THEORY OF MONEY
AND ITS PRACTICAL CONSEQUENCES

The quantity theory of money had a very great influence on the monetary evolution of several countries after the first world war, with effects that have not yet been altogether effaced. It can be formulated as follows: variations in prices are proportional to variations in the quantity of money, the former being the consequence of the latter.

This relation may be expressed in a mathematical formula: $MV = PT$, [1] where M = the quantity of money, V = the speed at which money circulates, P = the general level of prices, T = the volume of transactions.

The formula expresses a self-evident fact. It is obvious that the volume of transactions effected, the whole business turnover of a country, corresponds to the mass of settlements effected, in other words, the volume of money multiplied by the average number of transactions for which each monetary unit is used. But the formula says no more. It does not say whether it is the volume of money that commands the price level—or vice versa. Now, the advocates of the quantity theory claim that it does. For them, the speed at which money circulates and the material volume of transactions are invariable. This is the first mistake. On the other hand—and this is the second mistake—the theory assumes that the causal element, the prime mover in the changes that affect the monetary situation, is the quantity of money. This theory was contested even before 1914, but criticism grew after the first world war. It was based both on observation and on logic.

On *observation*: in point of fact, no strict parallel has been found between variations in the quantity of money and variations in the price level; moreover, in many cases the second phenomenon—itself often caused by variations in the exchange—preceded the first. French economists, Aftalion and Nogaro in particular, collected many examples of these discrepancies. [2]

---

1. Or rather $MV + M'V' = PT$, M and V standing for fiduciary money, M' and V' representative money.
2. In a work entitled *Monnaie, prix et change*.

Logic explains why this is so. The price level depends on demand, assuming for the moment that supply is constant. Demand depends on income. On the whole, and with certain qualifications that will be gone into a little later, the person whose income is increasing spends more. This variation in income means more to him than any change in the amount of cash he has in hand.

This may be illustrated by a concrete example. Let us suppose that the state, or a company, reimburses an individual for a holding of securities. From one day to the next he has more money at his disposal, but, as his income has not changed, it is unlikely that he will make any great change in his way of living. Let us suppose, on the other hand, that this same person hears that his salary is being doubled; it is probable that he will not wait till the end of the month before ordering some article he has wanted for a long time or looking for a new flat, etc.

Thus, it is easy to see why an increase in the quantity of money in many cases seems to bring about a rise in prices. When the budget of the state shows a deficit and the state issues money to cover the deficit, it profits those with surplus nominal incomes—the state buys more goods and services. Normally, if there is full employment, this increased demand brings about a rise in prices. But what creates the rise, what increases nominal incomes, is not the issue of money but the budget deficit, expenditure not covered by taxation. When the state spends the revenue from taxation—when the budget is balanced—the state restricts aggregate demand, for it reduces taxpayers' incomes by the same amount by which it increases them through its expenditure. Speaking very approximately, the price level is unchanged. On the contrary, with a budget deficit, part of the public expenditure is not compensated by a reduction in private expenditure.

FIRST CONCLUSION: THE EFFECT OF LOANS

The conclusion which follows from this analysis is easy to see. Any budget deficit must have an inflationary effect, even if it is not financed by the issue of money—if, for example, it is met by the product of long-term or short-term loans. [1]

At the same time the effects of loans and the effects of the issue of money are not always or entirely identical. Without going into all

---

. But, of course, in a period of under-employment the effect of expenditure financed by loan is salutary, as would also be the effect of expenditure financed by the issue of money.

the differences, some of which are psychological, though not the less real, one in particular must be mentioned. By reducing the quantity of money, loans tend to raise the rate of interest—a rise which reduces the demand for investment goods and consequently aggregate demand and inflationary pressure. But this effect is not as strong as the effect of taxation, which also reduces the quantity of money and, above all, which reduces private incomes as well.

With many qualifications, which cannot be entered into in detail here, it may be said that a budget deficit is an element in inflation, even if it is covered by loan.

France's financial policy offers many examples of the importance of this idea. It was because they believed that there was no inflation when the deficit was financed by loan that French governments after the 1914-18 war repeatedly relaxed their efforts to balance the budget, increased public expenditure, and had but limited recourse to taxation. The facts show the consequences of this mistake: a depreciation of French currency—with all the resulting economic and social consequences—graver than was really inevitable, and more acute than in other countries. [1]

SECOND CONCLUSION: FEATURES OF THE FIGHT AGAINST INFLATION

The same mistake led to the belief that the policy of fighting inflation consists essentially in reducing the quantity of money, or rather, one mistake being added to the other, of reducing fiduciary money only. So, after, the first world war, governments thought that they could arrest the depreciation of the currency—and revalue it—by reimbursing the advances of the Banque de France, even if this reimbursement was effected with the help of loan capital in a time of budget deficit. . . . Similar mistakes could no doubt be quoted from other countries.

Conversely, when Britain, after the first world war, wanted to revalue its currency, it understood that it must have a budget surplus, that

1. Between 1919 and 1920 the index of retail prices rose from 291 to 386 The total amount of money scarcely changed (it moved from 64.6 thousand millions to 66.6 thousand millions) But the budget deficit covered by loan was considerable: in 1919 the state borrowed 32 thousand millions, in 1920, 42 thousand millions.

We may also quote the period following the Liberation: between September 1944 and December 1945, the index of retail prices rose from 290 to 497. During the same period, the fiduciary circulation decreased and the monetary mass only rose from 871 to 1,013 thousand millions. But, during 1945 alone, long-term and short-term loans totalled 231 thousand millions.

Other examples could be quoted. See the article, 'Les Erreurs Techniques et Idéologiques in *Le Franc, Mythe et Réalité*. (*La Nef*, June 1953.)

is, it must reduce private incomes. The facts proved that this reasoning was correct. Whether Britain was right or wrong to revalue its currency is another question. What interests us here is that the necessary means of achieving this end were used because exact scientific reasoning was applied.[1]

THIRD CONCLUSION: TREASURY PROBLEMS

Finally, to take again the French example, a belief in the quantity theory may have another consequence, namely the attaching of too much importance to those 'treasury problems' which have played a leading role in French politics over the last 40 years. If there is really no inflation when loans are placed, the good government is the one that makes a success of these operations, the bad government is the one that fails, even if its financial policy is sounder. Obsessed with treasury problems, politicans, and the public too, are inclined to ignore the real problems, and not to concern themselves with a discrepancy between supply and demand while there is still time to do something about it.[2]

FOURTH CONCLUSION: THE ECONOMIC FUNCTION OF TAXATION

Another conclusion can and has been drawn from this analysis. It modifies the function of taxation, which is no longer basically designed to procure money for the state, but to reduce incomes and, therefore, demand. This idea is beginning to be recognized, at least since the last war. Several characteristic declarations may be quoted. In his Budget Speech on 14 April 1942, the British Chancellor of the Exchequer said: 'From the figures I have given I deduce that I must raise new revenue, which, measured in terms of money, will produce something of the order of £150 million. I deliberately used the term "measured in terms of money" to emphasize that my objective is not

---

1. Mr. Charles Rist, in a book entitled *La Déflation en Pratique* (published 1923), showed that an overbalanced budget, and not a reduction of the quantity of money, was the condition of any anti-inflationary policy.

   In a memorandum addressed to the government, Sir Basil Blackett, a comptroller of the British Treasury, expressed the opinion that consolidation was hardly possible while the floating debt was not yet materially reduced by a budget surplus.

   On the subject of budget surpluses in Britain, see the section devoted above to Britain's return to the gold standard.

2. In the previously quoted article, an effort was made to show that the whole of French politics after 1918 were dominated by treasury problems born of a false conception of money and of inflation.

simply the raising of money to finance the war, or any particular percentage of its cost, important though that is. It is also a paramount
duty to use the weapon of taxation as an aid to the other methods of
reducing civilian consumption in all but the most essential direction.'

On 12 April 1943, Sir Kingsley Wood, to justify an increase in taxation, emphasized the 'essential aim' of taxation—'the reduction of the
considerable volume of additional purchasing power created by our
war expenditure'. One could quote similar statements made during
and after the war by the President of the United States of America.
This view of the economic function of taxation does not correspond
only to a theory, to a way of presenting financial policy; it leads to a
bigger fiscal effort than the opposite policy. But to link inflation
solely with variations in the total of nominal incomes would be too
summary a view. The advances made in economics have brought us
—or should bring us—closer to realities.

ANALYSIS OF AGGREGATE DEMAND
AND THE FIGHT AGAINST INFLATION

Demand depends on income, but it does not vary in like proportion.
Keynes, like his predecessors, showed that this was so when income
increased. But a similar discrepancy occurs when income diminishes.
The 'viscosity' of demand works in the direction of a fall just as much
as in that of a rise. It is simply another aspect of the same thing:
the relative stability of people's habits, and therefore of the level of
consumption. This may occasion surprise. That a person whose
income is increasing may not spend the whole of the increase is conceivable. But how can a person who spends the whole of his income
spend more? To explain this, we must have recourse to what may
appear rather farfetched reasoning, but it will be readily accepted by
those who have gone through periods of penury or observed the too
rapid abolition of rationing and controls. In such a case we are
inclined to think—according to the classical reasoning—that the rise
in prices will restore equilibrium and that, if the state does not increase
demand by a budget deficit, this rise, once it has occurred, will have
no reason to go further. A selection will take place among consumers;
the less wealthy will have to reduce their expenditure, but, in the
long run, a new equilibrium will be achieved. It is by this line of
thought that orthodox economists reason that penury alone will not

cause a lasting disequilibrium and that the abolition of rationing during such a period presents no real disadvantage.

This idea and the applications that have been made of it are based on an error. They ignore the fact that the poorer people may not resign themselves to this reduction in demand that the rise in prices seems to impose. They may offer a higher price by spending more during the first days of the week or the month than they could if they spread their income equally over the whole corresponding period. In other words, they 'anticipate their income'. [1] By doing so, they increase demand and cause a further rise in prices. No doubt, at the end of the week or month they have to reduce their expenditure to offset the excessive purchases of the beginning. But, by this time, the producers and middlemen, whose profits have increased, may take the place of the defaulting wage earners and maintain the rise in prices. At the beginning of the next period, the same phenomenon repeats itself, the rise is set off again, and so on. The argument does not allow us to say that there is a stage at which the wealthy begin to reduce their consumption. The purchasing power of the wage earner, of course, continually diminishes. But this decrease is such that demands for higher wages cannot eventually be refused and in this way prices rise again with renewed vigour.

What is true of consumer expenditure is true also of investment expenditure. In periods when prices are rising, when the need for investment goods is particularly great, after war damage for instance, or during a period of economic expansion, entrepreneurs may increase their demand for investment goods in much larger proportions than would be necessary to satisfy the community's propensity to save. They may invest by depleting their treasury or by borrowing, thus causing an increase in demand, bringing with it a continuous rise in prices. Naturally, the speculation caused by the rise and the prospective rise in prices have the same effect.

FIRST CONCLUSION: NATURE OF ANTI-INFLATIONARY ACTION

It is understandable therefore that in periods of penury, such as after the two world wars, it is not enough to balance the budget; inflationary pressure must be fought more vigorously, either by an overbalanced budget or by any other means likely to reduce demand. This is why

---

1. See G. Ardant's *Problèmes Financiers Contemporains*, in which the author has tried to present in more detail this theory of anticipated income, which he considers essential to an understanding of the phenomena of inflation and to the perfecting of anti-inflationary techniques.

after a war, which considerably reduces production, the stabilization of the currency presents great difficulties and requires a more energetic policy than is generally adopted. This is one reason why, after the first and second world wars, various countries met with so many difficulties when they tried to stabilize their currency, why some of them had to take up the task repeatedly, and why the depreciation of currency was so acute.

One understands too how, throughout the world, the prospect of rearmament in 1951 caused a fairly considerable rise in prices, how some countries limited this rise by using vigorous anti-inflationary measures—rationing and an over-balanced budget—how those that did not adopt this policy, such as France, suffered a relatively severe depreciation of their currency.

Thus, an analysis of aggregate demand leads, in the first place, to the admission that, under certain circumstances, anti-inflationary measures, and especially a bigger budget surplus than would have been envisaged if expenditure were proportional to income, are necessary.

Applications of this idea may be quoted from England and the United States of America. Let us take a few typical statements by Chancellors of the Exchequer. Sir Stafford Cripps, in his Budget Speech, on 6 April 1948, had this to say:

'Last year there was a large budget surplus, which was in fact rather more than sufficient to secure that the money collected by taxation with other government revenue defrayed all the government's expenditure of every kind, omitting, of course, the sinking fund. I do not advance any view that this is a test which ought necessarily to be applied year by year in judging the adequacy of a budget. In this present inflationary condition a different and more stringent test is required.

'In spite of this large surplus, inflationary pressure has not yet decreased to any marked extent. In view of the factors mentioned, which would tend to increase inflationary pressure this year, we have to secure an exceptionally large budget surplus, big enough to yield a balance after all forms of government expenditure have been met.'

The Chancellor of the Conservative government, Mr. Butler, recognized the same principles in his speech of 11 March 1952:

'The accounts then show another big surplus in prospect. The question is, should I increase it, reduce it, or leave it broadly as it is?

'The answer depends on a proper assessment of what taxation has got to do. Its job is not merely to balance the government's expenditure. It has a part to play in so regulating the purchasing power available to the community as a whole that this purchasing power does not outrun the amount of goods and services available. My previous conclusion was that, in order to achieve our objectives, no more than the same amount of resources as last year can be spared for the ordinary civilian consumer at home. The question now is whether I need take action by way of taxation to prevent consumers seeking to buy in the coming year more than they have done this year.'

Similar ideas were expressed by the President of the United States of America. Let us quote, for example, his budget message for the year 1951-52:

'Even a balanced budget will not of itself serve to keep our economy stable during a period of rapidly rising defence expenditures. The full amount of inflationary pressure is not measured by the budget deficit alone, since this reflects only payments actually made. The Department of Defence alone will have been granted for the fiscal years 1951 and 1952 an estimated $112 billion of obligational authority for its military functions, and additional amounts will have been made available for foreign military-aid programmes.

'Bidding for manpower and materials, which pushes prices upward, begins as soon as procurement contracts to be paid from these authorizations are signed, even though expenditures may not take place for a year or more. Other positive stabilization measures, including allocations, and credit, price and wage controls, are essential to offset the inflationary pressures which are not reflected in the single figure of the budget deficit.'

SECOND CONCLUSION: NEW METHODS OF FIGHTING INFLATION

Advances in analysis also led to the discovery of new methods of influencing demand, that is, anti-inflationary measures different from those that the traditional technique had put at the disposal of governments.

Rationing

One of these was rationing. By limiting everyone's right to a certain quantity of consumer goods, it is possible to avoid the outbidding that shortages cause, and consequently to maintain the price level, while seeing at the same time that distribution is relatively fair. By this means too, it is possible to combat the effects of an extra demand created by the state, which, for various reasons, cannot be compensated altogether by taxation. The same system can be applied to the demand for investment goods.

Rationing is not a new expedient. The belligerents availed themselves of it in some measure during the first world war. However, it was during the last war, during the preparation for it in some countries, and just after hostilities, that this policy of authoritarian distribution became most general. In the countries in which it was applied most strictly and methodically, Great Britain in particular, the desired results were on the whole obtained. The rise in prices was relatively moderate and the government was spared uncontrolled inflation. The social effects of this policy are well enough known for it to be unnecessary to go into them here. On the other hand, in countries which abolished rationing too soon or applied it very imperfectly, the rise in prices was much greater and was attended by undeniable social unrest. If this measure was applied thus systematically in certain countries, it was largely because progress made in economic analysis had led to a more exact appraisal of the role and nature of aggregate demand. It was not by chance that during the war it was the economists of the Keynes school who contributed to the perfecting of the rationing system.

Compulsory Saving

The same scientific advances led to the devising of another procedure which respects the freedom of the consumer more than the previous one—that is what is called compulsory saving. Instead of reducing incomes by taxation, the state can oblige people to place a part of their income in a blocked account. In this way their purchasing power is temporarily reduced without their having the impression of being deprived of the stimulus of higher wages or profits. Later on, when production has reverted to normal, the blocked sums can be put at the disposal of their owners without danger, since the inflationary pressure will have disappeared. This is even a means of combating the depression that might follow an increase in production, and this first observation already shows the link between this idea and the analyses of the 'theory of employment'.

This device has many variants, depending on whether it applies to dividends, wages, or to all income. In Germany, the first provisions aimed at limiting dividends were enacted on 29 March 1934. Others were made in 1937 and in 1941. In Italy the limiting of dividends goes back to 1935. The regulations established at that time were modified later, in 1936 and 1940 in particular. In France, the law of 28 February 1941 had the same purpose. In Britain, a similar Bill was introduced by the Chancellor of the Exchequer on 23 May 1940.

The following passage from the statement of reasons supporting the bill gives a good idea of the nature of the measure:

'The rate of excess profits tax is high, but it leaves some of the surplus in the hands of the businesses that earn it. It is a timely provision, because it is a reasonable encouragement to practise economy in business as well as to intensify output. I believe that these excess profits are useful so long as they are retained by the businesses in question, but lose much of their value if freely distributed in the form of dividends. They will be of great use if they remain available to sustain industries during the very difficult period of adjustment that will follow the war. They are much less valuable if used for further distributions to shareholders, who may be tempted to devote much of them to the purchase of consumer goods. I therefore propose to take steps to limit the amount of dividends distributed by public companies for the duration of the war.'

The bill was not passed; instead, the rate of taxation on excess profits was raised from 60 per cent to 100 per cent. This fact reveals the possibility of choosing between two techniques with an identical purpose—to reduce demand.

We could select other applications of the system of compulsory saving. In Britain, the 1941-42 budget allowed for a reduction in the lower level of exemptions, but the amount of extra taxation levied in this way was placed to the taxpayer's credit in the savings bank, to be reimbursed to him after the war. A similar provision was made for a fraction (20 per cent) of the excess profits tax, which had been raised to 100 per cent. In Italy, according to a 1942 law, certain surplus profits had to be placed in government bonds at 6 per cent, blocked for the duration of the war. Similar measures were taken in Germany. Other examples of compulsory loans could be quoted.

Certain loan procedures, though voluntary, resemble the compulsory loan. For instance, what were called 'iron savings' in Germany. Payments were made regularly by the employer, who deducted them from wages and sent them to the savings bank. The wage earners were notified that these sums could not be withdrawn until after the war and then at a year's notice. Interest was paid on these deposits. In addition, they were tax free. So the advantages of this form of saving were substantial. What proves that it is not a matter of providing money for the state, as in the classical theory of loans, but of reducing demand by encouraging those who consume the most— the wage earners—to save their money, is the fact that the sums saved in this way might not exceed 26 Rm. a month.

109

In the Union of Soviet Socialist Republics certain loans, voluntary in theory, seem to have had much in common with compulsory saving.

The promoter of compulsory saving in Great Britain was the author of the 'general theory', J. M. Keynes, who suggested it as a means of limiting inflation, and later on of combating depression, in a pamphlet entitled, *How to pay for the War*, published soon after the war began.

Monetary Exchange Operations and the Taxation of Wealth

The technique of blocking purchasing power found another application just after the second world war, in the form of monetary exchange operations, which constitute an innovation in the financial policy of this period. [1] People were obliged to bank all the notes in their possession, notes that were not banked ceased to be legal tender. A part of these sums was immediately exchanged for new notes, the rest was placed in a blocked account. This freezing reduced purchasing power without reducing income or wealth. By itself, then, it was much less effective than taxation; but it was more effective than a voluntary loan. The frozen money was to be restored to its owners [2] after production had returned to normal so that the money would no longer have any inflationary effect.

But this technique had another advantage which may be considered more important. It made it possible to check upon the quantity of money in people's possession. Combined with the stamping of bearer-bonds and a census of other forms of wealth, monetary exchange made it possible to tax capital or additional riches, which in itself reduced capital and consequently demand.

Those whose enhanced fortunes were acquired by particulary illicit means punished themselves by not banking their notes, which thus lost all value. Because this measure was considered to be severe on capitalists, it enabled the government to be also stricter with other social classes, to limit wage rises for instance, to reduce public expenditure, etc. In this way the operation was part of a general anti-inflationary policy. The procedure may be said to have constituted an application of the advances made by economic analysis, so far as it aimed at acting directly on demand and by establishing a relatively high rate of taxation, at meeting the recognized need for a vigorous

1. An operation of this kind had been carried out by Czechoslovakia after the first world war. It did not stop prices from rising, but it helped to save the Czech crown from suffering the fate of the currencies of the other countries that succeeded Austria-Hungary. The experiment was an isolated one.
2. Or be used to pay taxes, or to be converted in part into securities.

fight against inflation. Its detractors, most of them classical economists, were therefore wrong to see in it a fallacious application of a quantity theory in summary form. As a matter of fact its first European application, in Corsica after the liberation of the island in October 1943, was nothing less than a laboratory experiment, designed to work out a new technique. Later, it was applied in many countries: Belgium (October 1944), France, the Netherlands, Denmark, Norway, Czechoslovakia (1945), Germany (1948).

The Union of Soviet Socialist Republics carried out an even more drastic operation of this kind at the end of 1947. [1] The French experiment is an exception in that there was no freezing, and consequently the census of wealth and levies of tax were less effective. On the whole, when it was strictly applied, this method contributed appreciably towards reducing inflation and price rises.

CLASSIFICATION OF ANTI-INFLATIONARY MEASURES

Summing up, analysis established two parallel categories of anti-inflationary measures: direct control over demand, indirect control by financial action.

Up to a point, the first series of measures can be substituted for the second, and vice versa. For instance, as regards consumption, rationing makes it possible to limit the effort to reduce demand by taxation. Inflationary pressure is still there, but it is restrained by controls.

Conversely, the adoption of an austere financial policy, the raising of taxation, an overbalanced budget, make it possible to relax controls, even when shortages still exist. That is why in Belgium the monetary exchange operation and the whole financial policy were able to go hand in hand with the fairly rapid relinquishment of authoritarian measures of distribution. In the Union of Soviet Socialist Republics, too, the 1948 monetary exchange was carried out at the same time as rationing was abolished.

The alternation of direct and indirect measures exists too in regard to investment. The indirect measures consist of raising the rate of interest, which induces businesses to forgo the less remunerative investments. Direct measures consist of prohibiting certain investments without authorization, building in particular, or of distributing the

---

1. Metallic currency was changed at the rate of 1/10, savings deposits at 1/1 up to 3,000 roubles, 2/3 from 3,000 to 10,000 roubles, and 1/2 above 10,000 roubles. The monetary operation was accompanied by the abolition of rationing and a fall in certain prices.

necessary raw materials, such as cement and metallurgical products, in an authoritarian way.

Restriction of the volume of credit, or of stock exchange issues, a restriction which implies a selection amongst borrowers, constitutes an intermediate system. In the early post-war years, the different countries on the whole made little use of the procedure of reducing the demand for investment by raising the rate of interest.

This was so in Great Britain. Some people saw in it an application of Keynes' theory. It is scarcely necessary to point out where this interpretation went wrong. Keynes suggested lowering the rate of interest as a means of combating under-employment. This recommendation certainly did not imply that the rate of interest should be kept low in a country with full employment.

Let us add that, when inflationary pressure is particularly strong, it is necessary to employ the different categories of measures for restricting demand simultaneously, for each has its disadvantages and its limitations. Then, again, they have to be co-ordinated. The necessity for co-ordinated action, making use of both economic and financial measures, is one of the clearest conclusions of this whole analysis. We shall see how far it is possible to do this, with the aid of appropriate techniques.

CONCLUSION

To sum up, the scientific advances which were based in part on the analysis of disturbances resulting from inadequate demand were applied to disturbances originating in a demand that was excessive.

Three main series of practical conclusions may be drawn from this: the necessity for stronger anti-inflationary action than was thought necessary before; the existence of new methods of fighting inflation; the necessity for co-ordinating them in an overall policy.

The various countries have taken this more or less into account. On the whole, the fact that the rise in prices was less marked during this war than during the first may be attributed to the application of these conclusions. Whereas between 1914 and 1919 Britain, which of all countries had made the greatest effort in the matter of taxation, covered barely 25 per cent of its expenditure in this way, the percentage reached 43 from 1940 to 1943, and more than 49 in 1943.

Although less favourable, the proportion still reached 36 per cent in the United States of America. [1]

These countries, particularly Britain, adopted far more systematic methods of fighting inflation than they did during the first war, notably measures for fixing and controlling the prices of consumer and producer goods. As a result, prices rose much less.

Index of wholesale prices: United Kingdom, 116 in 1914, 280 in 1919, 338 in 1920, 129 in 1939, 219 in 1944, 224 in 1945; United States of America: 110 in 1914, 231 in 1919, 253 in 1920, 124 in 1939, 168 in 1944, 170 in 1945.

Other examples could be quoted. [2]

Conversely, a few countries which did not control prices as a whole experienced a much larger rise, comparable to the one that occurred during the 1914-18 war:

TABLE 26.

Year	Egypt	Palestine	Portugal	Turkey
1939 (Jan.-June)	100	100	100	100
1944	328	340	250	427
1945	—	347	242	431

This progress in the fight against inflation accounts in part for the world not having known after this war anything like the 1920-21 crisis. Inflationary pressure, more contained, was relaxed gradually, production's recuperative powers being thus absorbed. This shows clearly that the fight against inflation is one of the conditions of the fight against under-employment. It is by resistance to the excessive speculation of 'prosperous' times that the repression can be kept within limits.

After the war, the countries that had made good use of the new techniques limited inflation much more than the others. On this point it is possible to compare the movement of prices in Belgium, where a monetary exchange policy was strictly applied, in France, where it was applied less strictly and in Italy, where it was not applied at all.

The relative weakness of price control and rationing in France and Italy must also be taken into account.

---

1. cf. L. Pommery: *Aperçus d'Histoire Économique Contemporaine*, Médicis, Paris.
2. In its sixteenth report, the International Bank of Payments said that an examination of the current situation would show that a great many countries had managed by effective price controls to forestall a rapid rise in prices such as occurred between 1919 and 1920.

TABLE 27.   Index of wholesale prices.

Year	Belgium	Denmark	France	Italy	Norway
1935-36	100	—	—	—	—
1938	—	112	100	100	100
1944	—	217	265	—	176.6
1945	—	213	375	—	177,1
1946	331	210	648	2 985	169.0
1947	355	232	989	5 158	175.2

Whatever the country and the period, the new procedures, in the main supported by economists trained in the analysis of aggregate demand, may be said to have shown their superiority over the traditional methods—these latter, it must be admitted, were weakly applied—which had the backing of the classical economists. [1]

---

1. In this matter, the controversy around the 'Belgian experiment' is significant, to mention no other examples.

CHAPTER IX

FORECASTING
AND CO-ORDINATION

In view of the progress achieved in the knowledge of the conditions governing economic equilibrium and in working out remedies for dealing with factors upsetting that equilibrium—either deflationary or inflationary—two practical problems naturally arise: how to forecast and appraise the economic situation; and how to co-ordinate economic and financial policy. The analytical method of the 'general theory', besides indicating the need for forecasts and co-ordination, also suggests certain ways of carrying out this policy. This is thus a field where theory and practice are particularly closely linked, each calling upon the services of the other. Much progress indeed still remains to be made on both planes; it might be useful to stress what still has to be done.

FORECASTS

One of the conclusions of the 'general theory' is that there is a fundamental distinction between the policies to be adopted in periods of full employment and under-employment respectively: measures suitable for one period are unsuitable for the other. For example, saving is to be encouraged in periods of full employment, discouraged in periods of under-employment. A budget deficit is alternatively commendable or regrettable. It might almost be said that changes in the employment situation cause a kind of reversal of the scale of values, so that good and bad no longer have the same meaning. Which shows how important it is to be able to appraise the economic situation. This in itself appears to be fairly simple. A high figure for unemployment points, generally speaking, to a deficient aggregate demand.

But we cannot stop there. Unemployment may be the result of

having had to reconvert certain sectors of the economy; it may also be caused by a shortage of certain essential commodities, raw materials or power. This sort of situation arose in France in 1945, and the fact that many people failed to interpret it aright may have been among the reasons why the proper measures of financial recovery were not taken.

Similarly there may, in underdeveloped countries, be unemployment whose solution, economically speaking, lies not in the employment policy adopted, but in other kinds of measures.

Further, the future state of a country's economy as well as its current position has to be taken into account. What is the outlook for the coming year, full employment or unemployment? It is on this that the state's action must be based. Since all measures require time to take effect, it is important to be able to plan them in advance.

The following example shows the importance of looking ahead. In 1937-38 there was a crisis in the United States of America, a crisis which, being of short duration, failed to attract much notice, although it was quite a serious one. Between 1936 and 1937, the national revenue dropped by 8 per cent, wholesale prices by 9 per cent, industrial output by 24 per cent, and private investment by more than half. The number of unemployed rose from 7,700,000 in 1937 to 10,390,000 in 1938. This recession may be attributed, to a large extent at any rate, to a number of measures taken at the wrong moment. In 1936, economic activity was normal. The unemployment figure was still high—7 millions—but it was hoped to reduce it fairly quickly. In face of this situation, administrative and banking circles began to fear inflation, and took a number of preventive measures. The figure for the compulsory reserves of banks was raised, thus reducing the possibilities for credit expansion. Bonuses to ex-servicemen were not renewed, and social security taxes were introduced, causing individual incomes to drop; all of which resulted in reducing the budget deficit and hence also the demand. As the outcome, banks sold their shares, rates of interest rose, and investment and consumption dropped.

Economists of today are amazed that such a mistake can have been made. 'Looking at the matter in retrospect,' writes one of them, 'it is hard to understand why the financial authorities were so scared by the spectre of inflation at a time when the unemployment figure stood at 7 millions; it is equally difficult to find a valid explanation of the sudden reversal in budget policy.'[1] The fact nevertheless remains. Having failed to assess the state of the national economy correctly,

---

1. Mr. E. V. Rostov, in a lecture delivered in Paris in November 1949.

the public authorities intervened at the wrong moment, thereby aggravating a depression the effects of which America was still feeling.

Counter-measures were taken in 1938—after which the change in the world economic situation as the result of rearmament and the war erased the effects of the mistake committed. This example confirms, none the less, the need to look ahead.

STATISTICS

One conclusion is self-evident, but there is no harm in stating it: the importance of information and statistics. The establishment of the Statistical Department (*Services de Statistique*), although its work is not confined exclusively to providing information on the evolution of the economic situation, was due largely to the need for knowledge regarding the state of economic equilibrium. [1]

ECONOMIC RESEARCH INSTITUTES

But the matter was not left there. Even before the first, but especially during and after the second, world war the problem of forecasting crises occupied the attention of theorists and practical economists alike. The economists, though at a loss to understand the causes of these crises, had noted their recurrence, together with the succession of phenomena by which they were characterized—fluctuations of stock exchange quotations, wholesale prices, retail prices, production, etc. A certain number of constants appeared to emerge. The following notion had therefore been evolved: would it not be possible by observation alone, and without seeking to explain them, to arrive at certain laws from which a method of predicting the future could then be deduced? Was it not by such means that the natural sciences had progressed?

It was this notion that was at the origin of various different methods, of which the most famous was the one called the Harvard method. The key indices were represented by three curves A, B and C. Curve A

---

1. Note however that it was in 1908 that the French Ministry of Finance decided to include tables of economic indices in its bulletin. The introductory article begins as follows: 'The extremely acute crisis at present raging in the United States raises the question of economic crises in general and of the possibility of forecasting their recurrence. There has even been talk in in Parliament of proposed observation methods for this purpose and of the desirability of research on this subject.'

117

was produced by the combination of a set of indices all referring to the stock market: stock exchange prices, total of shares sold, etc. Curve B represented the commodity market: prices index, steel production, etc. Curve C referred to the money market, the discount rates of the various bills.

It was noticed that, during recent years, these three curves had followed one another in a certain order. Thus, towards the end of the period of prosperity, curve A began to sag, while curve B only rose slowly, and curve C rose sharply. The crisis came at the moment when A was at minimum, B was dropping and C was at maximum. As has been pointed out, this may be expressed more simply as follows: it is when the Stock Exchange prices cease rising that the crisis is imminent; the Harvard forecast was in fact based on the forecast of Stock Exchange speculators. This method, introduced in 1917, at first gave good results; in 1919, it enabled the1920 crisis to be forecast: curve A began to sag before the end of 1919, whereas the drop of curve B did not begin until the middle of 1920.

This system enjoyed considerable success. Throughout the world, from 1920 to 1929, economic research institutes on the model of the Harvard one were set up: the Berlin Economic Research Institute in 1925; the Austrian Institute in 1926, the Louvain Institute of Economics in 1928; the Hungarian Institute of Economic Research in 1928, etc. But in 1928, doubts began to be cast on the soundness of this method. The curves no longer followed one another in the usual order. After 1924, curve A went on rising constantly, whereas curve B after 1925, and curve C after 1926 went on dropping: the Stock Exchange quotations rose continuously while prices in general dropped. The barometer was out of order, and the economists found themselves in the position of navigators whose compass needle veers round to all points of the horizon.

The curious thing is that this did not lead them to draw pessimistic conclusions. The scale of the speculation boom should have fore-shadowed the scale of the depression. This was generally speaking not so; and the 1929 crisis arrived like a cyclone which the meteorologists had not been able to announce.

Rightly or wrongly, the method was regarded as bankrupt. This was significant. It was the failure of empiricism, of the method which consisted in being content to observe phenomena, without attempting to explain them. This is a conclusive example of the need for digging down to root causes, as the physicist does when he seeks in the molecular structure the causes of statistical laws which he has been able to determine through observation alone. This is the method used by economic analysis when analysing aggregate demand and determining the factors governing its fluctuations. It is by studying these factors, in conjunction with the laws governing them, that economic disequilibrium can be forecast.

STUDY OF AGGREGATE DEMAND

Aggregate demand represents the sum of private consumption, investment, public expenditure and, in some cases, export surpluses. Some of these factors are known. Public expenditure is fixed by decision of the public authorities; so is taxation, which reduces private consumption. The other factors can be forecast with some degree of accuracy.

As a first approximation, private consumption is obtained by applying a certain coefficient—the coefficient expressing the value of the propensity to consume—to the sum of private incomes. Private incomes can be calculated with a fair degree of accuracy.

Private investment, factory construction, machine manufacture or stocking is more difficult to forecast, though it can be done within limits. It depends on prospective profit and on the rate of interest. The latter can be estimated on the basis of the quantity of money and money requirements, in particular money requirements for business transactions. The prospects of profit are more difficult to estimate, though it may be assumed that they will improve with a rise in prices and deteriorate when prices drop. Scientific discoveries, the opening of certain markets and the evolution of the political situation will also play a part; attempts can be made to forecast their effects.

The size of the balance of accounts may be anticipated, in so far as it depends on the gap between home and foreign prices, on the Customs policy, foreign currency holdings, etc. It is possible, by adding up all these factors, to estimate whether, other things being equal, the national economy will evolve towards rising prices and full employment or towards depression and unemployment.

The state thus needs a table showing on one side national production plus import surpluses, if any; and on the other side how these resources are used for private consumption, public or private investment, public expenditure and any export surplus. On the basis of this table, the state can decide what action to take: financial—or economic—measures, taxation, public expenditure, public investment, issue of money, credit.

The significance of this first table must not, of course, be misunderstood. Although, as a first approximation, the total for one side of the table may be higher than the other, or the anticipated aggregate demand may exceed the anticipated aggregate supply, the balance will nevertheless be redressed. Obviously, the community will not consume more than the figure for production plus import surpluses and drawings on stocks. But, unless production rises, or special action is taken by the public authorities, this balance will be achieved by a rise in prices, which will have the effect of reducing the consumption of certain categories of persons, cutting down investment or reducing public expenditure. It is moreover probable that the balance will continue to be repeatedly upset as a result of encroachments on future revenue, so that we are likely to witness not merely one rise of prices but a series of rises, constituting a constant increase in the general level of prices.

If, on the other hand, the first estimate of future aggregate demand falls below the figure for aggregate supply, i.e. roughly speaking, potential output, this does not mean that there will in fact be a discrepancy between the two figures. They will balance out by various adjustments to the terms of the equation, and in particular by a drop in aggregate production.

Thus, in one way or another, the balance between demand and supply is always established. Estimates may predict, *a priori* in the period under consideration, an excess of probable demand over probable supply, or vice versa. But the two figures will always be evened out, though this must entail either a rise of the general price level or a drop in aggregate production—both of which are undesirable. The action of the state must be resigned to prevent either of these processes from occurring.

It is incumbent on the state, when planning a financial policy, to estimate its repercussions, and adjust accordingly such factors in the first table as it is able to influence. Should it then appear that the balance has not been restored, that the level of aggregate demand necessary in order to guarantee full employment has either not been attained or has been exceeded, the state must then make further adjustments until it finally produces a table which represents a situation of economic equilibrium.

In other words, this table, which is called the economic or national budget, should be more than merely a basis for estimation; it can also contribute to the solution of the second practical problem: the planning and co-ordination of economic and financial policy.

CO-ORDINATION OF ECONOMIC AND FINANCIAL POLICY

The theory of employment shows that it is possible to affect the demand by means more numerous, and more varied than those of the classical technique. In addition to taxation, recourse can be had to compulsory saving systems, control of distribution, etc. Demand can be boosted by various financial devices: lowering of the discount rate, purchase of shares on the market, redistribution of incomes, public works, etc. A choice has therefore to be made between these different methods; a laxer financial policy requires stricter economic control and vice versa. There have been examples of this. In other words, all these measures must be co-ordinated. Otherwise, there would be a danger either of the foreign trade policy being counteracted by the effects of budgetary or credit policy; or, if all these methods were applied simultaneously, of over-shooting the mark, and passing from inflation to deflation, or vice versa.

Such co-ordination of course entails government action. The public authorities must realize that economic and financial policies are inseparable and that no single measure is effective except as part of an overall plan. There are however a number of technical instruments for guiding and executing the government's wishes: on the one hand, an administrative system; on the other, the preparation of programmes complete with figures.

ADMINISTRATIVE ORGANIZATION

Co-ordination being recognized as necessary, the government and administrative services must be organized accordingly. We do in fact find in various countries, especially since the second world war, co-ordinating bodies, whose aim, or at least one of whose main aims is to plan an overall policy designed to produce economic equilibrium. The following examples may be quoted:

In *Britain*, the responsibility of laying down economic policy devolves chiefly on the Treasury and its Economic Planning Staff, set up in April 1947. The office is responsible for general supervision of economic affairs, co-ordination of economic policy and preparation of overall plans. It also prepares investment programmes.

In the *United States of America*, the Employment Act of 1946, besides defining maximum employment as one of the aims of economic policy, set up two bodies designed to help carry out that policy.

The Council of Economic Advisers, consisting of three members assisted by a number of experts, forms part of the President's office. It is responsible for assembling accurate and up-to-date information on present economic evolution and trends and predictable future trends; and for analysing and interpreting this information with a view to deciding whether the said evolution or trends hamper or are likely to hamper the application of these principles. It also assesses the advantages of the various programmes and activities of the federal government, and recommends to the President such national economic policies as are calculated to encourage and facilitate free enterprise under the competitive system, eliminate or minimize the effects of economic fluctuations, and maintain the level of employment, production and purchasing power. Similar work devolves on the Joint Committee on the Economic Report, which is composed of seven members of the Senate and seven members of the House of Representatives. It is responsible for observing economic trends and considering whether or not the government should adopt certain economic policies.

In *Belgium* economic policy is co-ordinated by a ministerial committee for economic co-ordination, with a minister of economic co-ordination in charge of the secretariat. The preparatory work of this committee is carried out by an inter-ministerial economic commission, which is responsible for observing and analysing economic trends with a view to deciding whether government action is necessary, and if so, what the nature and scope of such action should be, and at what moment it should be taken.

The replies of various countries to the United Nations questionnaire on the maintenance of full employment showed that Denmark, New Zealand, the Netherlands and Sweden also had services for application or co-ordination of employment policy.

Further investigation should be undertaken in order to discover in each case whether the measures taken are adequate, whether the services provided are in a position to fulfil their duties, etc. All that concerns us is to emphasize that the governmental and administrative machinery of a number of countries does reflect the progress achieved in analysing the conditions of economic stability.

In most cases, the services in question either introduce or utilize another method of co-ordination—that of the economic budget.

THE ECONOMIC BUDGET

Any document designed to help forecast the economic situation should also provide the government with a co-ordinated policy, since the effects of all measures taken will be shown in terms of figures. Thus, if the measures taken to boost demand should be too drastic, this will be clear from the sum total of them. It will then be seen that it is useless to attempt to increase export, consumption and public expenditure simultaneously. Conversely, the plan should show whether a particular full employment policy is inadequate.

Private consumption can be reduced either through increased taxation or through restrictions on credit; these two methods are up to a point interchangeable, or they may be used in combination; but it is impossible to know what their effects will be without working them out in figures. Aggregate demand can be stepped up either by reduction of taxation or by expansion of credit, but to decide on the scale on which to apply each of these measures, they must be considered with reference to one another, etc.

This table is generally called the 'national economic budget', the 'economic budget' or the 'national budget'. The use of this term implies that, as with a budget, we have to proceed by process of comparison, and balance out two sums—that of the resources of the community against its expenditure. The use of the word budget also indicates that it is an estimate of a future situation.

The economic budget differs from the budget in the ordinary sense of the term in scale as well as in type. It is, in part, an estimate. Except that it adopts a certain economic policy, the government does not actually decide on the amount of private consumption, but only estimates it; the same applies to private investment. This does not mean that the government does not influence that consumption and investment—it does—but the action it takes, in a certain economic system at any rate, is not direct. Even in collectivist systems, incidentally, the state does not exercise direct and complete control over private consumption, but only over investment.

The following tables, based on the *Economic Survey* submitted by the British Chancellor of the Exchequer in March 1953, constitue an example of an economic budget for the year 1952; the figures for the preceding years enable a closer estimate to be made of the probable figures for 1953.

TABLE 28.   National production (in millions of pounds).

	1948	1952	1953 [1]
Salaries, wages and other emoluments [2]	7 972	10 456	11 048
Profits	+ 2 048	+ 2 582	+ 2 798
Rents	+ 381	+ 513	+ 571
Residual error	− 34	− 42	+ 66
Domestic revenue including depreciation and appreciation of stocks	10 367	13 509	14 483
Appreciation of stocks	− 325		+ 80
Foreign revenue	+ 176	+ 139	+ 156
Gross national revenue at factor cost	10 218	13 648	14 719
Plus indirect taxes	+ 2 020	+ 2 286	+ 2 369
Minus subsidies	− 571	− 419	− 358
Gross national production at market prices	11 667	15 515	16 730

1. Provisional figures.
2. Including the revenues of private enterprises.

TABLE 29.   Expenditure of the community (in millions of pounds).

	1948	1952	1953 [1]
Expenditure on consumption	8 379	10 403	11 029
Expenditure by the public authorities on goods and services	+ 1 760	+ 2 895	+ 3 098
Gross investment	+ 1 546	+ 2 060	+ 2 482
Exports	+ 2 365	+ 4 018	+ 3 853
Imports	− 2 383	− 3 861	− 3 732
Gross national expenditure at market prices	11 667	15 515	16 730

1. Provisional prices.

The economic budget may be said to constitute a translation into figures of the analysis of the employment theory.

Various Uses of the Economic Budget

Since it was the spectacle of depression and unemployment which first led to an analysis of total economic balance being made, it is understandable that the economic budget, at any rate in the Western world, should have originated from the desire of the public authorities to maintain full employment. It is natural, therefore, that it should be in the white paper on employment, published at the height of the war, that the British Government announced its intention to draw up a comprehensive table of the national output and of the use to which it was put. Similarly, in America, it was the Employment Act of 1946 that provided for setting up a Committee of Economic Advisers to plan a co-ordinated economic policy—which also, naturally, involves drawing up an economic budget.

Nevertheless, the first plans, or at any rate the first attempts at an economic budget, were based on other considerations: combating inflation, establishing economic controls, carrying out an investment or armament programme, co-ordinating economic and financial policy.

The Economic Budget as an Instrument for Combating Inflation

The same analytical method which provides a means of forecasting the possibility of a deficient aggregate demand also indicates if it is likely to be too large. All countries, in the immediate post-war period, were threatened by inflation; but the nature of the threat could not be understood without a comprehensive analysis, since the threat persisted even though the state budget was balanced, and though the public authorities refrained from resorting to the issue of currency. Individual propensity to consume was accentuated by the desire to purchase commodities which had been unobtainable during the war; and people were in possession of large sums of money accumulated during the war because they could not be spent. As against this increased private demand, combined with heavy public expenditure, the means of production had dropped, mainly owing to war damage, and stocks were practically nil.

This situation accentuated the economic importance of financial institutions—taxation, currency, and credit. The fact of their being recognized as a means of cutting down aggregate demand led to investigation of the contribution they could make to that effect.

Once again, we see how the evolution of science can influence technique. At the time when, in accordance with the quantity theory, the quantity of money was thought to constitute the main factor of inflation, the state paid special attention to the comparative evolution of monetary circulation and the level of prices. Recognition of the fact that price rises were due directly not to the quantity of money in circulation but to the state of aggregate demand led naturally to investigation of this latter factor.

Further, the force of inflationary pressure made it clear that a policy which consisted of applying various different measures in isolation was inadequate. The situation clearly called for the combination of various deflationary measures, no one of which by itself was wholly effective; experience had made this clear to a number of countries. Hence the advantage of a system which combined the various different measures, considering each in relation to the others, and estimating their total effect.

The economic budget has a further advantage: it brings home to the general public an idea which, though elementary, often tends to be forgotten—namely, that it is impossible to consume more products than actually exist, that the national output, plus imports and stocks, constitute a common pool whose total restricts the amounts available to the various recipients; and that no amount of financial juggling can alter this self-evident truth. The point was stressed by various statesmen, Sir Stafford Cripps, for instance; and it is doubtless one of the reasons why the statesmen in question preferred a method which enabled them to bring home to the general public the need for the sacrifices they were being or would be asked to make. The explanation should be in simple terms such as to reconcile technical difficulties with the machinery of a democracy.

It is therefore understandable that the first attempts to plan an economic budget, in the post-war world, should have been anti-inflationary in purpose.

The British *Economic Surveys* contain what are in fact economic budgets. They take a variety of forms but they all aim at detecting inflationary pressures, and discovering means of combating them. It is no coincidence that these tables should have been drawn up with such extreme care in a country which has fought hardest against inflation.

In the United States, the reports of the President and of his economic advisers contain no numerical estimates. None the less these documents, which are based on the aggregate supply and demand tables for the preceding period, and which seek to forecast the factors which may operate in the ensuing period, do in some sense constitute a tentative economic budget. The main concern of the official economists is to detect threats of inflation and to arrange preventive measures.

In France, the first economic budget, which was drawn up in the guise of a national balance sheet at the end of 1947, set out deliberately to calculate the 'inflationary gap'. Incidentally, it led the public authorities to make a special fiscal levy designed to reduce an anticipated surplus aggregate demand.

The framing of economic budgets in Norway and the Netherlands may be attributed to the desire to co-ordinate the action of the public authorities in order to reduce aggregate demand. But the steps taken to draw up tables representing the forecasts of the public authorities and the co-ordination of their financial policy cannot, in any of these countries, be considered the result of inflation only.

The Economic Budget and Control of the Economy

The institution of economic budgets was facilitated by the fact that governments, in the face of wartime or post-war economic conditions, had attempted to exercise direct control over production, consumption and trade. This took various forms. Some measures were designed to introduce arbitrary control over the distribution of commodities amongst consumers, and of power and raw materials amongst enterprises. For this purpose, the government had to estimate the total quantity of commodities or raw materials available—or at any rate of the essential ones—whose distribution had to be controlled. It also had to decide how all these resources were to be used. A number of equations had to be drawn up in order to ensure that the aims selected were not incompatible. It is thus no mere chance that this method of calculation and presentation was applied most thoroughly in those countries which attempted to control their economy, such as Great Britain, Norway and the Netherlands. [1]

However, the use of this kind of technique is not necessarily bound up with a state-controlled economy. The elimination of economic control means substituting one set of measures for another, exchanging economic measures for financial ones. The effects of this change have to be calculated.

Let us take an example. In the event of a larger aggregate demand, or a drop in production due to war, poor harvests or some other cause, two kinds of solution are possible. Demand can be reduced by means of rationing and by controlling distribution of raw materials and power. This system has no effect either on revenue or on purchasing power; it merely suspends, partially, the right to make use of them. Conversely, it is possible to leave people the right to purchase what they wish, but to reduce their incomes and, therefore, their ability to purchase, by means of taxation. The same two opposite methods can

1. Note that, in the Netherlands, the Central Planning Bureau, set up in 1946, was placed in charge of an economist of repute, Professor Tinbergen.

be applied to investment; the government can either restrict investment directly, by forbidding certain types of work or making it obligatory to obtain government permission for building; or can leave individuals free to build when and as they wish, but discourage some persons from doing so by raising the rates of interest.

Whatever the method adopted, the effects must be calculated. Inaction is also tantamount to a solution, but a bad one—inflation.

The Economic Budget as a Means of Carrying Out an Investment or Export Programme

The decision to institute an economic budget may be taken, not because of the need for controls in a period of shortage, but for entirely different reasons, and at a completely different historical juncture; it may be the result of deciding to embark on a programme of investment, export, rearmament, housing, etc.

After the war, various countries realized that great efforts would have to be made both for reconstruction and for the improvement of their equipment. They realized also that it was not enough merely to draw up investment programmes, include the necessary credits in their budget, or provide for certain loans. If nothing more were done, there was a danger of their decisions remaining a dead letter. As a result of the pressure of other demands—the demands of consumers, of individuals wishing to invest money in programmes not ranking as top priority, and the demands of the public services in general, there was a danger that the demand for commodities required for the equipment most vital to the country might not be fully met. Unless provision were made to balance aggregate supply and aggregate demand, price rises, accentuated by the orders for capital investment, might well reduce the results obtainable with a nominal total of budgetary or bank credits. It became clearer than ever before that any general programme of investment must be accompanied by a drop in consumption or a reduction of certain types of private investment. In order to carry out an investment programme, it is necessary to calculate both the figure for national production and the amount to which private consumption and general state expenses can be cut. The difference between these two figures represents the maximum sum which can be spent on equipment. In this respect, as in others, the economic budget gives a clear picture of the economic facts forming the background of financial phenomena.

In addition to other reasons for using this technique, the Netherlands and Norway were motivated by the desire to carry out an investment programme; the United States of America was engaged on an armaments programmes. In France, the Commission du Bilan National concentrated on determining the inflationary gap, and the first attempt at an economic budget came, at a very timely moment, in 1947, to show that inflation constituted an obstacle to the success of the plan.

In a country whose very existence depends on foreign trade, the main purpose of introducing the technique of a national budget has been to ensure a certain minimum of exports. Faced with the difficulties of the post-war period, British statesmen found it necessary to calculate by exactly how much national production must be increased, and private consumption and public expenditure reduced, in order to ensure a minimum of exports.

The Economic Budget as a Means of Reducing Arbitrary Financial Administration

Finally, the economic budget constitutes a means of restricting the arbitrary element in financial administration, thus partially offsetting the effects of the disappearance of the checks operating under the classical system. Although the principle of the balanced budget was not always respected, it was never infringed without misgivings. But for the adoption of the economic budget, which introduced a new principle—that of economic equilibrium—the scrapping of the principle of balancing the budget might have resulted in the institution of a hand-to-mouth system. In so far as the volume of national production, the volume of private consumption and investment and the size of the balance of payments are taken as data, the size of the state budget is calculated no less accurately than when the principle of the balanced budget is applied.

The introduction of the economic budget also serves to offset the disappearance of the check represented by the gold convertibility of currency. Although the automatic operation of the gold standard failed to prevent the adoption of hand-to-mouth policies, it did at least make it impossible for that kind of policy to be pursued indefinitely. A substitute for this mechanism has therefore to be found. In the absence of a commodity standard which has not yet been worked out, or an international currency system subject to a large number of conditions not at present existing, the economic budget constitutes a kind of straitjacket for economic and financial administration.

Governments accepting these restrictions cannot resort to the issue of currency to cover a budget deficit; nor can they continue to count on credit expansion in order to carry out an investment programme in conditions liable to cause inflation. Operating on the basis of a balanced budget estimate, governments can only increase public expenditure or investment by increasing taxation, by limiting certain forms of credits, or, when this is possible, by lifting certain restrictions operating against the development of national production.

Of course this mechanism, as already indicated, is not completely effective. Mistakes can be made, figures can be falsified. But, with an economic budget as with an ordinary budget, the extent to which estimates can be miscalculated, in one direction or the other, is limited. Even supposing the various terms of the equation to be correct, the public authorities may deliberately misinterpret the resulting directives. But it would at least be a step forward if it were impossible to exploit ignorance or confusion in order to embark on a hand-to-mouth policy.

One of the aims of the economic budget, as of budgetary systems in general, is to rule out contradictory decisions and impart a certain uniformity to public policy. If, in the past, the authorities had been forced to give the results of their decisions in terms of figures, it would have been less easy for them to take mutually contradictory decisions, to attempt to increase both consumption and investment simultaneously, to strive to obtain an export surplus without cutting down the sums earmarked for domestic requirements, to step up public expenditure without limiting amounts available to other recipients, etc.

Considering the advantages of the economic budget, it may appear surprising that it has hitherto been relatively so little used. [1]

Amongst the main countries where an economic budget is drawn up and published are Great Britain, Norway, the Netherlands, the United States of America and France.

In *Britain* the economic budget forms the real framework both of financial policy, the budget proper, and of the government's economic policy. It also, as we have seen, constituted a means of informing the general public of the need for and significance of the measures taken and the sacrifices called for.

In *Norway*, the economic budget has existed since 1946. Its main

---

1. At any rate in countries which have kept the capitalist system either entirely or in part. As regards the Union of Soviet Socialist Republics and, generally speaking, all countries ruled by a collective system, the problem of the economic budget will be dealt with in a separate chapter.
   Concerning its application in non-collectivist countries, we may refer especially to a book by Dumontier *Budget Économique et Comptabilité Nationale* (P. U. F., 1951) and to the various official documents published by governments.

purpose has undoubtedly been to ensure fair distribution of products in short supply amongst the various categories of recipients.

In the *Netherlands* likewise, the economic budget was an outcome of shortages and of the need for reorganizing the whole national economy, after the paralysis of war and occupation. The Central Planning Bureau, the body responsible for drawing up the economic budget, was established at the beginning of 1946, under the supervision of Professor Tinbergen, an economist of repute. The Dutch national budget is prefaced by a global plan containing an assessment of needs and resources. The comments submitted in 1946 by the planning bureau provide a practical example of how to use a plan of this type.

There were, in theory, three possible ways of dealing with the economic problem of the Netherlands:

1. To reduce the demand for investment goods by cutting down power and transport programmes, and to expand supply by using more international credit and liquidating more foreign holdings.
2. To increase the number of workers, prolong working hours, recruit foreign labour, and alter the salary scales.
3. Rationalization, standardization, development of technical research, redistribution and improvement of the land, organization of professional training, recovery of stolen property, reparation for damage and, finally, emigration.

Each of these methods provided a possible solution, in that each constituted a unified plan. The planning bureau proposed, however, to reject the first for technical reasons, the second for psychological reasons; and to adopt the third.

In the *United States of America* an economic budget—in the form of a table of estimates—appears to be drawn up, but it is not published. The reports of the President and his advisers are based only on forecasts of future trends, not backed up by figures. [1]

In *France* the first economic budget was drawn up at the end of 1947 by the Commission du Bilan National. A decree of 31 March 1950 established a committee of experts to draw up the nation's economic accounts, every year for the current and the coming year.

There are various reasons why the technique of an economic budget was never generally applied. The fear that it might facilitate an interventionist economic policy doubtless had something to do with it. In so far as the use of the economic budget results in 'exploding' the contradictions of any economic and financial policy, it does not

---

[1] At any rate such figures as do appear in these reports are incomplete.

recommend itself to the public authorities. Further, this method is a new one, and the theory of economic equilibrium underlying it has not yet been generally accepted. Nor must we underestimate the importance of another factor—the difficulty of applying it. Here again the help of economics has to be sought in order to solve problems of technique.

Problems of Application

In estimating the probable volume of private consumption, the author of the economic budget bases his calculations on the figure for private incomes, which can be ascertained with fair accuracy. He has then, in accordance with the indications of the analysis, to multiply this income by a certain coefficient, translating into figures a psychological phenomenon—the propensity to consume. What shall this coefficient be? The practical expert has to consult the economists on this point. On the basis of a set of statistical investigations, it can be stated, with a fair degree of accuracy, that a certain average income, distributed in such and such a way, and varying by a certain percentage, should correspond to a certain level of consumption.

Economists are however forced to observe that the propensity to consume varies from one social class to another. That of wage earners and heads of firms, farmers and tradespeople, etc. is different. By drawing a distinction between these social categories, we are able to ascertain more accurately what changes in consumption will occur as a result of a given change in the national production. In other words, the practical expert has on this point to consult sociologists as well as economists. It is for these reasons that attempts have been made in certain countries, France in particular, to draw a distinction between the incomes and consumption levels of the different classes of society.

The economic budget must also estimate how heads of enterprises will react to fluctuations of the economic situation. The effects of a certain move—an armaments programme, for instance—which causes an appreciable though limited increase of aggregate demand, may be considerably amplified by the expectations of entrepreneurs. They may build up stocks in anticipation of difficulties in obtaining supplies; or install plant in preparation for orders, so that the aggregate demand rises much more sharply than the mere increase of state expenditure would have made likely.

The economic budget necessarily assumes that the possibilities of expanding production are known. It is essential, in order to assess the effects of an increase of demand, and to calculate the resulting rise in national income, to know what stocks of labour, raw materials, power and in some cases metallurgical products are available. It is of course possible that though there are workers unemployed they cannot be used for lack of power—such was the case in France, for example, from 1943-46; or that investments cannot be increased for want of metallurgical products. It is, in short, a case of making allowance for a phenomenon which should logically have been foreseen but which became doubly apparent as a result of war conditions—the existence of 'bottlenecks' in the economic system as a whole. To detect existing bottlenecks and predict future ones, we have to estimate the quantity of labour, power, and metallurgical products required by each industry and by agriculture in order to attain a given output figure. It is possible, by adding up the various sets of figures representing firstly the labour, and secondly the power or metallurgical products required for production, to make an overall estimate of the power, labour and metallurgical products required for a given aggregate production. In other words, we have to draw up a stock balance (*bilan-matière*) as the Union of Soviet Socialist Republics and Britain do, and as various other countries with systems for controlling the distribution of certain raw materials or means of production are doing or have done. However, tables of this kind are not necessarily part of a controlled distribution system; they are also an essential part of the machinery for working out the estimates contained in the economic budgets of liberal economic systems.

It is not sufficient merely to investigate past and present bottlenecks. The most acute shortage afflicting an economy at any given moment may conceal other shortages which will become apparent as soon as the original one is remedied. The truth is that the problem is more abstruse than appears at first sight. Every industry is dependent on all other industries or on imports. If, therefore, we ascertain what a given industry—machine construction, for example—has to purchase (in terms of value) from each of the other industries and from agriculture: and the wages it has to pay its workers in order to attain a certain production figure, our knowledge of the current situation and ability to forecast trends will be improved. Naturally our table must be based on the present situation, for which sufficiently accurate statistics are assumed to exist; also on the assumption that the technical conditions of production remain more or less stable. These figures may be collated and submitted in the form of a double-entry table, of which a rough, deliberately simplified example is given below.

The vertical columns for the branches of production show the purchases made by this branch from other branches and the sums paid, in the form of wages or profits, to individuals operating in that branch. For example branch 1 has, for a production of 90 (this production is of course expressed in value), to use products from branch 2 to a value of 30, and products from branch 3 to a value of 20. Further, the wages paid for transforming the products purchased from branches 2 and 3, and the profits made on the production add up to 40.

		Branches of production [1]			Individual firms	Investments	Total
		1	*2*	*3*			
Branches of production [1]	1		10	20	60		90
	2	30		10	40		80
	3	20	15		25	50	110
Individual firms		40	55	80			175
Investments					50		50
Total		90	80	110	175	50	

1. Branches of production: the branches in question are, for example, agriculture and industry but they can be subdivided into different sectors: mechanical production, electrical equipment, etc.
   The sectors 'individual firms' and 'investments' are similarly subdivided.

The column representing individual firms gives figures for purchases of consumable goods made by individual firms from each of the branches 1, 2 and 3; and for the savings drawn by individual firms from their incomes and used for financing investment.

The investment column gives figures for purchases of equipment and for stocks

If we take the horizontal columns corresponding to the various branches of production, we see for example that branch 1, whose total production is estimated at 90, has sold products to the value of 10 to branch 2; of 20 to branch 3; and of 60 to consumers. The horizontal column for individual firms gives the sums made available to individual firms by each of the three branches of production. The origin of these sums, totalling 175, is as follows: 40 from branch 1, 55 from branch 2, and 80 from branch 3. Finally, the horizontal column for investments gives figures for the amounts of capital obtained from savings and used for the financing of investment.

The process of subdivision will, naturally, have to be pursued beyond the three main branches, extending to the main sectors of industry. The table must also give an estimate of exports and imports, and of state revenue and expenditure.

Such, again greatly simplified, is the form of economic accountancy proposed and used by the American economist Leontieff, [1] and the origins of which can easily be traced back to the stock balances (*bilans-matières*) of the Union of Soviet Socialist Republics. [2]

The table, since it gives data for the past, shows the ratio between the production figures of the various branches; and the distribution of consumers' purchasing power between the various products. It is thus possible to draw up a table of estimates, with figures which are mutually compatible. It is not possible, for example, to forecast an increase of production in any particular branch unless the other branches can supply the necessary materials. In other words, this table should show more accurately than the stock balances do (though these will continue to be useful) what bottlenecks exist in industry, and what volume of industrial production can be attained.

It also provides more exact figures of certain ratios which must be known in order to prepare the economic budget. It assesses what effects an increase in consumption—and accordingly in production— will have on investment, since it indicates what plant must be purchased or factories built in order to raise the production of any given branch. It also gives a detailed picture of how increased investment will affect firstly consumption and, secondly, other forms of investment.

The United States used this method in carrying out its rearmament programme in 1950 and subsequent years. [3]

---

1. For a more detailed account of this method, see the article by Leontieff 'A New Analysis of Economic Facts, the "Receipts-and-Payments" Method', in the review *Scientific American;* a translation, by Mr. Hoppenot, was published in the April 1952 number of *Banque.* See also the relevant chapter of Mr. Dumontier's book, quoted earlier.
2. cf. Bettelheim, *Soviet Planning,* p. 100 et seq.
3. This does not mean that the method may not be used for other policies as well.

These advances of technique indicate that, in addition to problems of total equilibrium, there are also problems of partial equilibrium; the analysis of the latter problems, which we can do no more than mention here, represents a field for the future progress of economic science, technique and policy alike.

CHAPTER X

THE PROBLEM OF EQUILIBRIUM
UNDER A COLLECTIVIST RÉGIME

Under a collectivist régime, the volume of production and its distribution between private consumption, investment, and general state expenses are decided by the public authorities. This control of the economy would seem, in principle, to exclude all possibility of underemployment, or of production falling short of effective demand. The government decides what is to be produced and its decision is presumably aimed at guaranteeing full utilization of all the resources of the country. It also allocates the resources as between investment and consumption, so that it both intends and is in a position to ensure that no commodities or manufactured products are wasted for lack of consumers, and that the investments considered necessary for economic progress are made.

There are however grounds for wondering whether disequilibria or at any rate phenomena similar in some respects to the anomalies occurring in capitalist society have really been banished; and whether, consequently, similar preventive measures may not have to be envisaged.

The consumers' freedom of choice, which the maintenance of money is specifically designed to safeguard, may be expressed by a degree of abstention. Individuals may not wish to buy all the commodities available to them. The state can dispose of surplus production by cutting prices, and it must of course bear the consumers' reaction in mind when fixing the volume of production for the ensuing period. The effects of this kind of price cut are incidentally not the same as they might be in a capitalist régime, in that such cuts do not normally cause those responsible for production to anticipate further price cuts, so accentuating the depression, as happens during crises in a capitalist economy.

A collectivist state may also counter under-consumption either by reducing taxes or by increasing wages. In this respect its action is similar to that of any other government which reduces taxes, taxes on consumption in particular. Note, however, that a collectivist state is able to achieve the desired result more easily, since it is not forced to reckon with a time-lag before tax cuts affect the price levels, etc.

The collectivist state can also increase investment,[1] and, since it controls investment, has no need to fear the reaction of entrepreneurs, who may, in a capitalist society, refrain from investing in the fear of prices dropping and profits falling.

In short, the collectivist state, which is able to raise both consumption and investment, cannot permit a lasting discrepancy between the supply and demand of goods. The measures it employs to prevent such a situation arising are obviously identical, in substance and sometimes even in form, with those taken by capitalist states pursuing a policy of full employment. They are more effective and more speedy because the state does not have to reckon with the reactions of entrepreneurs. Its action is more direct.

The total state estimates may, however, prove erroneous. The state may, in order to correct errors of assessment, have to make drastic changes in prices or wages. The greater the error, the greater the risk of its hindering the execution of the plan. Even under a collectivist system, therefore, it is desirable that both the increase of products made available to individual consumers and the reactions of consumers shall be estimated as accurately as possible.

Nevertheless, it is the opposite kind of disequilibrium in a collectivist régime which raises the most serious problems. It is indeed clear, both logically and from experience, that fairly acute inflationary phenomena may appear. The sum of the total wages paid may be markedly higher than the total value of consumer goods available. This situation may be due to a variety of causes—to an over-optimistic estimate of the expansion of production, for example. The aggregate demand may thus exceed the aggregate supply. The state can remedy such a position by controlled distribution of products (rationing); by raising prices, which may be done through a tax on consumption; by reducing wages through a tax on income; by introducing a compulsory saving system with compulsory non-negotiable loans; or by encouraging voluntary saving. All these measures are identical in substance and sometimes also in form with those used by any régime which has to restore economic equilibrium in the face of too big an aggregate demand. Otherwise, consumers would be unable to obtain the products they required, and a black market system, with higher prices, would spring up.

---

1. This chiefly affects the future, since products intended for consumption cannot as a rule be used as equipment.

The effectiveness of many state measures varies according to where they are employed—in a capitalist régime or a collectivist one. In the latter, an official rise in prices will quickly liquidate the surplus aggregate demand, since it eliminates a certain fraction of the purchasing power, which is not re-utilized. In the capitalist system, on the contrary, an increase of prices, whilst reducing the demands of one class of the population, raises those of the producers and intermediaries, whose incomes rise in proportion to the rise in prices.

In view of the above, the collectivist state, like the capitalist state, must attempt to avoid a gap between aggregate supply and demand. The measures taken to redress the balance—raising prices or cutting wages—may need to be more drastic than if the situation had been foreseen and steps taken to prevent the gap ever opening.

The volume of consumption must therefore be fixed in relation to the volume of individual income, minus taxation, i.e. the volume of wages multiplied by the coefficient for the propensity to consume. If there is reason to suppose that individuals will not spend the whole of their income, this coefficient may be less than one. It may also be higher than one. In a collectivist régime where money is used, it is always possible that individuals may wish to spend in excess of their present income, either by encroaching on future income or by using money accumulated during previous periods and not needed to cover their money requirements. [1]

An assessment will therefore have to be made of the propensity to consume, which is related as in capitalist régimes, to private income, but not necessarily in direct ratio. This means that a collectivist state must, in order to prevent economic anomalies, use financial measures designed to increase or reduce the aggregate demand. It will, similarly, use a table showing the total supply and demand, split up into various different sections so that their fluctuation, and the effects of measures used to establish a balance, can be more accurately assessed. In other words, the collectivist state will draw up a national economic budget consisting partly of estimates and partly of decisions. The main difference between this budget and the economic budget of capitalist countries is the predominance which the former gives to decisions.

It may be considered that the 'balance of the money incomes and expenditures of the population' of the Union of Soviet Socialist Republics constituted a sort of economic budget. The circumstances

---

1. This phenomenon may occur after a period of rationing, after a war for example. This explains why the Union of Soviet Socialist Republics carried out a currency reform accompanied by a levy on wealth, in conditions similar to those in several other countries.

which revealed the advisability of drawing up this plan are significant. After 1930, in the absence of any budget of this kind, the volume of consumer goods had become inadequate for the demands of the population. This was due mainly to the fact that the increase in production scheduled for the first five-year plan had not been achieved. The production of consumer goods therefore fell short of the demand.

In order to offset the effects of this under-production, the Soviet Government had introduced a rationing system. As this controlled distribution system was gradually discarded, starting with the abolition of bread cards at the end of 1934, it became apparent that a plan showing on the one hand the total money incomes and on the other the utilization of those incomes in the form of public expenditure on consumption or 'accumulation' goods was eminently desirable. [1]

The actual plan of course serves, amongst other things, as an economic budget, since it estimates, and determines, national production and its distribution between consumption and investment. In order, however, to decide whether consumption can be maintained at the figure predicted, it is useful to be able to draw a clear picture of the volume of individual incomes, and to investigate whether the volume of consumer goods will, at current prices, be equivalent to that proportion of those incomes which individuals desire to spend on consumption. Any document showing the conditions of total economic equilibrium must rest on a discrimination between production, incomes and consumption. Any estimate or overall decision, whether in the form of a plan or of a 'balance of money incomes and expenditures of the population' requires figures for the volume of production attainable in the various sectors of the economy. In order to obtain figures indicative of the true situation, allowance must be made for the resources of each sector, the possibilities of altering them, and the relationship between the various branches of production. This is the function of the 'stock balances' used in the Soviet economy [2] which may, moreover, be regarded as the model for Leontieff's method of economic accountancy.

A distinction must also be drawn between the various categories of income holders, since the propensity to consume—or at least the types of articles demanded—may vary from one category to another.

The maintenance of freedom of choice for consumers, whose reactions must therefore be predicted—they are free, as money is in use, to spend more or less than their total income, more or less than forecast—

---

1. In the words of Margoline, quoted by Bettelheim, it is no mere coincidence 'that the increased concern for drawing up a balance of the income and expenditure of the population . . . coincided with the abolition of the food card system' (quoted by Bettelheim in *Soviet Planning* p. 114).

2. On the subject of 'stock balances', cf. Bettelheim, *Soviet Planning*, p. 100 et seq.

is not the only reason why collectivist régimes have to face the problem of maintaining a total economic equilibrium. It follows also from the nature of things. The mere fact of deciding that a certain quantity of articles shall be produced does not automatically put that decision into effect. Manufacturing may be impossible for want of certain essential materials; or the quantity of labour earmarked for such production may be inadequate because the productive capacity of the workers has been overestimated. Similarly, a volume of power calculated in theory as sufficient may in fact not be so.

TOTAL DISEQUILIBRIUM
AND THE AUTONOMY OF ENTERPRISES

Disequilibrium may also be due to the system of production adopted, the structure of enterprises, and the regulations to which they are subject. When a collectivist régime grants enterprises, and factories in particular, a wide measure of autonomy with a view to encouraging the efforts of directors and workers, the conditions of production may differ widely from those planned for. The scale of such discrepancies will of course vary according to the degree of initiative left to the directors. In cases when they have a certain latitude as regards recruiting staff, directors of firms may select one type of labour in preference to another; or may even engage a larger staff than provided for. They may also purchase one type of power instead of another.

In so far as the collectivist system seeks to encourage the initiative of heads of enterprises and of staff, and to stimulate their output by giving them an interest in the results obtained, or even by introducing a certain measure of competition, their estimates may be upset by the attitude of factory managers.

This is another possible reason for a discrepancy between aggregate supply and demand. To give an example, let us assume that factory managers realize that it is to their advantage not to use their lorries to the extent planned, so as to reduce the petrol item in their costs. This will result in the refineries showing an unforeseen drop in fuel sales, so that they are left with surplus stocks, and may be obliged to leave a proportion of their productive plant and perhaps also of their manpower idle. Even if the workers concerned continue to receive full pay, the problem of how to use this labour, or even reclassify it, will still arise. Alternatively, the pay of workers in the refineries concerned may be reduced, but only by a certain amount—otherwise it will cause such wage discrepancies as to arouse discontent, or lead to a general drop in wages liable to bring in its train a sharp drop in consumption.

These are mere hypotheses. Our main purpose is to emphasize that, when either producers of consumers are allowed a wider measure of economic freedom, more detailed estimates will be essential, since the maintenance of equilibrium depends on individual reactions.

THE PROBLEM OF TOTAL ECONOMIC EQUILIBRIUM UNDER COLLECTIVIST AND CAPITALIST RÉGIMES

Generally speaking, even though the collectivist economy may adopt many of the mechanisms of liberal economy, certain differences will remain. There are three chief reasons for this.

1. The factor of the inequality of incomes and consequently of savings will differ between the two types of régime, even when a collectivist system has a wide range of wage scales. Since savings cannot be converted into producers' goods, they will presumably be smaller. Consequently, the mechanism of underconsumption will operate less than in a capitalist régime.

2. Certain processes which make the anomalies of a capitalist régime cumulative should not operate in a collectivist régime. In the case of inflation, we should not encounter the phenomenon of encroachments on income which, in a capitalist régime, creates an extra margin of profit to the benefit of sellers, who are able to increase their consumption and to some extent constantly 'relaunch' the process of rising prices. Conversely, there is no reason to suppose that, if the state decides to lower prices, this will necessarily entail further price drops; although it is possible that, when a state introduces regular price drops every year, they will be anticipated by individuals, who will, temporarily, restrain their demand. Subject to this reservation, a collectivist state appears to be able, more easily than a capitalist state can, to introduce price cuts without reducing production.

3. The main difference between a collectivist state and a capitalist one lies in the attitude to investment. A capitalist state wishing to step up investment in order to absorb the whole of a surplus of

production over consumption may take certain measures—reducing the rate of interest, for example—but they may prove inadequate. There then remains the method of public works, but this often has the disadvantage of discouraging private enterprise. A capitalist state depends very largely on the attitude of private entrepreneurs, over whom it has no direct control.

A collectivist state, on the contrary, even if it allows managers of factories wide latitude at the executive level—and it seems that this is essential for satisfactory results—retains, in principle, control over investment. It could hardly be otherwise, since individuals cannot own the means of production. It is therefore an essential part of this régime that all large-scale investment [1] shall be controlled by the central authority. In this way, the state, by its control over the volume of investment, wields a vital instrument for adjusting economic anomalies.

It is clear from this brief survey that a collectivist economy is better equipped to raise the aggregate demand to the required level than to reduce a surplus demand. It is possibly better equipped than a capitalist state to combat inflation as well as deflation. Its chief asset in this respect is that it is able to rationalize institutions, introduce a fiscal system more nearly fraud-proof than is possible in a capitalist régime and, consequently, to exercise control over incomes dependent on personal position and market conditions, leaving individuals only such sums as are considered necessary in order to encourage them to work and to use their initiative and organizing ability.

The sole purpose of this very brief summary is to emphasize that the problems existing in widely different types of economy present a striking similarity; and to point out that, generally speaking, the same problems, risks and basic difficulties occur in collectivist and liberal régimes alike, despite differences in legal structure, institutions and delegation of responsibilities.

It is thus not surprising to find that both types of régime have adopted roughly the same methods; and that the progress of economic studies is applied in this field as in others.

---

1. Managing directors may have charge of minor investments, build up stocks subject to certain limits, equip buildings and even purchase certain machinery.

CHAPTER XI

THE FUTURE OF THE FULL EMPLOYMENT POLICY

When we pass from experiments belonging to another period of history —the period before the second world war—and examine more recent events and look forward to the future, a number of observations suggest themselves.

The first point is that the repercussions and effects of a set of ideas which were officially accepted, at the end of the second world war, by a large number of governments and international institutions cannot be ignored.

But, by a kind of paradox, at that very moment the immediate economic situation, which, during the war and the early post-war years, was characterized by full employment, made the application of these ideas appear less urgent. Nevertheless, as the war recedes further into the past, and especially if the prospects of a stable peace improve, the problem of under-employment does and must arise. It has lost none of its importance.

At the same time, the existence of improved methods of analysis and observation leads us to query whether the employment policy is indeed as completely effective as some of its advocates believe. Or, at least to question whether this policy can be fully effective until more definite progress has been made in the practical application of economic analysis.

OFFICIAL ACCEPTANCE OF THE PRINCIPLES OF FULL EMPLOYMENT

The importance of the fact that governments and international institutions have made the achievement and maintenance of full employment one of their main aims must not be underestimated. [1] We have only to remember the scandal provoked by the declaration of the Republic in 1848 on the right to work, in order to realize how far we have travelled. It was due to the attempts of scientific analysis to prove that full employment was a possibility that the United Nations Charter adopted its achievement as one of its aims:

'Article 55. The United Nations shall promote:

'(a) Higher standards of living, full employment, and conditions of economic and social progress and development . . .'.

'Article 56. All members pledge themeselves to take joint and separate action in co-operation with the Organization for the achievement of the purposes set forth in Article 55.'

The Universal Declaration of Human Rights, adopted by the United Nations General Assembly on 10 December 1948, proclaims 'the right to work, to free choice of employment; to just and favourable conditions of work and to protection against unemployment'.

A number of international organizations, such as the United Nations Economic and Social Council, are designed to promote the execution of this policy. The Economic and Social Council and the United Nations have also established other bodies to help attain this aim.

Similarly, since the end of the war, a number of governments have made full employment one of their main objectives. In this connexion we may quote the British white paper on employment policy, which was published as early as May 1944, i.e. at the height of the war, just before the Normandy landings. This white paper opens as follows:

'The government accept as one of their primary aims and responsibilities the maintenance of a high and stable level of employment after the war.'

Mention may be made in the same connexion of the Australian white paper 'Full Employment in Australia', dated 30 May 1945; and the Canadian white paper on employment and income. The Canadian white paper stated that the government had made it abundantly clear that one of the primary aims of its policy was to maintain a high and stable level of employment and income, and so to raise living standards.

Similar declarations appear in certain laws: the New Zealand Act of 1945 and the United States Act of 1946, both on employment.

The preamble of the United States Act is however less downright: 'The Congress hereby declares that it is the continuing policy and responsibility of the federal government to use all practicable means. . .

---

1. cf. A. A. P. Dawson, 'The United Nations and Full Employment' in the *International Labour Review*, May 1953.

to co-ordinate and utilize all its plans, functions and resources for the purpose of creating and maintaining, in a manner calculated to foster and promote free competitive enterprise and the general welfare, conditions under which there will be afforded useful employment opportunities, including self-employment, for those able, willing and seeking to work, and to promote maximum employment, production and purchasing power.'

These are mere declarations. However, these countries and certain others have set up machinery for applying and co-ordinating employment policy. In any case the very fact of stating that this policy is necessary—and hence also feasible—makes it impossible for governments to adopt a negative attitude on certain points, on pain of deliberately provoking revolt amongst the working people. Here, again, they would not have taken such a step had not the 'general theory' convinced them that this policy represented something more than a Utopian dream.

A more detailed examination confirms this impression and we find official documents listing various means of combating unemployment accompanied by analyses which might in some cases almost have been lifted from the work of Keynes or his followers.

Even before the war, in 1937, the International Labour Conference adopted recommendations on recourse to public works as a means of ensuring employment. [1]

These recommendations contained a clear definition of the part played by public investment as a means of offsetting the inadequacy of private demand, and of the need for encouraging this demand by an appropriate monetary policy. The conference stressed, in this connexion, the need for setting up in every country a national co-ordinating body to collate information and encourage preliminary preparation for certain works. Note that, from that time onwards, several governments were considering this problem: Sweden, the United Kingdom and Canada, for example. The international conference also emphasized the need for international collaboration in the matter of public works. The British white paper contained a definition of the main methods of controlling aggregate demand, i.e. consumption and investment, based mainly on Keynes' analysis.

---

1. cf. an article published in the *International Labour Review*, for December 1938, entitled 'Public Works as a Factor of Economic Stabilization'.

THE ECONOMIC AND SOCIAL COUNCIL ENQUIRY

It also became apparent that an international definition of the methods of applying the employment policy was needed. At the request of the Economic and Social Council, a questionnaire was sent to members of the United Nations, concerning the measures they were taking, or might take to achieve or maintain full employment. [1]

The replies to this questionnaire fall into three categories: (a) replies from countries whose economy is centrally controlled and run in large measure by the state. As we shall see, these countries regarded the questionnaire as being of no interest; (b) replies from industrialized countries which, unlike the first category, are concerned with abolishing unemployment as one of the main dangers besetting them; (c) replies from economically underdeveloped countries. These countries are not seriously concerned with unemployment caused by fluctuations of demand. Their main problem is the chronic shortage of employment for the available manpower, due to economic backwardness. They are concerned with increased the productivity and living standard of the population.

Note however that the economically underdeveloped countries may feel that repercussions of an economic depression occurring in more advanced countries: their difficulties are then accentuated by a drop in their exports.

The importance of the employment policy of the economically advanced countries—where private property exists—is therefore not confined to those countries.

All the replies, despite their variety, have a common feature: no government any longer bases its policy on a belief in the effectiveness of the classical mechanisms. All recognize the need to exercise control over the main factors of aggregate demand.

REPORT OF THE EXPERTS

Parallel with this enquiry, the Economic and Social Council decided, in face of the slackening of business activity in 1949, to set up a group of experts to prepare a report on national and international measures for achieving full employment. Their report was published at the end of 1949. It is based on an analysis of the employment theory and sets out to outline the practical measures for applying that theory.

---

1. An analysis of the replies received was published in 1949 under the title *Maintenance of Full Employment*.

Subsequently, further investigations were made and further enquiries sent to governments.

EVOLUTION OF THE EMPLOYMENT
PROBLEM SINCE THE WAR

In the period since the beginning of the second world war, the nature of the employment problem has changed. During the war, full employment was achieved, and even the belligerent countries were short of labour. This situation continued during the early post-war years. Aggregate demand was very high both for consumer goods, which had been in short supply as a result of the war, and for investment goods; owing to the needs of reconstruction and re-equipment. The main concern of governments was to meet inflationary pressures, which excluded the possibility of unemployment. In 1949, however, when there was a return to normal production, and when individual firms had replaced their stocks, there was a certain slackening of economic expansion, even a slight recession. [1] This, however, came to an end shortly before the Korean war, which, in conjunction with rearmament, launched a new wave of inflation.

For the past few years, nevertheless, there has been a fairly high rate of unemployment in certain countries (in Belgium, between 1949 and 1952, the number of unemployed averaged between 150,000 and 170,000; or 7 to 8.6 per cent; and in Italy from 1947 to 1951 there were between 1,600,000 and 1,700,000 unemployed); but on the whole the main countries have not had to apply the conclusions of the employment theory. There would therefore be no point in investigating applications of the theory during this period as we have done for the earlier period.

However, an easing of international tension in combination with the completion of reconstruction might raise the problem of full employment again in acute form. It may therefore be questioned whether the various countries would be capable of dealing with it.

---

1. In the United States, the unemployment figure in 1949 stood at 3,395,000.

DIFFICULTIES AND LIMITATIONS
OF THE EMPLOYMENT THEORY

A study of the experiments made in the period 1931-37, of the discussions about problems of economic stability, and of the theoretical analysis itself, leads us to wonder how effective the various remedies which, in combination, constitute the employment policy really are.

The criticisms which can be and have been levelled against the theory and policy of employment are too numerous to be taken in detail. They may, however, be divided into two main categories:

The first group point out that the mechanisms proposed are inadequate; especially as their effects depend on the attitude of private entrepreneurs and of the population as a whole. The second group, on the contrary, concentrate on the adverse effects which the employment policy has, or might have, on the stability of currency and the functioning of international trade.

Roughly speaking, the first set of criticisms may be said to come from the opponents of a 'liberal' economy, the second from its supporters.

FIRST SET OF CRITICISMS

The very nature of the employment policy, with its concern to retain the maximum of liberal mechanisms, and to sanction intervention of a general character only, may restrict the effectiveness of the policy in two ways.

Each of the various measures envisaged by the employment policy may provoke reactions running counter to the desired result. The use of taxation—or any other method—for the purpose of levelling incomes and so boosting consumption may have the effect of damping the initiative of entrepreneurs especially as regards improving equipment. Any rise in consumption may thus be neutralized by a fall in investment.

A decrease of the rate of interest may fail to stimulate private investment if heads of firms have lost confidence and fail to react to the drop in the price of money. Keynes himself admitted that this weapon might prove ineffective.

There remain public works, but these—according to the employment theory—operate mainly indirectly, by stimulating consumption and private investment. Their effects, moreover, are liable to be offset by the attitude of entrepreneurs, who may be apprehensive lest state inter-

149

10

vention in economic affairs, in the form of building or other works, may interfere with a sector hitherto regarded as the domain of private enterprise. There is a danger that a state works policy extending beyond the traditional province of the highways department may smack of socialization. This may incite individuals to reduce their private investments still further. In such case, the increase of public investment may give rise, contrary to all expectations, to a drop in private investment.

It is possible that something of this kind may have occurred in America, and that this is the reason, firstly, why President Roosevelt's budget deficit policy did not cause a sharp increase in private investment; and secondly why, despite strenuous efforts, the unemployment figures were still very high in the United States of America in 1935 and 1936. It is perhaps also the reason why full employment is more easily achieved through war, or even through an armaments policy, than through a programme of expenditure on welfare projects.

This is one of the points on which the supporters of a collectivist economy criticize the full employment policy. In a collectivist economy, the central authorities do not have to reckon with the reactions of entrepreneurs: the directors of factories, who are their counterparts, are obliged to increase their production and investments in accordance with instructions given them. There is no question, in principle, of their psychological reactions constituting an obstacle.

This explains why, at the time of the enquiry in 1948 the Secretary-General of the United Nations merely received from the Union of Soviet Socialist Republics a brief communication to the effect that 'there is no unemployment in the Union of Soviet Socialist Republics, and that economic stability is guaranteed'; and that 'consequently, the problem specified in the resolution of the Economic and Social Council of 3 May 1948 ... does not arise'. The Government of the Byelorussian Soviet Socialist Republic sent a similar communication. The Czechoslovak Government, whilst stating that unemployment did not exist, gave a more detailed reply, including the following sentence: 'All economic activity is directed by a uniform economic plan which aims at developing the maximum economic operations; it is therefore impossible that in some branches or in some areas a decline in the demand for labour should set in which could not be made good under the plan in relation to branches or areas by other means which are at disposal for regulating the labour market....'

The fact that the employment policy is a relatively liberal one imposes another kind of limitation. It is in the nature of this policy to apply general measures, which cannot prove effective against economic anomalies of a partial character. In the case of a depression in a particular region or industry, an increase of the aggregate demand may easily fail to improve this particular situation—or else the increase of demand needed will be so drastic that it leads to inflation and a continuous, accelerated rise of prices in other sectors of the economy. It is true that there is, during inflation, full employment in all sectors, but it is achieved at the price of destroying normal trade machinery.

Classical economic theory had exaggerated the role of partial economic disequilibrium in economic crises. According to this theory, unemployment in a particular region or industry was due to individuals —wage earners—refusing to be transferred, as the need arose; due, in fact, to the economic system being too rigid. Although there may be some truth in this theory, and although it does account for the difficulty of cutting down unemployment below a certain figure, it does not explain the scale of crises and depressions.

It may be pointed out, at this juncture, that there is every reason to concentrate at present on this kind of phenomenon. It is the business of economics to investigate the nature of these phenomena, and propose remedies. It is possible, for example, that the balance of supply and demand, and the balance of public receipts and expenditure in each region, need closer investigation. The state should certainly make more effort to introduce greater flexibility, and encourage transfers of personnel and changes of occupation. This is a vast field in which it is to be hoped that progress will be achieved through both theoretical analysis and practical measures.

This is however not a reason for ignoring the danger of anomalies affecting the economy as a whole.

The first category of objections indicate that state intervention may in some circumstances have to be more drastic than might at first be supposed, since state investments will have to compensate for a very sharp drop in private investment. In other words, in the event of private enterprise failing to operate in the field hitherto regarded as its prerogative, the state will have to step in. The matter may be stated in somewhat different terms. There do exist methods for achieving nearly full if not total employment and avoiding the acute depressions to which the world has been subject in recent years. But all these methods involve a certain reduction of capitalist profits. This is true of cutting the rate of interest, and true also, obviously, of the method of levelling incomes; as for public works, they inevitably appear, rightly or wrongly, to constitute a menace to capitalism.

The question is therefore whether the capitalist power, and in particular the wealthiest categories, will consent to have their profits

reduced in this way.   Economics cannot answer this question—it is to
sociology and political science that we have to turn.

SECOND SET OF CRITICISMS

Another category of criticisms concerns the repercussions of the full
employment policy on the monetary system and hence on international
economic relations.   That splendid instrument of classical economics,
that international currency—gold—whose movements guaranteed the
equilibrium of international economic exchanges, and whose existence
protected every individual against the arbitrary power of the state,
helpless in the face of its movements; gold, that mechanism so beloved
by Ricardo, has been thrown overboard by the application of the
employment theory.

ARBITRARY POWERS IN ECONOMIC
AND FINANCIAL ADMINISTRATION

Monetary expansion, which is necessary in order to lower the rate of
interest and permit an increase of public expenditure, is difficult, sometimes impossible, to achieve without abandoning the gold convertibility
of currency.   This is not obviously true, and it is possible to envisage
retaining a system of convertibility, of currency, though at a rate
varying with the fluctuations of the economic situation.   But that is
not the point.   The opponents of the employment theory argue that
it introduces an arbitrary element into economic and financial administration.   They assert that it is both illogical and dangerous to count
on the wisdom of governments.   It is all too tempting to use monetary
expansion as a convenient means for avoiding stringent financial controls.   Whenever the state budget fails to balance, the state will be
able, instead of introducing economies or imposing taxes, both of which
are unpopular measures, to quote the policy of full employment as an
excuse for maintaining the deficit and resorting to the issue of currency
to finance that policy.   Similarly, the scrapping of convertibility, or
the introduction of machinery for adjusting the parity of currency,
eliminates outflows of gold and the export of capital, which otherwise
stand in the way of any policy that threatens the owners of wealth.

All this is incontrovertible.   But, if we do not regard state intervention as necessarily to be deplored, the problem may be summed up as
follows: is it possible to find a financial system compatible with full

employment whilst at the same time limiting the arbitrary element, which, it must be admitted—whatever our view of the ideal form of society—governments tend to abuse.

There are, *a priori*, three different types of solution:

The first is to substitute, for gold, another form of currency consisting of a set of commodities, so that an increased demand for currency is reflected in an increased production of copper, iron, zinc, etc. This theory, which has been advanced by certain economists, will need to be further analysed and practical proposals formulated for giving it practical effect.

The second method—which may be combined with the first—is to substitute for gold some other international currency which can be issued in amounts varying with changes in the economic situation. This arrangement also would be arbitrary, but, being international, might be less so than one controlled by national governments.

A third method is to seek mechanisms for compelling the public authorities to explain their action, and draw attention to threats of inflation: this is the technique used by the national economic budget. Though it does not solve the problem completely, it has the advantage of actually existing. We shall return to it later.

THE FULL EMPLOYMENT POLICY AND INTERNATIONAL TRADE

As things are today, the employment policy has another aspect: it may cause a restriction of international trade. The 'general theory' showed that a limitation of imports may, in certain circumstances, have positive advantages; it resolved the doubts of those economists who had observed, albeit with regret, the restrictions put upon foreign trade.

It had to be admitted that, in accordance with these analyses, complete autarchy as applied in Hitler's Germany did constitute a means of ensuring full employment. Without going to such extremes, monetary expansion, which is a necessary condition for lowering the rate of interest, may, as we have seen, be incompatible with the maintenance of the gold standard. That this is so, and that a particular country is obliged, in order to eliminate unemployment, to quit the international market is due to developments in the world economic situation. In an expanding world, the need to guarantee full employment does not involve cutting down commercial exchanges with foreign countries.

The way to avoid autarchy is therefore by achieving full employment on a world scale. The same measures which have been recommended for application on the national scale should also be applicable internationally. Means must be found, in the event of a threat of depression, of effecting a monetary expansion that will avoid a drop in prices, reduce the rate of interest and promote investment. Measures must be taken to encourage the wealthiest communities, those with the strongest inclination to save, to invest their money abroad. The establishment of the International Monetary Fund and of the International Bank for Reconstruction and Development might have served this kind of purpose. The author of the 'general theory' allotted them an important role in the achievement of world-wide full employment. However, the system finally adopted is closer to the classical theories than to Keynes. Moreover, the funds at the disposal of the two bodies are not large enough to enable them to exercise more than a temporary influence on international exchanges. On the other hand, the importance of the question of full employment has been realized by the United Nations experts, who, in investigations carried out considerably after Bretton Woods, aim at eliminating restrictions on imports in the wealthiest countries with a surplus balance, and at encouraging these countries to invest abroad. These measures are parallel to those which the full employment policy proposes at the national level: the elimination of restrictions on imports encourages the development of consumption; the promotion of foreign investment is designed to compensate, on a world scale, for the fact that the consumption of the wealthiest countries is too low. Some proposals have gone further in this direction, and consider equalizing resources throughout the world at the level of the most favoured countries. Thus Prebish, in his work on the relationship between the American economy and that of the underdeveloped countries, has transposed to a world scale measures which reflect the social conflicts existing within countries. Point IV aims at providing at least a partial solution of this vast problem. It is understandable that this plan should have attracted the attention of disciples of Keynes, and that politicians such as Mr. Bevan should have laid such emphasis on the importance of a comprehensive and systematic policy for assisting the underdeveloped countries.

Without going into detail, we would merely say that, theoretically speaking, these admittedly more complex questions have, to date, received less attention than the question of the conditions of full employment at the national level.

CONCLUSION

Economists or practical experts trained in analyses of the employment theory have adduced another series of criticisms, or rather observations which, unlike certain others, are constructive and deserve special attention. They point to the difficulties of passing from a state of under-employment to full employment. Whilst the present economic situation is known, its future evolution is hard to forecast. There is a danger that the remedies employed may be inadequate or too drastic, or may cause inflation by launching a wave of uncontrollable speculation. These dangers are all the greater in a rigidly controlled economy. An increase of purchasing power too slight for certain sectors of the economy may prove excessive for others.

These observations lead to a number of conclusions.

The first is, of course, the need for eliminating any obstacles to the reconversion of the economy. In France, the reports of the Commission des Comptes de la Nation emphasize the vital importance of a policy of this kind. [1]

The second is that attention must be paid to problems of partial equilibrium, to the use of methods, modelled to a certain extent on Leontieff's, for studying those problems; and to the widely varying applications of those methods. In this field, very little has yet been done.

The third conclusion is the importance of working out methods of combating inflation. Countries which feel that they are powerless to control inflation are especially chary of policies of full employment. The credit, budgetary and fiscal policies must be defined, and must be made sufficiently flexible to enable the state to take measures to modify aggregate demand in the shortest possible time. All these are pre-requisites for a policy of economic expansion. To put it metaphorically, we cannot recommend increasing the speed of a car whose brakes are unreliable.

In other words, the problem of equilibrium must be taken as a whole; and it is not surprising to find that the same private individuals, experts, administrators and governments have waged or won the battle against both inflation and unemployment. This indicates the complexity of the problem of economic equilibrium and also its importance.

Is a capitalist economy or a mixed economy capable of achieving full

---

1. See *Rapport sur les Comptes Provisoires de la Nation des années 1951 et 1952* (Report on the Provisional Accounts of the Nation for the years 1951 and 1952), France, Imprimerie Nationale, 1953.

employment? This is a key question, social stability depends on it. The workers are no longer prepared to tolerate long-term mass unemployment of the kind they have known in the fairly recent past. Governments understand this, or they may at least be supposed to, and some have entered into pledges of a fairly categorical nature. This is one of the first results of the progress of economics. Peace in the ordinary sense of the word also depends on full employment. If foreign markets were really essential for the elimination of unemployment, this would be a constant incitement to imperialism—unless it were interpreted to indicate the need for systematic and large-scale aid to underdeveloped countries. Finally, it must not be forgotten that mass unemployment formed the basis of the dictatorial régimes which brought about the last war.

PART II

THE PROBLEM
OF CHOICE

CHAPTER I

GENERAL REMARKS

Choice is one of the basic problems of economic life. It arises from the fact that available resources are limited in relation to man's desires. This explains, also, why the problem becomes especially acute in periods of scarcity. The problem of choice is in fact a double one; it arises in two fields: consumption and production.

As regards consumption, it may be stated as follows: how can the maximum satisfaction of each individual be ensured? This is the question posed by every individual when wondering what arrangement of his finances will be least disagreeable to him, whether he should give up his car or his country house, cut down his expenses on food or change his flat, purchase a new article of clothing or a wireless set, etc.

As regards production, the entrepreneur asks himself how best to use his means of production. Peasants wonder whether to buy a horse or a tractor, to use one type of manure or another, to plant apple trees or pear trees.

Communities as well as individuals are faced with this question. Shall they spend more on housing or on education, build new roads or new railways, encourage mining research or the construction of dams, etc.?

All these problems appear to belong to the realm of common sense, of empiricism. They are all individual cases where, it would seem, all that science can do is to express in fine phrases what a man does of his own accord without thinking about it.

This is not in fact the case. It is of course true that certain institutions, certain techniques designed to facilitate choice—currency, which can be exchanged for any type of product; taxation, whose rate can be varied so as to increase or diminish each individual's resources—have been discovered more or less spontaneously, without the aid of any theoretical analysis. Gyges, if he was indeed the inventor of money, had no economic advisers; nor had the Pharaohs, who established one of the most perfect fiscal systems known to history.

For all that, the importance of economic analysis must not be underestimated. Man does not make the best choice as naturally as certain philosophies would have us believe. Unconsidered decisions, excessive preoccupation with the present and failure to draw a comparison between possible solutions are more frequent than any other kind of behaviour. The same is true to an even more marked degree of communities or, if we prefer it, of their rulers. To engage in the simultaneous pursuit of contradictory aims is doubtless the most natural way for statesmen to behave.

History shows very clearly the connexion between scientific analysis and the improvement, or even discovery, of the institutions and techniques for facilitating choice. Moreover, we shall see that not all the implications of the progress of economic theory have yet been fully understood or, at any rate, applied.

EVOLUTION OF EVENTS AND OF ANALYSIS

The backwardness of science in this respect, and the even greater backwardness in the applications of science, require explanation. Society for a long time allowed man little freedom of choice and, we might even say, little desire for choice. As a result of transport difficulties, the persistence of a closed economy and the force of tradition, the individual tended to use the commodities which were available, as his parents did, or his neighbours. Society imposed on him, without his realizing it, its own scale of values—closely bound up with religious, moral and political conceptions—so that it was difficult for any economic system to develop independently of the influence of theology and ethics. In a more conscious fashion, rulers restricted individual freedom of choice by their vetos, regulations and general policy, based partly on their own personal interests and partly on their conception of the common weal.

It was not until a fairly late epoch that free exchange was instituted. The legal system still bears traces of this primitive stage, when commercial transactions were rare, and had to be authorized by witnesses and legal instruments. For all this, there were a number of people who realized there was profit to be made by acting as middlemen, selling the surplus products of one party to other parties in need of them. These men had of course to contend with the obstacles raised by tradition, custom and laws. As transport improved and individuals became more independent of their environment, middlemen more influential, the conflict between the system of controlled consumption and production and the desire to expand exchanges emerged more clearly.

PROBLEM OF CHOICE IN THE CLASSICAL ECONOMY

The desire to cast off controls was not unknown to what we regard as the beginnings of economics—the works of the Physiocrats in France, of Adam Smith and his followers in England. These men tried to show that the individual was the best judge of what gave him the greatest measure of satisfaction, and of how to organize production most advantageously. Their system was here contrary to the procedure in force at that time. They pointed out that, when the state required industrialists to produce certain types of manufactures, forbidding the manufacture of very light materials or of materials of certain dimensions, it was claiming to be a judge of something of which it knew nothing. The individual, the consumer, knew better than the state what he liked. It was for him to decide whether he wanted materials of this or that type, manufacture or dimension. It was the demand of the consumer, which would guide the producer and induce him to manufacture those articles which, since they sold best, brought him the most profit.

To do otherwise was to fail to recognize that utility is simply and solely a reflection of man's desire. For each person, the most useful thing is that which he desires most. The only way of achieving the greatest satisfaction of the largest number is by allowing freedom of choice.

The same argument was applied to production. It was considered that the individual was the best judge of how to organise his work, when to rest, harvest, sow or manufacture. Animated by the desire for profit, he knew better than the state which method of production to select.

Such was the classical theory of economics. Thanks to the machinery of the market, and to the free initiative of individuals, manufacture and sale will proceed under optimum conditions. Even so, competition must be free, so that each individual will be able to manufacture the articles other people want to buy, and to purchase what he wants after comparing qualities and prices; and so that the producer will be forced to manufacture as cheaply as possible simply because, unless he does so he will be supplanted by someone able to undersell him.

APPLICATION OF THE CLASSICAL SYSTEM

This system may be said to have been applied in all the institutions adopted in Great Britain during the eighteenth century. In France, during that period, there was a conflict between the advocates of what was called the control system and the upholders of the new theories which found favour in administrative circles. The aim of the *Intendants* (administrators of provinces), in abolishing statute labour, was to set free the individual to arrange his time and work as he thought best. Their application of Colbert's regulations was half-hearted because they wished to leave producers free to choose the best methods of manufacture, and consumers free to purchase what they preferred.

The combination of theory and practice and the effects of one on the other were very marked in the work of Turgot, an economist, author of a number of books on economics and a disciple of the Physiocrats, some of whose theories he did not, however, accept. Turgot attempted, first as *Intendant* of Limoges and later as Comptroller-General of Finance, to put the new ideas, which mature reflection had convinced him to be the most just, into practice: abolition of the guilds, abolition of statute labour, free marketing of grain. His work was undone when he fell from power, but was revived at the time of the Revolution. Little by little, the system of free trade was instituted in countries which were casting off the vestiges of the feudal system or of state controls. The entire economic reform of the world in the nineteenth century in the most 'advanced' countries may be regarded as an application of the theory of free choice; and economists like Ricardo, J.-B. Say and Bastiat were untiring in their support of the progress—in their view all too slow—made by the public authorities. But scientific analysis was still incomplete; subsequent progress of great practical significance enabled it to be filled out.

THE MARGINAL ANALYSIS

The marginal analysis led to important advances. It derived from a kind of logical contradiction. Classical economics had equated utility with human desire. That which men desired most strongly possessed the greatest utility value. But the early economists could not but notice that certain objects which were very useful, and recognized as such, fetched nothing or very little on the market; whereas other less useful articles sold at very high prices. It was of course possible to explain this by drawing a distinction between value in use and value in exchange, but this did not account for the contrast between the two. To talk of scarcity value was tantamount to admitting that the value of an article did not depend merely on utility. In fact, the exchange value or price of an article depended much less on utility than on the cost of production; and it was the cost of production which tended to control not perhaps the current price of an article, which varied with the fluctuations of supply and demand, but at any rate the 'normal' price, which remained relatively stable despite market fluctuations.

It is thus natural that, in those countries where the economic system founded on exchange had made the most progress, economists, in attempting to paint a truer picture of the facts, build up a coherent system, and account for the first phenomena to strike the observer— i.e. the mechanism of the market and the establishment of prices— should have established a connexion between the value of an article and the cost of production or, more precisely, the labour expended on it. It is not surprising that this analysis should have been used by persons interested in workers' conditions. They pointed out that, since value was based on labour, the profits made by entrepreneurs were not only morally questionable but also contrary to a kind of economic logic. Marx, and his predecessors, applied to industrialists the same kind of argument that Ricardo and the English industrialists had applied to landowners.

It is understandable also that the 'classical' economists should have taken fright at these conclusions and attempted to counter them by reviving and extending the concept of utility and choice on which the liberal system of economy, in certain countries at any rate, had been based. But this could not be done unless the apparent contradiction between use value and exchange value could be resolved. Liberal economics had to explain the paradox whereby the most useful articles had little or no market value. The theory which related value to cost provided an answer, an answer which was both awkward for the current system, in that it revealed the existence of unearned incomes, and unsatisfactory as regards theory because it failed to explain why so much labour was expended on certain types of object.

The difficulty of resolving the problem of choice in the domain of public works had led an engineer of the Highways Department in

France in 1844 to propose splitting up the production of each commodity into portions of decreasing utility. However, this theory, which was designed only to increase the efficiency of the public services, did not recommend itself to the ruling classes. It was not until the second half of the century, when socialist theory had made advances and theorists had adopted the Anglo-Saxon definition of value, that economists returned to this method of analysis. They stressed the importance of the psychological law according to which the satisfaction afforded by successive instalments of the same commodity diminished progressively, as the need for it becomes less and less acute; the first glass of water quenches a man's thirst, the last is merely used to water the flowers in the garden. It is the final utility of an object, the limit or marginal utility, which determines the price it will fetch: the value of each unit of the commodity is equal to its marginal value, the value of the final use to which it can be put. This analysis, representing the application to economics of the method on which differential calculus is based, revived the concept of subjective utility; and enabled value in exchange to be substituted for value in use.

The main result of this was to show that the best means of procuring the greatest satisfaction both of individuals and of the community as a whole was by equalizing marginal utilities. Let us take an example to explain this idea. A man can buy a certain number of shirts and a certain number of pairs of shoes. Let us suppose that, after buying two shirts and two pairs of shoes, he has enough left to buy either another shirt or another pair of shoes: if he decides on the shirt it means that, for him, the third shirt and the second pair of shoes have the same marginal utility. In this way, the individual equalizes his marginal utilities.

APPLICATION OF THE MARGINAL ANALYSIS

Some people have regarded this theory as having no more importance than to provide a sort of explanation, a pseudo-scientific picture, of the facts. After all, the individual does not need a theorem to be made out of this simple common-sense idea: namely that, in order to achieve the greatest possible happiness, he has to sacrifice the superfluous to the essential. This theory had nevertheless a practical purpose. It represented a fresh justification of the system of free competition which, as can easily be shown, guarantees the equalization of marginal utilities.

The marginal analysis could therefore be used as an argument against any system of controlled distribution, since such systems did not automatically equalize the marginal utilities. It showed, even more clearly than the classical doctrine, that any régime which dispensed with the mechanism of commercial exchange could not possibly achieve the greatest satisfaction of the greatest number. Retrospectively, as it were, it explained and justified all progress in the direction of free exchange.

Some of the conclusions which were drawn, incidentally, went further than the premises warranted: there was nothing to prove that private ownership of the means of production was an essential condition for equalizing marginal utilities; nor was it certain that individuals would always be able to recognize what was most useful for them, or that all essential commodities could always be obtained by way of exchange.

Nevertheless, the method of the marginal analysis does lead to a better understanding of the nature of the problem of choice and the means of solving it. It indicates that it is expedient, in principle, and in the absence of indications to the contrary, to permit individuals to equalize their marginal utilities through the mechanism of exchange. It suggests that reforms affecting production should leave the consumers' freedom of choice intact.

As we shall see, these advantages have in certain circumstances been regained, by what may be called the process of rediscovery of the natural mechanisms of choice. But at the same time the progress of scientific theory has shown what conditions are essential in order that these mechanisms may have the expected result; and what obstacles may prevent them from operating. A set of practical deductions have been or could be drawn.

One of the most interesting points of this analysis is its application to the domain of public economy. There are in fact circumstances in which these natural mechanisms cannot operate. This happens when the community has to decide on the allocation of public expenditure or when it controls production and exchanges, distribution of imports, investment, etc. In such cases, we have to ascertain what conditions shall govern the choice of the community, or rather of the rulers of the community in order to guarantee the greatest satisfaction of the greatest number and the maximum efficiency of production.

It does not appear to be possible to leave the choice to be decided by the competition between purchasers, sellers and producers, which results in providing every individual with the articles he most desires and eliminating the least efficient producers. In the absence of this natural machinery are we to resort to arbitrary control, or can we find some guide? Economics is beginning to be aware of this problem. It is incumbent on economists—and they have already done this in certain fields—to suggest to the public authorities techniques derived from the marginal analysis, techniques which may be called considered mechanisms. It is, perhaps, in this field that both theory and technique still have farthest to go.

A. *The natural mechanisms*

CHAPTER II

REDISCOVERY
OF THE
NATURAL MECHANISMS

As a result of state intervention, war economy and, *a fortiori*, the experience of the collectivist economy, economists have been able to 'rediscover' the advantages and methods of operation of the natural mechanisms, which have, therefore, influenced economic and financial policy.

FIRST EXAMPLE:
THE LAW OF SUPPLY AND DEMAND

The first reaction of governments faced with overproduction or scarcity phenomena has often been to resort to fixing prices. Minimum or maximum prices were fixed. It soon became apparent that this method, which disregarded the elementary principles of economics, came up against natural reactions. Whenever prices failed to reflect the supply and demand position, they were not respected; transactions were made at a different rate or, if control was exercised, trade deserted the official market. The examples of this state of affairs are too conclusive and too well known to need mentioning.

The public authorities were therefore forced to take steps to influence the conditions of supply and demand. They could, in periods of overproduction, purchase the surplus, and keep the price at the level they wished by reducing supply. But this method also ignored elementary economic laws. The effect of keeping prices too high was to perpetuate the excess of supply over demand. The French administration of wine and tobacco is a characteristic example of this. There remained one other method: to take official steps to control the actual volume of production, by restricting the area planted with vines, for example. It is gradually being realized, however, that the only really

167

effective way of balancing supply and demand is by fixing official prices at a figure approximating to the prices the commodities in question would naturally fetch. In this way products which are unprofitable— the most expensive ones—the marginal products, in other words, tend to disappear. Consumption is stimulated, and equilibrium restored.

The same kind of process occurs in periods of scarcity. It soon became clear that, in order to maintain prices at a level not based on market conditions, demand would have to be restricted by rationing. The ration card system gradually came to replace the system of fixing prices. Simultaneously, supply had to be controlled, and producers obliged to put their goods on the market or deliver them to the official distributing agencies. A whole collection and distribution machinery was thus built up.

The whole of this organization may be regarded as an application of the basic principles of economics. Similarly, many countries found that the restriction of rents lead to reducing building, unless the state intervened to take the place of private initiative. Faced with a housing crisis, the public authorities finally had to resort to raising rents—to the market system, in other words—or to state building projects.

In these different senses it is true to speak of the rediscovery of the natural mechanisms; and in another sense as well.

SECOND EXAMPLE: MONEY

One of the drawbacks of rationing is that it fails to give optimum satisfaction, encourages waste, and restricts production of the most useful commodities. A person who is entitled to a tobacco ration at a relatively low price may not be a very keen smoker; if the ordinary market system were operating, he would not buy tobacco, but now, since he can get it cheaply, he smokes, to the detriment of those of his fellows who are keener smokers than he is. He can of course exchange his tobacco ration for the sugar ration of his neighbour, whose tastes are different. But this may be awkward; and situations such as these emphasize the advantages of the natural mechanisms. Rationing prevents the equalization of marginal utilities on which the achievement of maximum satisfaction depends.

The same sort of effects are evident in production also. A producer is obliged to sell the whole of his output at a fixed price and, since that price is relatively low, he has no encouragement to increase his production, or to produce luxury goods, as he would under a free market system. Controlled collection and distribution may thus perpetuate shortages.

This has led to consideration of the advantages of the money system. The importance of money, which enables the individual to choose, to give priority to the commodities he desires most—or, to use the language of the economists, to equalize marginal utilities by a series of adjustments—has become fully apparent. This rediscovery of the utility of money has doubtless been responsible in some measure for the two lines of action followed by the public authorities.

EVOLUTION OF THE RATIONING SYSTEM

One of these was to work out a rationing system which was similar to the money system, and to restore the greatest possible measure of freedom to the consumer. This was the purpose of introducing what may be called the multivalency of ration cards. Instead of having a sugar card, a jam card and a sweet card, every person may receive a card entitling him to a certain quantity of sugar products.

He will then choose sugar or jam according to his tastes. Similarly he will be able, with his fats card, to choose between butter, cooking fats or margarine. One of the countries whose economists have had the greatest practical influence, Great Britain, is also one of those where the use of multivalent cards has been most widely adopted. The greater the multivalency of a card the closer its resemblance to money, with which it would, in the end, coincide.

In order to ensure smooth distribution, there has naturally to be a system of 'handing on' ration cards. The retailer obtains his provisions from the wholesaler, the wholesaler from the producer, by handing on the cards received from his customers, so that these cards constitute a kind of currency, and cheques can be used to facilitate circulation. It is even possible, if the authorities issue cards in excess of the commodities available, that there may be positive inflation, identical with money inflation. This happened in France.

Nevertheless, cards inevitably lack some of the advantages of money—unless the system of multivalency is carried to a point where cards can buy everything, so that they acquire the characteristics of real money.

THE RETURN TO MONEY

The drawbacks of distributive systems have however in certain cases led to a return to the use of money as such. A typical example of this occurred in the Union of Soviet Socialist Republics.

During the period following the seizure of power by the Soviets, the period of 'war communism', money tended to disappear. This was largely the effect of inflation, and of the need for rationing and controlled distribution; but it was also due in part to theoretical concepts. Various methods for abolishing money were envisaged. In June 1920 the Central Executive Committee of the Union of Soviet Socialist Republics instructed the Commissariat for Finance to study a system of payment without money. The following year, the Commissariat proposed the use of a labour unit, the *trud*.

But the Soviet Government realized the drawbacks of the non-existence of money. Under the NEP policy, a series of measures restoring the monetary economy were taken: certain public services ceased to be free of charge; taxes, payable first in kind and later in money, replaced requisitioning; workers were paid in money instead of in kind, etc. Between 1922 and 1924, a new form of money, the *chernovetz*, was introduced. Subsequently the Union of Soviet Socialist Republics, like the capitalist countries during and immediately after the war, had periods of rationing which reduced the importance and the function of money. But—and this is a very important fact—it never disappeared completely. The Soviet economy—like that of other collectivist régimes—is based on the use of money. It therefore differs in an important respect from the socialist régimes dreamed of at the time when no country had yet abandoned capitalism. In a collectivist state, the maintenance of money allows the individual to exercise his choice and to decide how, out of the various possible ways, to spend to his greatest satisfaction the wages he receives.

It was for the same reasons that the various countries which had adopted rationing were induced, gradually, to abandon it. The fact of restricting the role of money served to emphasize its usefulness. This was one of the reasons for the various measures which were taken to prevent or halt inflation and restore the freedom of the consumer.

It is difficult to ascertain how far scientific analysis was responsible for this evolution. The part played by money as an instrument of choice appeared, or rather reappeared, very clearly in theory as well as in practice.

Whilst recent events—combined with the progress of analysis—have led to a rediscovery of the advantages of the natural mechanisms, the progress of economics has also shown that it is not as easy as is commonly believed to ensure that these mechanisms operate ideally. Certain obstacles have emerged, and the study of these obstacles has led to a number of practical conclusions, several of which are already being applied, or very soon will be.

CHAPTER III

OBSTACLES TO THE OPERATION
OF THE NATURAL MECHANISMS

The early theorists were inclined to believe that, if only state intervention were abolished, the natural mechanisms would operate in perfect conditions. With the advance of science, it has become evident that this was an over-simplified view. The economists have admitted that the capitalist régime, left to itself, does not constitute a complete and perfect competitive system; and they have emphasized the effects of the fiscal system, which may prevent the weeding out of the less productive enterprises. Similar observations have been made since the very beginning of the study of economics; but the course of events, which has been characterized by an increase of the obstacles to perfect competition, leading to what has been called the rigidity of the economy, has caused economists to turn their attention once again to this kind of phenomenon. Another factor is the startling progress which has been made since the first world war in the analysis of the price mechanism. Whilst these studies cannot be said to be entirely responsible for the series of measures taken during the past few years for the purpose of restoring free competition—or at any rate proclaiming the intention to do so—they did probably have a certain amount of influence; the form of certain anti-trust laws and fiscal reform plans may be traced directly to scientific progress.

The official attitude of the United States Government since the Sherman Act provides perhaps the most direct indication of the belief in the possibility of restoring the conditions of competition. Measures such as the abolition of cartels in the German and Japanese economies, as well as the principles proclaimed at the Havana Conference and accepted by a large number of countries, point to the same thing. This is thus a typical example of the influence of scientific theories on practice. The effectiveness of these measures may be questioned and it is possible that the subsequent progress of the analysis may reveal their defects more clearly.

MONOPOLY AND IMPERFECT COMPETITION

The phenomena of monopoly or imperfect competition have led to two different developments. [1]

On the scientific plane the economists, after starting with somewhat over-simplified theories, arrived at a much more complex analysis of both the phenomena and their consequences. This progress was due in part to the evolution of the situation—but only in part, for science often lags a certain way behind events.

On the practical plane, the attitude of the state was influenced by the changes and improvements in economic analysis, as well as by those of the economic environments. The negative attitude of most governments in the nineteenth century reflects the scientific ideas of the age —as well, of course, as the relative strengths of various forces. The large number of the 'anti-trust' laws and the very measures envisaged for putting this legislation into force are an indication of the 'discoveries' of certain contemporary economists as well as of the fluctuations of the economic environment.

Finally, the other solution to the problem of monopolies—nationalization or permanent control by the public authorities—may be considered to derive, in part, from a study of the economic and social effects of the restrictions upon a competitive system.

THE CLASSICAL CONCEPT OF MONOPOLY
AND ITS PRACTICAL CONSEQUENCES

The classical concept may be stated as follows:

The advantages of a liberal economic system are linked with competition. As a result of competition, a drop in cost prices is followed by a drop in selling prices. An enterprise which finds that, thanks to technical progress, there is a margin between the cost and selling prices of its products will be induced by the profit motive to reduce its selling prices, in order to increase its sales and turnover by an amount more than compensating for the loss in profit on each article.

---

1. *Documentation Française* in 1953 published a series of articles under the general title: *Combinations and Monopolies in the World*. Two volumes dealt with the anti-trust laws in the United States of America; one with industrial agreements in France; others with each of the main countries. They thus give a large number of practical examples. The volume on France contains a bibliography. We shall confine ourselves to mentioning the following works on the phenomena of imperfect competition: *The Economics of Imperfect Competition* by Joan Robinson; *The Theory of Monopolistic Competition* by Chamberlain; J. Marchal's book in French *Le Mécanisme des Prix* (The Price Mechanism) sums up the findings of economics on this subject.

Other enterprises are obliged to follow suit, for fear of going under. Those unable to do so go out of business. As the result of a process of true natural selection, only the best, economically speaking, survive. Thus a competitive system forces enterprises, in their own interests, to make technical progress and enable consumers to share in the benefits resulting.

But this only happens where the competition is real. Liberal economists recognized long ago that, when there are monopolies, individual interests no longer coincide with those of the general public. The monopolist can raise the selling price of his articles above the cost price. It is true that his turnover will then drop, but the drop is more than offset by the increase of his margin of profit. Moreover, he has less incentive to improve production methods; so that monopoly results in a fairly low volume of production at relatively high prices.

Liberal economists, however, continued to advocate the capitalist system as opposed to state intervention, despite the risk of factors of this kind. They maintained that monopoly situations were exceptional, 'monstrous' phenomena so rare that they could be ignored. In fact, when one enterprise obtains a monopoly, the exceptional profits it makes lead to the setting up of other enterprises desirous of making similar profits: with the result that the very advantages which accrue from monopoly have the effect of establishing, or restoring competition.

This is the reason given for the fact that, until the first world war, there were very few laws on industrial agreements. For a long time, the only such laws in existence were the Le Chapelier Law of 14-21 June 1791, according to which 'citizens of the same calling and profession ... may not concert together or adopt any agreement designed to promote their common interests'; and Article 419 of the Code Penal,[1] which also figured in the Belgian Penal Code of 1867.

But facts showed that economists who believed the restrictions on competition to be few were mistaken. As the nineteenth century wore on, and in particular after 1870, monopolies, trusts, agreements between producers, the so-called cartels, became more and more numerous. This was true of Europe, and particularly of Germany where, by 1905,

---

1. Article 419 of the Code Penal ran as follows: 'All persons who, by deliberately spreading abroad false or libellous rumours, offering prices in excess of those asked by the sellers themselves, or promoting meetings of or agreements between the principal holders of any one merchandise or commodity to refrain from selling the said merchandise or commodity, or from selling them below a certain price; or who, by any fraudulent ways or means whatsoever, shall cause the prices of goods or merchandise, or of public money or bills, to rise or fall below the prices which would have operated on the market in conditions of natural and free competition shall be liable to a term of imprisonment of at least one month and at most one year; and to a fine of from 500 to 10,000 francs. Offenders may further be sentenced by the court to be placed under police supervision for a period of at least two years, and not exceeding five years.'

there were 385 cartels containing 12,000 of the largest enterprises; but the real paradise of combinations and agreements was North America. After the end of the War of Secession, and during the years 1880 to 1890 in particular, the development of the American economy was marked by a degree of industrial and financial concentration unparalleled in the rest of the world. The early captains of industry, Vanderbilt, Rockefeller, Carnegie, John Pierpont Morgan, used their first profits to buy other businesses, or to ruin their competitors. Veritable battles took place, battles of tariffs or stock exchange battles, with the winner carrying off the monopoly of an industry: in 1879, Rockefeller controlled 90 per cent of all transport and all the refining of petroleum products. Carnegie was in the process of acquiring the monopoly of ironsmelting. In 1880, Morgan attempted to gain control of all railways—and very nearly succeeded. Other trusts were springing up in every possible field. The control of many branches of production was in the hands of two or three groups.

The reaction of the public authorities to this state of affairs varied from country to country. In some, where the process of industrial concentration and agreements was widely developed, they made no move at all. Except for a short period, the German law on coalitions (1870) was never applied. Cartels were regarded in Germany as a means of keeping a check on the economy and facilitating the application of the dumping policy which was considered necessary in order to dispose of a constantly expanding production.

Meanwhile, the country where industrial concentration was most widespread and most spectacular—the United States of America— passed, in 1890, the Sherman Act, declaring illegal 'every contract, combination in the form of trust or otherwise, or conspiracy in restraint of trade or commerce among the several states . . .' and condemning 'every person who shall monopolize, or combine or conspire with any other person or persons, to monopolize any part of the trade or commerce among the several states, or with foreign nations. . . .'

The wording of this act was obviously a reflection both of the phenomena characterizing the evolution of the United States of America, and of the implicit, or explicit, belief in the accuracy of the classical analysis according to which any restraint on free competition leads to the restriction of production and the rise of prices. Another striking point about this law is the general and summary nature of its text. It is clear that its authors recognize two economic phenomena—competition and monopoly—which are completely distinct and between which there is no middle way.

Monopoly being a clear cut though exceptional phenomenon is not difficult to define. In this respect, the Sherman Act closely reflects the view of classical economics at that time. [1] It indicates the same attitude as the Le Chapelier Law, and it derives from the same remark of Adam Smith, who had pointed out that meetings between heads of the same branch of industry always spelled danger for the public. The nature of the law was doubtless responsible to some extent for the half-hearted way in which it was applied. The result was that it had little effect on the growth of the monopoly movement between 1890 and 1910.

At the beginning of the twentieth century, and down to the 1914 war, there were several other examples of anti-trust legislation: a Canadian law in 1889, and laws passed in Australia and New Zealand between 1906 and 1910. Generally speaking, however, these laws were few, and their application was half hearted because of the general attitude towards monopolies.

Broadly speaking, it is not until after the first world war that the advance of economics is paralleled by legislation on agreements and the restriction of competition.

NEW THEORIES AND PRACTICES REGARDING MONOPOLIES AND IMPERFECT COMPETITION

Scientific theory developed along two lines: on the one hand economists asked themselves whether the idea of monopolies being unmitigatedly harmful required revision; on the other, they were forced to admit that imperfect competition was much more prevalent than classical theory assumed.

Opinions Regarding the Effects of Agreements and Monopolies

Arguments in favour of the concentration of economic power fall into two different categories.

The first reflects the concern to limit production and price drops. Economists pointed out the drawbacks of over-production, and the need for matching production to consumption: this view was particularly prevalent during the 1929 slump and the depression of the ensuing

---

1. As has been written: 'Those people who regarded this as an artificial phenomenon, and one which would always be exceptional, thought it quite unnecessary to accompany the legal definition of the infractions penalized by the law by detailed provisions designed to reduce the loopholes. People knew very well, after all, what an industrial agreement or an attempt at a monopoly was: something easily recognizable, standing out from the average, and generally condemned; something that the courts would have no difficulty in spotting'. *United States of America, Anti-Trust Laws*, vol. I, p. 67 (*Documentation Française*).

years; and it inspired or justified a series of laws favouring industrial agreements—or sometimes even making them compulsory. The most significant step was that taken by the New Deal in the Codes of Fair Competition. Thus the NRA, as mentioned above, suspended anti-trust legislation. This was the concession made to business circles in return for their acceptance of the social measures of the Roosevelt codes.

During the same period, laws designed to permit governments to make certain agreements compulsory were passed in a number of countries: Germany, Italy, Great Britain, Belgium, etc.[1] Generally speaking, this type of agreement cannot unreservedly be admitted to have advantages except in an economy showing a natural tendency to unemployment. With a systematic full employment policy, on the contrary, acts which are aimed primarily at cutting down production and maintaining or raising price levels cannot be approved. Many of the arguments adduced in favour of industrial agreements during the period between the two world wars may be considered to have been rendered invalid by the progress of economics; all the same they exercised a considerable influence on the policy of states, in particular as regards 'corporatist' trends. Here again, there is reason to believe that the progress of economic analysis has undermined the theory and prevented application of this type of economy.

Economists have, however, pointed out that certain industrial agreements may have the effect of influencing conditions of production or sale and reducing cost prices.[2] Restricting competition may make it possible to cut down on advertising and sales drives; it may lead to standardizing products, making factories specialized, and setting up joint research bureaux and laboratories.

The classical argument that the monopolist will normally raise his selling price considerably above his cost price still holds good; but, if agreements enable the cost price to be lowered, it is not impossible that the selling price may in the long run be lower than it would be in a competitive system. Is this in fact the case? Is this possibility a probability? Economists are not at present able to answer this question, since research has not yet been carried far enough. Analysis however shows that some of the acts resulting from industrial agreements—perhaps even certain agreements themselves—can reduce pro-

1. In France, no general measures were adopted, but agreements affecting certain sectors of the economy were instituted by the public authorities (sugar, footwear, peaches, potassium, etc.).
2. We are not concerned here with war-time legislation which, in various countries and in various ways, set up special groups to distribute products in short supply, prevent wastage, and ensure prompt execution of government orders, etc.

177

duction costs; but this does not mean that all the dangers of such agreements are eliminated.

This view may be taken as an explanation or vindication of certain compulsory agreements designed to improve conditions of production. An example of this is the British Coal Mines Act of 1930, the purpose of which was not only to restrict production, but also to reorganize the industry by the merger of firms too small to be efficient. In France, the Centres Techniques Industriels (Industrial Methods Bureaux) established by the law of 1948, provide a central machinery for carrying out technical research for which individual enterprises lack proper facilities.

However, the recognition that some of the consequences of agreements might be favourable has also had other results. It has led, not unnaturally, to legislation which attempts to discriminate between the various types of agreements, not condemning all outright, but, on the contrary, even encouraging certain types—subject to control. In order to draw this distinction, the public authorities have had to set up special courts or commissions of enquiry to advise the government, in particular when referring cases to the special courts.

The United States of America, in 1914, had passed a law instituting the Federal Trade Commission vested with investigatory powers; its decisions required the endorsement of the judiciary.

Germany, in 1923, passed a law setting up a cartels court, with power to annul agreements which were contrary to the general interests. The government wielded similar powers in certain conditions.

The British Monopolies Act of 1948 set up a commission of enquiry. It is the duty of this commission, at the request of the government, to investigate activities of heads or groups of enterprises as regards restrictions on free competition, and to report whether they are harmful or dangerous to the general interests. The government, which is not bound to accept the advice of the commission, may issue a declaratory decree of illegality, which requires parliamentary ratification. Infringements of such decrees may be referred to the courts.

In Canada, a commissioner, assisted by an administrative staff, exercises permanent supervision over agreements.

In the Netherlands, recent legislation has made it compulsory to register agreements; and has established a special commission, but its findings are not binding on the Minister, who is empowered to declare certain clauses illegal.

In the Scandinavian countries (Sweden, Norway, Denmark) agreements have to be registered and made public. In Norway and Denmark there is, in addition, a price control commission, with power to give instructions to enterprises designed to prevent the evils of coalition.

In France, a decree of 9 August 1953 'on the maintenance or re-establishment of industrial and commercial competition' forbids, in principle, all practices designed to restrict free competition by preventing the lowering of cost or selling prices. This veto does not however apply to any practices which can be shown to result in improving markets or furthering economic progress. Infringements of this law, as well as applications for exemption, are referred to a technical commission on agreements. In accordance with the advice of this commission, the Minister institutes legal proceedings, where necessary.

Many countries are in the process of drafting legislation designed to serve a similar purpose, namely to discriminate between the harmful and useful effects of agreements, eliminating the former and encouraging the latter.

Analysis of the Phenomena of Imperfect Competition and its Practical Consequences

The progress of science, especially in the last thirty or forty years, has led economists to admit that there exist, between competition and pure monopoly, a whole range of intermediate situations.

The existence of a very large enterprise whose sales amount to, say, 20 per cent to 30 per cent of the total market upsets the mechanism of competition. The number of customers that an entreprise of these dimensions can attract away from other enterprises by lowering its selling prices varies in inverse proportion to the number it already has, and is very small. In the extreme case of monopoly, as we have seen, an enterprise cannot increase its sales except by drawing on new purchasers. The same kind of situation tends to arise with very large enterprises. In other words, the concentration of enterprises as a result of technical progress tends naturally to reduce competition.

This kind of situation arises from the mere fact of one large enterprise existing, even if its rivals are small or average sized. But when the entire market is controlled by a few large enterprises—a situation which is called oligopoly—another, more complex phenomenon emerges.

Economists have long discussed the conditions governing the establishment of prices on such a market; for a long time they overlooked the most likely explanation. Every large enterprise is aware that, if it lowers its prices in order to attract customers away from its competitor or competitors, these will follow suit by lowering their prices, with the result that this kind of competition will not, in the long run, benefit any of them. It is better not to do this. In this way, without any kind of agreement, the conscious interests of every enterprise lead to keeping prices fairly high and restricting production, i.e. to a situation identical with or similar to that generally regarded as due to monopoly only. The same kind of results are produced by the indifference or ignorance of consumers, and the partitioning of markets due to transport costs.

A tradesman has his own customers, who do not readily desert him. Proximity, habit and good neighbourly relations tend to prevent them from changing their shop so long as price differences do not exceed a certain amount. The result is that prices may be considerably higher than cost prices. Why should an individual tradesman lower his prices? The number of customers he would attract away from his rivals by doing so would be very small. Conversely, he would lose only a few of his customers if he put his prices up.

Advertising may operate in a similar way. A producer can, by persuading purchasers that his product, his brand, is superior to others—actually very similar—count on a certain number of fairly steady customers who will not transfer their custom even if his prices are noticeably higher than those of his rivals. If his rivals act likewise, so that the market is split up as it were into a number of compartments, all selling prices will be higher than normal cost prices, since they include fairly large advertising costs, plus a substantial margin of profit. We may therefore ask—and this is the conclusion certain economists have reached—whether the system of imperfect competition is not in fact the most prevalent, and whether perfect or near-perfect competition is not exceptional.

Analysis of the economic situation of a market dominated by a small number of enterprises, i.e. oligopoly, began in the first half of the nineteenth century, but in a very sketchy way; economists gradually succeeded in obtaining a more accurate picture of the possible effects of giant enterprises or groups of enterprises. As investigations advanced, economists began to emphasize the importance of customer reaction, of partitioning the market and of advertising.

The general theory of imperfect competition was worked out in the main by two economists, an American, Edward Chamberlin, and an Englishwoman, Joan Robinson. Both took as their starting point actual conditions and set out to discover the laws operative in a world situation characterized by restrictions on competition. Thanks to this approach, a much more realistic one than that of the classical economists, who were prone to base their arguments on an artificial and ideal world, they were able to contribute to the knowledge of the mechanism governing prices. The present legislation on agreements is based on the recognition that there in fact exist, in the economy of countries supposedly living under a system of free competition, numerous and important factors conducive to imperfect competition. This partly accounts for two trends discernible in this legislation:

Firstly, the sheer number of the laws which have been or are about to be passed. As opposed to the position at the end of the last century, there are now few countries having no law on agreements and most of those which have such laws are preparing to introduce changes.

This is no doubt partly a result of the Havana Charter, which pledged signatory states to adopt legislation to restrain monopolistic practices and restore free competition (Charter signed by France in 1947). It is also, of course, the result of a process of economic evolution towards greater restrictions on competition. But there is reason to believe that the kind of analysis made by Chamberlin and Joan Robinson has had something to do with it. These and other analyses have moreover helped to bring about the adoption of laws specifically directed against one or other of the obstacles to free competition.

As early as 1914, prior, therefore, to these analyses, the United States Congress had adopted the Clayton Act, specifically forbidding a number of practices restricting free competition: discriminations in price, discriminatory contracts for sale of goods, contracts for compulsory sale, sharing in deals, holding corporations, etc. We might also quote other examples in recent legislation—the prohibition of special low prices, for instance.

ANALYSIS OF MONOPOLIES
AND OF THE POLICY OF NATIONALIZATION

The 'rational' basis for nationalization and, ultimately, for the transfer to the community of all the means of production may be found in large measure in the observation and analysis of monopoly situations. This is understandable: the superiority of the private ownership system, according to the exponents of liberalism, derives mainly from the advantages of competition. Anything which reduces competition upsets the whole system of free enterprise.

Classical analysis could imply state seizure of monopolies or the exercise of very strict control over them. If liberal economists failed to draw this conclusion it was because they assumed that monopoly phenomena were exceptional and unnatural, and could not last. Directly it was recognized that monopolies were much more prevalent and lasting than supposed, the problem of transferring them to the community was bound to arise.

Social reformers inevitably used this argument. Lenin, in his *Imperialism, the Last Stage of Capitalism,* published in 1917, stressed the significance of the transition from competition to monopoly, which he regarded as one of the most important phenomena—if not the most important—of capitalism at the time. Reformism uses the same arguments.

There are in theory two possible ways of dealing with a monopoly. The first is by restoring competition—this is the aim of anti-trust legislation. The second is by nationalization. Economic analysis questions whether the first method is always desirable; there are in fact certain sectors of industry in which agreements, concentration and even monopoly may have advantages. The second way is to recommend nationalizing an enterprise or subjecting it to permanent control in cases when conditions of production or technical requirements make monopoly inevitable. Thus the preamble to the 1946 French Constitution proclaims the following principle: 'Any property or any enterprise which has or acquires the characteristics of a national public service or *de facto* monopoly must pass under the ownership of the community.'

In fact, nationalization, both in France and abroad, has been applied mainly—but not, it is true, exclusively—to branches of production operating under highly centralized control or in monopolistic conditions.

In the United Kingdom, Labour policy emphasizes the need to nationalize certain industries where competition no longer operates, so as to retain the advantages of monopoly without its drawbacks.

We are not of course claiming that nationalization or collectivization has occurred mainly as a result of the progress of economics. It is nevertheless true, and the line taken by propaganda proves it, that the findings of the analysis of monopoly or imperfect competition do provide one of the strongest arguments for either anti-trust legislation or a policy of nationalization or state control of large sectors of the economy.

CONCLUSIONS

A purely economic study of monopolies and agreements does not cover the whole problem. Sociology and political science have also a contribution to make. It has become evident—many years ago, but more particularly owing to recent events—that monopolies can influence social and political life as well as price levels and production. Their financial and economic power may upset a country's domestic policy; they may support imperialist and bellicose ventures. In this connexion, the support of the German *Konzerns* and the Japanese trusts for the policies which led to the last war cannot be overlooked.

Realization of these facts may lead either to a policy of national-ization—such as was adopted in France after the Liberation, a policy based not on economic considerations alone—or to a very extreme anti-trust policy. The measures taken by the allied authorities in Germany and Japan after the war may be quoted as an example of the latter policy. The allies adopted a policy, which they pursued with varying degrees of thoroughness, of abolishing the cartels; there was however, subsequently, a tendency to reverse it.

With these reservations, the policy of nationalization and the existence of a growing body of anti-trust legislation, covering a wider variety of cases and revealing a greater flexibility of approach, may be attributed in some measure to the progress of economics in its analysis of the phenomena of imperfect competition, which is now recognized as being a common state of affairs, and not merely a rare exception, as was thought in the past.

FISCAL APPLICATIONS OF THE ECONOMIC ANALYSIS

Certain fiscal reforms which have been proposed or carried out are a direct result of the analysis of the advantages of competition and of the mechanism of the market, or rather, of the conditions without which this mechanism cannot operate properly. In order to show the full significance of these reforms, it may be useful to recall the main argument of classical economics in favour of taxation.

In order to obtain resources and to adjust the position of certain social classes, there are two kinds of measures open to the state: it may requisition individual property and services by various different methods—straightforward requisitioning, statute labour, forced labour, compulsory military service, etc. Or it may require individuals to supply a certain commodity, preferable money, to be furnished as they think fit, by sacrificing those forms of consumption to which they attach least importance or by performing additional work at the time which suits them best.

Taxation is therefore the best way of preserving individual freedom of choice. It allows individuals to rearrange their expenditure so as to restore the equality of their marginal utilities and costs; whereas state requisitioning might deprive them of the commodity to which they attach the most importance, or force them to perform additional work at the time most inconvenient to them. Taxation thus belongs to the same category of mechanisms as trade and money. It is for this reason that taxation was often in the past regarded as a means of curbing and mitigating the rigours of state intervention. In a country like France, one stage in the evolution of medieval society was the replacement of statute labour owed to the nobles by the payment of fixed dues; the same process of evolution led the monarchy to restrict the right to exact hospitality and benevolences—or at any rate to make several attempts to do so; to make it possible to buy exemption from military service; and finally, under Charles VII, to establish a permanent army financed by the King and by a permanent system of taxation.

It was no mere chance that one of the aims of the policy of so staunch a protagonist of economic liberalism as Turgot should have been to abolish all forms of requisitioning of either persons or commodities, including statute labour, requisitioning of saltpetre and all contributions designed to furnish supplies for the King's coronation and even to abolish the militia.

Even so, we must consider what form of taxation best preserves individual freedom of choice. In this matter, the latest research has shown the importance of fiscal neutrality and its influence on economic productivity. This view may be challenged by those who believe in the virtues of certain forms of state intervention; but there is no denying the drawbacks of any kind of 'guidance' exercised on the basis of chance legislation inefficiently applied or on a superficial assessment of the commodity situation, as opposed to a deliberate government policy aimed in a particular direction. In this sense we may consider that the 'productivity and fiscality' commission which has broached the problem in France, did right to proclaim fiscal neutrality as the first condition of a system of taxation conducive to increasing the productivity of the economy as a whole.

Two conclusions of this analysis require stressing: the adverse economic consequences of fiscal fraud; the need to reform certain taxes on production and trade.

ECONOMIC CONSEQUENCES OF FISCAL FRAUD

Fiscal fraud does not result only in decreasing the receipts of the Treasury and preventing public charges from being evenly distributed. It also directly hampers economic activity by giving those who commit fraud an advantage over more honest tax payers. It therefore prevents both the weeding out of the less efficient enterprises and the optimum use of individual means.

The economists. or statesmen of the eighteenth century realized and deplored the effects of fiscal fraud. This led them to condemn certain forms of taxation, such as the salt tax, which diverted a large part of the country's vital resources to contraband. It was for the same kind of reason that the Commission des Comptes de la Nation, in its report on the 1951 budget, pointed to the effects of fraud on economic output. It emphasized that 'tax inequalities constitute an important factor of unfair competition'. Assessing the economic effects of legal privileges and fraud respectively, it points out that these two kinds of inequality 'both equally tend to upset normal trade relations between the various sectors of the economy and between enterprises of different sizes and types within the same sector'.

In other words, the reduction of fiscal fraud is essential to ensure that the mechanism of the market functions satisfactorily. The above observations. and the campaign against fraud which should logically ensue, constitute a typical application of the analysis of the conditions essential to enable the system of free competition to guarantee freedom of choice in the production field.

It is however possible that legislation, even when correctly applied, may itself have the effect of hampering the natural mechanisms of choice and hence diminishing the output of the economy.

FORMS OF TAXATION INTERFERING WITH FISCAL NEUTRALITY

We must, if we wish to preserve producers' freedom of choice, consider what forms of taxation are most likely to upset this natural mechanism. Taxes applying to certain products only come, of course, within this class. although they may be more convenient to apply than certain others, since they affect only a small sector of production or trade and are thus simpler to supervise. The objections of economists to this form of tax was based on the concern to preserve the freedom of choice. For similar reasons the early economists criticized the salt tax, which discouraged farmers from using salt, a product useful for improving land and raising cattle.

We find an echo of this objection in the criticism provoked by a recent proposal to impose a single tax on power. On the face of it, this tax presents, or at any rate appears to present, the great advantage of simplicity. That explains why the French Ministry of Finance ordered a thorough investigation of its economic consequences. The following passage from the report of the 1952 Commission on Fiscal Reform shows very clearly on what economic principle this tax was rejected.

'It is amply clear that a tax on power will have the effect of limiting its use.

'The idea that power can be taxed with impunity arises from the false assumption that producers will be unable to avoid using a certain quantity of power. It assumes, firstly, that price changes will not affect demand, and that enterprises will be impelled by their own impetus to go on producing under the same conditions as before. More than that, it assumes that the present forms of power will not be replaced by others. Alcohol, for example, a fuel which in present economic conditions cannot compare with petrol, may suddenly become profitable to use. It is not relevant here to discuss the advantages and drawbacks of alcohol, but it may be pointed out that its production is very costly. This means simply that a whole number of production factors would be switched from more advantageous uses to the production of alcohol. The profits made by individual enterprises would be matched by a drop in the nation's productivity.

'Again the use of tractors in agriculture is risky because there are many farms whose precarious profits hang mainly on the price of fuels. A rise or drop of a few francs in the price of petrol causes very many small or average-sized farms to give up motorized machinery or adopt it, as the case may be. We may confidently forecast that the use of motorized machinery would cease to be profitable immediately if the price of the fuel used in agriculture were increased by the proposed tax on power. We can easily see what changes in the organization of agriculture this would produce and, without hazarding any opinion of the merits or otherwise of these changes, we may confidently state that, if they occurred too rapidly, they would be extremely dangerous. To avoid this danger, should we tax alcohol or animal power? Or, on the contrary, remove the tax on mechanical power employed in agriculture? What then becomes of the beautiful simplicity of the system?

'The same points which are particularly striking in the case of agriculture are also true of a large number of other economic fields. There are many cases where it only just pays to use a machine.

'Nor must we forget, finally, that power is not used only for the production of other commodities: it is also a commodity in itself. This is true of the electricity used for lighting houses, the coal used for domestic heating, and the petrol consumed by tourist cars. Nor is this a negligible quantity, since it represented, in 1949, 22 per cent of the total consumption of electricity and 25 per cent of the consumption of petroleum products. What shall we do in this case?

'Shall we accept the change of prices thus imposed on the consumer on the assumption that his *total* income and his *total* expenses remain the same? If we do, we may expect to see houses lit with candles and constantly underheated.'[1]

It may be supposed that the economic disadvantages of special taxes confined to one product, one branch of activity or specified means of production were responsible for attempts made to impose general taxes on production, consumption or income. This trend made its appearance in the nineteenth century, with the gradual introduction of systems of income tax tending to cover all types of income. The main reasons for the introduction of this type of tax may be traced to the change in the economic environment, and the desire for state intervention in the distribution of wealth. But there is reason to believe that the increased application of a type of tax designed to cover all sources of income was also largely influenced by concern to avoid interfering with the natural cause of economic activity.

It may also be supposed that reasons of this kind contributed to the success, during the 1914 war, of the general taxes on business transactions, consumption and production. It is of course true that the turnover tax owed its success mainly to the high figure for public expenditure and the need to find new resources to draw on. It was impossible to obtain these resources solely from the classical forms of taxation, levied on a few products only, partly, no doubt, because it was seen that, when raised above a certain level, these taxes upset and distorted both consumption and production.

Whether this was explicitly stated or only obscurely felt, or whether these general taxes were introduced for reasons which had nothing to do with the concern for avoiding upsetting the natural course of economic activity, the fact remains that they do possess this advantage.

We have however to consider whether the advantage is an absolute one, and whether taxes of this type are in fact neutral taxes of the kind regarded by economic analysis as the most favourable to productivity. There is no room here to go into details of this complex analysis. but we may mention one form of tax which had led to a characteristic development: the tax on business transactions.

---

1. *Report on the Taxation of Power,* drawn up in conjunction with the Statistics and Financial Research Institute of the Ministry of Finance and Price Control, *Annex II of the General Report of the Commission on Fiscal Reform,* Imprimerie Nationale, 1952.

Evolution of the Tax on Business Transactions and the Problem of the Tax on Added Value

The tax on business transactions, generally called the turnover tax, is one which upsets the mechanism of the market by leading heads of enterprises to choose one form of activity in preference to another not for its economic, but for it fiscal advantages. This explains why it has led to reforms or proposed reforms based directly on scientific analysis. It was only shortly after the introduction of the tax on turnover—which, generally speaking, dates back to the first world war—that the economic disadvantages of an eminently convenient tax transpired. It was observed that taxing every business transaction meant over-taxing products which were sold in the largest numbers, giving an advantage to chain enterprises. Chain enterprises were thus favoured, not for their economic but for their fiscal advantages.

A number of measures were taken to eliminate these drawbacks. One was to exempt from taxation certain stages of sale—wholesale trade sale, for instance. This system is as present applied in West Germany and Italy.

Another measure was to tax products at one stage only, the production stage for instance, or the wholesale stage. Such, broadly speaking, is the system used in Great Britain and America at the present day, except that only a certain number of products are taxed. In France, the single tax system introduced from 1924 onwards was based on the same conception; so was the tax on production, which in 1936 was substituted for the turnover tax system. In 1939 however, the tax on business transactions was restored though the tax on production was still retained.

Understandably the 'productivity and fiscality' commission, set up specially to investigate how the fiscal régime was hampering the development of the economy, concentrated mainly on these two taxes. This commission defined and explained the theory of fiscal neutrality, one application of which it proposed to introduce immediately. [1]

The commission begins its report with the following words:

'One of the conditions essential to the development of productivity is free competition. The most productive enterprises must fix market

---

1. Though we do not claim to be able to name the 'sources' of this plan, we may mention Thomas A. Adam's proposal to the United States of America in 1921, and Paul Studenski's book *Toward a Theory of Business Taxation* (1940). In France this system was proposed by the rapporteur of the above-named commission, Mr. Lauré, Inspector of Finance, whose book *Taxation of Added Value* (1953) deals with the principle and application of this tax.

prices at a low level for the improvement of the general standard of living, instead of the least productive enterprises fixing them at a high level.'

The commission therefore opted in favour of neutral taxation, and made many proposals to that effect. The most important relate to the taxation of production and turnover. As regards the tax on production, the commission drew attention to one of its most serious disadvantages: the over-taxation of investment. A machine-manufactured product carries a double tax: the tax on the product, and the tax on the machine at the time of its purchase. The removal of the tax on investments, decreed by the French Government in 1953, is designed to correct this drawback, and represents an obvious application of the above analysis.

Another more general application of the principle of fiscal neutrality is the proposal to replace the complicated system of taxation of production plus taxation of business transactions at present used in France by a new type of tax—the tax on added value. This tax would be levied from every enterprise on the basis of the difference between its sales and purchase figures. In this way a product would be taxed, at every stage, in proportion to its added value. On arriving at the final stage, of sale to the consumer, it would have been taxed only on its retail sale price.

The French Government laid great emphasis on the tax on added value in the fiscal reform proposals submitted to Parliament in 1952 and 1953. Although these reform proposals do not adopt the suggestions of the commission, they are strongly influenced by them.

In Japan, the report of the Shoup Mission on fiscal reform [1] also recommended levying this tax, on a local scale. The plan adopted by the Japanese Government, which was to be carried out at the end of 1953, is based on this idea.

This new type of tax, not yet applied anywhere, but which there is reason to believe will figure in future taxation systems, may be regarded as a typical example of the application of economic analysis to the conditions for optimum choice of manufacture and sale methods.

---

1. cf. *Report on Japanese taxation by the Shoup Mission*, Tokyo 1949.

SHORTCOMINGS OF THE NATURAL MECHANISMS

Perfect competition and an ideally neutral fiscal system are not enough in themselves to guarantee the optimum choice and, at the same time, to give maximum satisfaction to the largest number. Other conditions are also necessary. The classical school of economics tended to believe that these conditions were automatically fulfilled, but this is by no means obvious. The optimism of the first economists and of the politicians who heeded them was based on a number of premises which were not at first clearly expressed, and which were only to be expressed gradually as they came up against criticism.

The first series of premises may be stated as follows: profit rewards any effort that is useful to the community, and is proportionate to this usefulness. This presupposes the absence, or at least the rapid elimination through competition, of unearned profits. On this assumption, indeed, a man's remuneration is proportionate to his labour or his savings; both benefit the whole community. All activity favourable to the community is profitable to the individual; at any rate, activities that do not fulfil this condition are an exception. All innovations, economics or organizational changes made by the head of an enterprise bring him in a substantial profit; on the other hand, anything that improves the remunerativeness of an enterprise, and increases the profit of its head, represents an advantage to the community.

The second series of premises may be summarized as follows: man's behaviour is rational; he asks for what is most useful; he produces under the most suitable conditions; he invests wisely in what should bring the biggest return.

All these premises have been called in question by economic analysis, which will accept none of them as completely true. [1]

---

[1] Among those who have made such analyses we might mention in particular the American economists whose work has been summarized by G. Pirou in his book *New Trends in Economic Theory in the United States.*

INDIRECT PROFITS FROM CERTAIN ACTIVITIES

One of these premises was stated and later refuted by the father of liberalism, Adam Smith himself. He pointed out that the individual could not derive direct profits from certain activities, even though they were very useful to the community, because their utility was too diffuse to make recovery in the form of sales possible. The example he gave was that of reafforestation, which improves the climate of a whole area, regularizes the flow of water, protects the land against erosion, gullying, etc. It is not possible for a person who plants trees to be paid by all those who benefit from his action. It is therefore logical that the state should bear this kind of expenditure, the usefulness of which can only be paid for by taxation. In the view of the classical economists, this was the main, or some would say the only, justification for state interference. However, not all the possible deductions were made from this argument; orthodox economy strictly limited state interference, because it did not take account of all the indirect consequences of certain expenditures.

UNEARNED PROFITS: 'RENT'

But very soon, in the early years of the nineteenth century, economics made a second discovery—one that provoked something of an intellectual outcry, and challenged a whole system of values. This was what came to be known as the 'theory of rent'. It is usual to quote Ricardo, who was the first to state the theory, or who, at any rate, stated it most clearly. He applied it to land, pointing out that there was only one type of land the cultivation of which provided its owners with profit proportional to their work; and that was marginal land, i.e., the least fertile land, the last to be cultivated. The sale price of its produce is equal to the cost price of this marginal land. It cannot be less, because cultivation would then cease. Thus the owners of more fertile land receive more than cost price, the difference between sale price and cost price being what Ricardo called 'rent'. 'Rent' is therefore unearned profit. The very machinery of an economy based on private ownership contains, therefore, the seeds of injustice; and since property is inherited and grows through the savings of the rich, it is obvious that the injustice tends to increase. The inequality of wealth, of which 'rent' is one of the causes, leads to another result which is in conflict with the classical optimism. In the absence of an even approximate equality of incomes, the rich can consume, in excess of their needs, what are for the poor necessities. It is therefore impossible to talk, in these conditions, of the greatest satisfaction of the largest number being achieved.

Different kinds of conclusions could be drawn from this analysis. Logically, the supporters of liberalism ought to make war on all unearned profits; and some of them drew that conclusion. Certain mid-nineteenth century economists, e.g. John Stuart Mill, advocated the abolition of inheritance, essentially a form of unearned profit. This idea has, indeed, had much to do with the relative importance attached to estate duty, the first tax to be applied on a graduated scale.

The above analysis could, of course, lead to 'rent' being taken over by the state (that is indeed what certain reformers proposed) or to the taxation of incremental value, as happened in Britain under the Lloyd George government in 1910. In a general way, the recognition of the phenomenon of inequality of incomes, and of its origin and consequences, led to the system of a graduated tax on capital or income which has characterized the fiscal laws of numerous states since the middle of the nineteenth century. Needless to say, this evolution coincided with a political development, the advent of universal suffrage, which gave a share of political power to the mass of the people. This method of reducing inequality was prompted by the desire to reconcile the mechanisms of the liberal system with certain aspirations towards social justice. Thus the establishment of a graduated income tax became the great ambition of those who in France called themselves Radical-Socialists, and who aimed at combining the functioning of the natural mechanisms with a certain tendency towards equality. [1]

After the first world war, and especially as the result of the 1929 crisis, the most important premises on which liberalism was implicitly based came under the searchlight of criticism. They were challenged from various sides, notably by numerous American economists, [2] who, themselves or their pupils, were later to become supporters of Roosevelt and the New Deal.

---

1. In this sense, one may say, income taxes represented a kind of tribute to the economic virtues of liberalism.
2. Veblen, J. M. Clark and Slichter, among others.

CONSEQUENCES OF THE DEVELOPMENT
OF JOINT STOCK COMPANIES

The premise according to which profit is merely a remuneration of effort useful to the community has been challenged not only by the existence of unearned incomes derived from 'rent' and inheritance, but also by developments in the very structure and management of enterprises. Economists [1] have noted that joint stock companies are not, in fact, managed by their shareholders, but by a small number of business men or 'managers', who, though in a minority, can, by various processes which we need not detail here, secure control of important businesses. And they can manage them in their own interests, which do not necessarily coincide with those of the bulk of the shareholders. This cleavage between ownership and profit undermines the functioning of the liberal mechanism described by Adam Smith, for whom (as was more or less the case everywhere in his day) the head of the business was owner and manager at the same time.

This analysis led some of these authors to conclude that where the owners had become passive, the community should take upon itself to direct such businesses. Others concluded that it was necessary to modify the laws governing joint stock companies so as to make it compulsory for the shareholders to exercise a certain control over the managers; to make them more responsible; and to establish a degree of supervision by the public authorities. In this sense the evolution of legislation concerning joint stock companies in the different countries may be considered as having some connexion with certain economic analyses.

Finally, there were those who insisted that, even if human behaviour were as rational as the classical analysis assumed, the search for profit and the improvement of the well-being of the community were not necessarily synonymous. Numerous examples were given of the discrepancy between individual interest and the general interest.

---

1. cf. in particular a book by two Americans, Berle and Means, *Modern Corporation and Private Property*, 1934.

TRANSFER OF CHARGES FROM THE ENTERPRISE TO THE COMMUNITY

It was observed that an enterprise could rid itself of certain charges by shifting their burden onto the shoulders of the community. Let us take a typical example: that of a factory emitting unpleasant, if not positively harmful fumes. It could spend money on suppressing this smoke, but it would gain nothing in return, even though the whole neighbourhood benefited by its suppression. Similarly, unhealthy working conditions, which require the community to supply medical treatment or assistance, are an example of how charges are shifted onto the community. An enterprise does not bear all the charges and expenses it incurs. This shows that one of the premises of classical economics is contrary to the facts. This analysis may lead to new legislation making an enterprise bear all the expenses for which it is directly responsible. Such may be the economic basis for legislation on industrial accidents.

The above drawback still applied when such expenses are spread over, with each enterprise paying a contribution proportionate to the wages it pays to its workers. The entrepreneur thus has no direct interest in looking after the health and security of his workers. In order to give him that interest, his contribution will have to be made proportionate to the expenses for which he is responsible, for instance (as is done in France), by relating his contribution to the number of accidents occurring in his factory.

Needless to say, another conclusion may also be drawn from the above: the community may introduce measures calculated to protect the health of the workers, or of neighbours, through certain regulations regarding cramped or insanitary premises, labour conditions, etc.

COMPETITION AND PROFIT FROM INNOVATIONS

The argument that the profit motive and the general interests coincide may be challenged in yet another way. When the entrepreneur uses a new process, or embarks on research, sometimes very costly, or manufactures new machinery, he benefits from his inventive effort or organizational improvements only until his competitors begin to imitate him; since, once the new techniques have spread, a fall in prices will deprive him of his temporary advantage. It is true that the patent laws protect the benefits accruing from the exploitation of new ideas for a reasonable period. But not everything can be patented. This applies, for instance, to innovations in the realm of organization. In these conditions, competition may actually operate against the progress of production and the satisfaction of the greatest number. [1]

IRRATIONAL BEHAVIOUR

So far, we have been assuming that man acts rationally, and seeks to further his own interest. But contemporary economists, with the aid of psychologists and sociologists, have now questioned this assumption.

The head of an enterprise does not always act as classical theory expects him to. He may be motivated by a taste for fine work ('instinct of workmanship'), or by a desire for power. Keynes has dwelt particularly on the influence of irrational impulses, the taste for adventure or, conversely, the unreasonable fear of risk evidenced in the management of businesses, more particularly as regards capital investment.

The whole machinery of the stock exchanges, where investments should be decided on with reference to prospective yield, is according to Keynes put out of gear by that element of speculation which makes stock exchanges more like gambling dens than centres of economic calculation.

Special attention has also been paid to the psychology of the consumer. The consumer's choice is not guided by a careful examination of the quality and price of the various articles available. Advertising has been the object of much research; the consumer can be diverted from goods which would give him the greatest satisfaction and be made to believe in the virtues of certain articles which are dearer, but no better than others, and that advertising can, by multiplying man's desires, also increase his dissatisfaction. In any case advertising represents an important part of business costs. While it is favourable to the community when it tells people more about the variety of goods available and encourages competition, it represents a useless charge when it merely directs demand towards one particular brand instead of to another equally good one.

---

1. This idea was stressed by Schumpeter in his latest book *Capitalism, Socialism and Democracy.*

GAPS IN THE NATURAL MECHANISMS
IN TIMES OF SHORTAGE

During war—the first world war and more especially the second—and in the period of shortage following the war, another of the classical theories came into prominence. It was not, it is true, explicitly expressed; but it may be said to have been recognized by implication.

The natural mechanisms do not work easily in times of great shortage. This is true particularly of a shortage of consumer goods. The rich are, in such a case, able to eat up all the food, not only the surpluses, but even the essentials needed by the rest of the community. This situation would rapidly become quite intolerable. It can be remedied in one of two ways. Incomes can be levelled by the application of steeply graduated taxes. In this way, everyone keeps his freedom of choice without anyone being starved to death. But this solution presupposes a complete equalization of incomes; even a small disparity is sufficient to expose a certain group of people to fresh privations.

On the other hand, complete equalization might tend to destroy incentives to work, as well as making it impossible to base wages on the quality of the work done and the effort exerted.

In such cases, therefore, it becomes necessary to ration essential goods; each person receives a certain quantity of ration points enabling him to buy certain quantities of bread, meat, fats, textiles, etc. This is the 'besieged town' system, and has to be applied to countries at war, occupied countries, and even certain neutral countries.

The same arguments are used in favour of controlling producers' goods. In the first place, because of shortages, only the manufacture of essentials can be allowed. If there still remains some inequality of wealth, building materials, for instance, must not be allowed to be used for building luxury homes at a time when more essential needs cannot be satisfied. But there is another consideration. The operation of the natural mechanisms involves a certain waste. These mechanisms are based on individual enterprise and the elimination of those who make mistakes. Thus a badly sited factory must in theory go bankrupt, and be abandoned. The buildings, and in some cases the plant as well, become useless. Such is the price paid for individual initiative; and, in a general way, for progress—a point rightly stressed by classical economies. Even so, the fact remains that competition, like natural selection indeed, does imply a certain wastage. This waste has always been criticized by Socialists, who use it as one of their arguments against the liberal economy. But the criticism becomes unanswerable when the means of production are in very short supply. Then even the smallest waste is shocking. Obviously, in war-time, the limited means of production must be used for producing goods directly needed for the war, and for making the indispensable minimum of goods required by the civilian population. It may also be argued that even in peace-time, when needs are great (whether for reconstruction or for rapid building up of an industry deemed essential to an underdeveloped country), the regulation of production i.e. the limitation of abolition of the natural mechanisms becomes essential. That is why, during war preparations—in those countries which give them top priority—as well as in war-time, systems of control have been set up for the distribution of raw materials, compulsory production, introduction of licences for setting up new factories, enlarging industrial plants, etc.

Nor is it surprising that, after the war, the need for reconstruction, or the concern of impoverished countries to industrialize themselves should have led to the adoption of similar measures. Thus various countries have devised plans regulating distribution of fuel and power; or plans for capital investment and import programmes. The same reasons which led the Union of Soviet Republics to adopt its five-years plans are now leading other countries to embark on investment programmes.

But the increasing intervention of the modern state in investment plans has another explanation. Economic research into the gaps and obstacles created by competition shows that it is in the field of capital investment that the natural mechanisms work least efficiently, and are apt to be most harmful to the community. It is bad enough when an entrepreneur runs his business in a manner incompatible with the general interest. But it is worse still when this happens in matters that affect the whole economic future of a country. And it is probably in the field of capital investment that this risk is greatest. In this matter Schumpeter's analyses supplement those of Keynes. It is in the field of capital investment that planning has the most solid advantages to offer.

CHAPTER V

ANALYSIS OF THE NATURAL MECHANISMS AND STATE INTERVENTION IN ECONOMIC AFFAIRS

May it be said that the intervention of the state in economic affairs is a consequence of the foregoing analyses?

In a way, we are tempted to say not. The conflicting interests which led, at various times and in various countries, to the triumph either of protection or of free trade; the social and political movements which resulted in labour regulations; the increased taxation of incomes, even nationalization; wars (their preparation or their consequences) complete with the introduction of rationing and the control of production and prices; and the various phenomena which led to collectivization in several countries—all these phenomena seem, at first sight, to stem from causes which have no connexion with the patient labours of a few learned men.

It is not as simple as that. Firstly, the facts underlying all these happenings—this fundamental difference between the economic world of the early nineteenth century and that of the twentieth century, in all countries (for there is no country where state intervention has not increased) cannot but be attributed in large measure to the imperfections of liberalism. It was partly because, in some fields, the search for profit produced results which seemed contrary to the general interest that public expenditure increased; and partly because the natural mechanisms did not entirely eliminate the inequality of fortunes and the poverty of the working class that governments felt compelled to restrict the freedom of the labour market and to use taxation as a means of controlling the distribution of wealth. It was because it seemed impossible to trust to the free interplay of supply and demand in times of shortages that all countries at war—and others as well— introduced strict distribution regulations. The desire to combat the ill effects of economic disequilibrium went hand-in-hand with the wish to correct the imperfections of the competitive system. A sort of inner logic gradually modified the structure of society.

198

But in this evolution itself an element of conscious rationalization can be detected. Those who wished to change the structure of society found in the analysis of the natural mechanisms arguments they were quick to use. The theorists and leaders of the Socialist movement, besides denouncing the unemployment resulting from capitalism, remarked on the monopolistic character which part of the economy was beginning to assume, and indicted all the contradictions between the search for profit and the general interest. They pointed to the 'waste' of the competitive system, the poor use made of individual skills, the blind destruction of natural wealth, the transfer to the community of charges that should be borne by the heads of businesses, etc.

The admission by bourgeois economists that there was an element of truth in all this weakened their defence. The fact that, during the nineteenth century, a relative but still unmistakable liberalism held its own for so long, and successfully repelled so many assaults, must be attributed to some extent (how far it is hard to say) to liberalism's intellectual framework. But once this framework had been undermined by economic analysis, a kind of guilty conscience made it increasingly difficult to resist the 'encroachments' of the state.

In the nineteenth century, the theory of 'rent' and the study of unearned profit, became one of the arguments supporting a graduated taxation, increased death duties and the introduction of income taxes. In the twentieth century, we cannot ignore the influence of certain men who, in the United States of America, denounced and challenged some of the premises of classical economics. They reappeared in President Roosevelt's brains trust, and their influence on the New Deal is unquestionable. In many other countries similar currents of ideas gave rise to policies known as 'planned economy'. It is worth noting again that in Britain, a number of economists took an active part in organizing the war-time and post-war economy.

The ideological basis of a planned economy is the assertion that the search for profit and the general interest do not coincide; and the desire to replace the search for profit by the search for utility. However, the development of this theme has led to a good deal of confusion —a confusion of ideas which has contributed to the blunders made in the shaping of economic policies. Analysis alone should help towards better practical results. It reveals the weaknesses in the attitude of nineteenth and even some twentieth century governments, which believed in the virtues of natural mechanisms and confined themselves, though somewhat uneasily, to correcting some of their worst effects. Thus they were protectionist while still believing in free trade; they regulated labour conditions though still believing freedom to be the

199

most advantageous for the workers; they brought influence to bear on the distribution of incomes although they believed in a natural tendency towards an ever-growing equality of wealth.

Analysis also makes it possible to draw a distinction between deliberate state intervention, and state intervention rendered necessary in times of shortage. This point deserves stressing since, owing to the fact that a controlled economy gained ground in war-time and continued for some years after the war, when shortages necessitated compulsory distribution, public opinion has naturally tended to confuse a planned economy with rationing. Those who recognized the need for a certain amount of state intervention were regarded as supporters of systematic control, which in practice was meddlesome and often clumsy. It must be admitted that the economists did not do all they should have done to clear up misunderstandings. They did not point out that the advantages of the mechanism of choice in the field of consumption and, within limits, in that of production, were so great that this mechanism should have been retained until resources became so blatantly inadequate that its drawbacks outweighed its advantages.

Nor was sufficient attention paid to the question why, in countries where economic progress had been retarded, the so-called under-developed countries, the taking over by the state of important sectors of the national economy could proceed so quickly. For a long time it was not realized that, in these conditions, the disadvantages of state management were counterbalanced by the elimination of the waste inherent in the natural mechanisms—waste which was perhaps of minor importance in times of relative plenty, but extremely serious when the means at a country's disposal were severely limited. Such reflections might have made it easier to understand why, contrary to forecasts, collectivism developed first in the poorest and most backward countries; and why progress in those countries should have been much greater than liberal economists had expected.

Finally, analysis enables us to distinguish between the two different processes by which the state can intervene in order to correct the imperfections of the natural mechanisms.

The state may take over the economy with a view to replacing the search for profit by the search for general utility. Private enterprise, motivated by the search for profit, is thus replaced by public enterprise, guided by the desire to serve the general interest. Such, in the first analysis, and subject to subsequent reservations, is the collectivist solution.

As against this, the liberal, or one might say neo-liberal, solution consists in an attempt to make the search for profit and the search for utility coincide.

We may start by a scientific examination of the various omissions and shortcomings of the natural mechanisms, and then attempt to see what remedies can be applied in each case. Methods may be challenged. For example, an enterprise wishing to transfer certain charges to the community may instead be made responsible for them itself. That, for example, is the purpose of the system of making the contributions of each enterprise for industrial accidents dependent on its percentage of accidents in the past. The fiscal system and the social security system can be revised so as to make each enterprise pay what it costs, or at least approximately what it costs, the community. In many countries attempts have been made to graduate the taxation of vehicles in accordance with the wear-and-tear each type of vehicle inflicts on the roads.

The fiscal system may likewise be based on a steeply graduated taxation of unearned income. The levying of high death duties, and the system of discriminating, as many countries do, between incomes of different origins corresponds to the same ideas. It may be possible to go even further in this direction. Of course, by correcting the inequality of incomes, taxation may increase the demand for popular goods, reduce luxury buying, and so direct production itself towards the satisfaction of the needs of the largest number.

There remains the question of correcting the irrational character of human behaviour. In the case of the consumer, it is possible to impose a heavy tax on the least useful articles and reduce the taxes on those for which the need is most legitimate. These measures could be accompanied by others calculated to restore the conditions of normal competition: legislation against industrial agreements and against restrictions on competition; or the adoption, in matters of taxation, of the principle of fiscal neutrality.

The systems of controlled (*dirigé*) economy, which represent an intermediate—or mixed—solution, consist, or should normally consist, of a series of interventions aiming not only at preserving the capitalist management of property, but also at leaving the individual a field for free action. In principle, the management of an enterprise remains free, but the state, through a number of measures, modifies the conditions in which it is run. These measures are based on the criterion of usefulness instead of on that of profit. The state decides on the usefulness of such and such imports. It provides foreign exchange only for the expenditure it considers most useful, and penalizes, by means of taxation, the production of articles regarded as superfluous, if not actually harmful; it fixes certain prices, profit margins, etc. Measures of this kind may often have serious drawbacks. They tend to modify the natural mechanisms and, if clumsily applied, may defeat their own ends.

But here too economic analysis may serve a useful purpose, not only by warning against ill-considered policies, which overlook the secondary repercussions of the measures adopted; but also by making it easier to see in what sectors there is the greatest danger of a discrepancy between utility and direct profit.

In this connexion, special attention must be paid to capital investment. As we have seen, the investments most useful to the community are not the most profitable to the investor; they may indeed become less and less profitable as they become more generalized and, accordingly, more useful. Moreover, some investments which are in fact profitable, may not appear so to the individual. On this point, it is useful to remember Keynes' analyses of the psychology of capitalists. We may, therefore, well wonder whether state intervention should not concentrate mainly on the field of investment.

The most recent economic analysis might therefore lead to a distinction being drawn between the usual management of enterprises, which gains from being as free as possible; and the administration of investments, which requires guidance, supervision and support from the state. This idea is being more and more widely accepted. Investment plans are no longer the prerogative of the collectivist state. They are to be found in other countries too, so much so that those countries are obliged to modify their credit policy and make it hinge partly on considerations of general economic interest and no longer be guided solely by the traditional criteria of solvency.

We do not claim that all these developments are due to analysis of flaws in the natural mechanisms. But analysis may well be assumed to have had some effect.

B. *Considered mechanisms*

CHAPTER VI

THE PROBLEM
OF CONSIDERED CHOICE

When we seek the 'economic' explanation of growing state intervention in production and trade, we find two forces at work: to balance aggregate production and consumption; and to ensure the best use of the resources of the community. These two aims operate in conjuction, and any particular customs, fiscal or control policy may reflect both at the same time.

Passing from the aims of a policy to consider the measures used for carrying it out, it may be useful to refer, on more general lines, to earlier analyses; and to note the profound difference, at least at first glance, between two kinds of state intervention.

1. One kind respects the mechanism of the market or aims at ensuring its operation. This covers measures by the state to ensure fair business deals, eliminate monopolies, enforce the principles of fiscal neutrality, tax enterprises according to what they cost the community, etc.

   Similarly, we may say that certain forms of intervention designed to restore equilibrium by adjusting the aggregate demand—by lowering or raising the rate of interest, for instance—do not distort the natural mechanisms of choice. This is the reason why the Anglo-Saxon countries prefer this form of state intervention. A social policy which imposes heavy taxes on the largest incomes may also be said not to upset the natural market mechanisms; which explains why systems like these have been able to originate in an essentially liberal society.

2. Other forms of intervention are, in principle, of a different character. Their aim is to substitute the utility motive for the profit motive, either by placing production under state control, or by less drastic measures such as the expansion of state expenditure, making state authorization compulsory for private investments, fixing import

quotas, controlling foreign exchange, rationing, exercizing control over credit, etc.

In all these cases, the state decides what it considers most useful. It authorizes certain imports and forbids others; encourages certain investments; uses the funds of the community for certain works and certain subsidies designed to encourage the activities deemed most useful; and grants loans or interest rebates to interprises considered to be most essential. In all fields the criterion of utility is substituted for that of profit.

But at once the question arises: how can we assess what is most useful, and how can we make our choice? Governments sometimes refuse to make the choice and try to do everything at once. The result of such a policy is inflation, one of the root causes of which is perhaps merely the inability of the community to make a choice. The very occurrence of inflation implies incidentally that a choice has, all the same, been made. For the rise in price affects the balance of demand and supply. But, by dimishing the resources of certain social classes, it leads to a choice that is not in accordance with social justice.

The question therefore remains: how can the basic problem of public administration, the problem of choice, be solved? Economists long disregarded this problem, or rather one group, the advocates of state intervention, underestimated, not to say ignored the difficulty; whilst the other group emphasized that, without the mechanism of the market, the state would lack all reliable indications and be unable to make a perfect choice. Liberal economists used the difficulty of making a collective choice as one of their main arguments against any control by the public authorities over production or consumption.

Some of them attempted to prove that it was impossible for a collectivist economy to make rational calculations. The problem was raised as early as 1902 by a Dutch economist, Pierson, in an article entitled 'The Problem of Value in the Socialist Community'.

After the 1914-18 war, with the socialist movements of that time (some of which died fairly rapidly whilst others gave birth to the Soviet State), these questions were raised again. In 1920, the Austrian economist, L. von Mises, published an article on economic calculation in a socialist community. He pointed out that money calculation, i.e. the use of a common denominator, was essential in order to enable the most efficient means of production to be chosen. He noted that a socialist community could make this kind of calculation by using money, organizing a separate system of accountancy for every sector of production, and allowing commercial exchange between the various sectors. But he thought that exchange relations could only be instituted on the basis of the private ownership of the means of production. Hayek, in his contribution to a collective book entitled *Controlled Economy in a Collectivist Régime,* published in 1938, stressed the same idea.

Speaking of the impossibility of rational calculation in a collectivist economy, these writers concluded not that such an economy was impossible but merely that its output must, owing to the defects of the choice mechanism, inevitably be much lower than that of a liberal economy. Production would not concentrate on the commodities for which there was the greatest popular demand; the most efficient methods of production would not be adopted, etc. There is no denying that these writings were useful because they demonstrated the difficulty of choice when the natural mechanisms are wanting.

A number of writers holding different views have also investigated the conditions of optimum choice; mostly in relation to studies of planning. In this connexion, the article by O. Lange, published in 1936 and 1937, 'On the Economic Theory of Socialism' [1] should be mentioned. His view may be summed up as follows: taken over a long period, a planned economy resembles a competitive economy. The prices of consumer products have to be left free to find their own level on the market; so do wage-rates. On the basis of these prices, enterprises can proceed to make an economic calculation, i.e., to decide on the least costly means of production, and on the quantities to be produced.

This view has provoked various criticisms; [2] but the very people who criticize it proceed in their turn to define the means of solving the

---

1. 'On the Economic Theory of Socialism' in *Review of Economic Studies,* October 1936 and February 1937. For a study of these theoretical problems as a whole, cf. Bettelheim's book *The Theoretical and Practical Problems of Planning,* Paris 1946. There are of course other works on this subject but many of them, in Russian, are not accessible.

2. From Bettelheim, who writes: 'In our view, Lange's conception is open to criticisms. It implies setting up not a planned economy but a pseudo-competitive economy, although the conditions for a competitive economy (a large number of firms, which are independent of one another, and none of which can, by its decisions alone, appreciably affect the total quantity of supply or demand) do not exist. This is one of the objections which A. P. Lerner made to Lange's theory, and which the latter has not, in our view, satisfactorily refuted.

'On the other hand, even if the economic control mechanism proposed by Lange were workable, it could only be operated through a series of *a posteriori* adjustments (a corollary, in our view, of his conception of value) and not on the basis of a plan drawn up in advance. This mechanism therefore allows all the wastage of energy resulting from these adjustments to continue, instead of cutting it to the minimum.

'Finally, the mechanism proposed by Lange excludes the possibility of rational economic budgeting in those sectors of the economy whose products are not designed for sale (and these sectors are becoming more and more numerous with the expansion of the sphere of socialist consumption), since, without sale, there cannot—from Lange's point of view—be rationally established prices. Nevertheless, even in these sectors, it must be possible to calculate what combinations of production are economically the most profitable'. *The Theoretical and Practical Problems of Planning,* page 7.

problem of choice in the light of growing state intervention. We should add that these studies have kept pace with experiments carried out in collectivist countries, which have been forced by political considerations to face this kind of problem and seek a solution.

Nevertheless, the analysis of these problems cannot yet be said to have been carried far enough. Certain problems such as that of the functioning of the public sector of a non-collectivist country; and that of the best conditions for selection of public expenditure still remain largely unexplored. [1] In our view, the general policy to follow in solving all these problems is to set up considered mechanisms representing a transposition of, or, if we may put it that way, an imitation of the natural mechanisms or at least of what they should ideally be.

The general principle governing the investigation of considered mechanisms has been or can be applied in many fields: administration of public enterprises, methods of drawing up the budget, use of economic budgets in the national accountancy system, and the method of planning investments.

---

1. The importance of this kind of problem has been demonstrated by investigation into the conditions of optimum functioning of the public services. G. Ardant has attempted, in a series of studies, to give a definition of both theory and application, notably in his book *State Technique*; and in an article entitled 'The Theoretical Significance and Practical Scope of a New Technique: Assessment of the Efficiency of Public Enterprises and Services', *Revue Economique*, July 1952.

CHAPTER VII

ECONOMIC ANALYSIS
AND THE MANAGEMENT
OF PUBLIC ENTERPRISES

The fact of the state's taking over the whole or a part of production does not necessarily involve the complete disappearance of the natural mechanisms, even in this domain. Provided the use of money is retained, it is possible for state enterprises to sell commodities or services which the workers, who receive money wages, can buy. In these conditions, the customers exercise a kind of control, in the same way as they do in a liberal economy. The state will not be able to sell unless the purchasers are satisfied with what it offers; the public can show its preferences, which the state will normally have to take into account.

Some of the motives which exist in a liberal economy are however lacking. The very fact of transforming a private enterprise into a public one eliminates the search for profit, which impels the private entrepreneur to seek the best methods of production. Nationalization also excludes another motive, the fear of bankruptcy, which, in a liberal system, eliminates the least productive enterprises and forces the others to improve their methods. Another of the mechanisms of liberal economics—competition—also disappears. Finally we may ask whether, without the pressure of the market which tends to bring down selling prices to about the figure of cost prices, there is any rational basis for fixing the tariffs of public enterprises.

State management has of course its own compensations. It enables certain joint services to be organized, and advertising expenses to be reduced; when there is a state monopoly, the volume of production and the prices can be fixed in accordance with the general interest.

The community does however run the risk of the manager's being uninterested in business and neglecting to administer it efficiently. There is the risk of enterprises continuing to exist when insufficiently productive even without its being realized that this is so; the state may also fix selling prices arbitrarily at too high or too low a level—

in short, state management is constantly open to the threat of inefficiency. It is true that communities can exercise control, the sort of
control which every owner has over his manager, and it is not
surprising to find control being reinforced whenever the managers
of public enterprises are inefficient or suspected of being inefficient.
But control has its drawbacks. It may accentuate one of the basic
weaknesses of public management, discouraging managerial initiative
and, by extension, that of the workers at all levels. Moreover,
control does not prevent arbitrary decisions, particularly with regard
to the fixing of prices. It is our view that, in order to solve the
main problem of management by socialist states—a problem which
exists to some extent in all countries where a sector of the economy
is nationalized—investigations must be along the following lines: an
analysis must be made of all the various mechanisms of liberal economy, and methods of replacing them must be sought. This leads
to the partial re-establishment of the natural mechanisms in the form
of considered mechanisms.

This is the solution towards which the nature of things tends to
impel the public authorities both of states which have collectivized the
whole of the economy, and of those where only a certain sector is
nationalized. That this process has not yet gone far enough is due
no doubt to the fact that the problem has not yet been investigated
thoroughly enough, or too little attention has been paid to the findings.

All such considered mechanisms as are conceivable demand more
details of the output of public enterprises—determination of their total
yield, calculation of the cost price of products manfactured, according
to categories, factories and even down to workshops. It may seem
surprising that so much importance is attached to problems of
accountancy; but it will be less surprising if we remember that the
progress of the economy in general has gone hand in hand with progress
in assessing results.

The three main principles to be followed are these:
1. Calculation of the total output of every enterprise, an operation
   which both results from and determines its financial autonomy.
2. Re-establishment of a kind of competitive system as between
   factories or workshops.
3. Rational price control based on accurate details of cost of production.

FINANCIAL AUTONOMY OF PUBLIC ENTERPRISES

A series of developments, some dating far back into the past, others fairly recent, some occurring in predominantly capitalist systems and others under collectivism, have demonstrated that the structure of state industrial or commercial establishments must be modelled on that of private enterprises, i.e. they must have a minimum of administrative and financial autonomy.

THEORY OF INDUSTRIAL BUDGETS
AND THE EVOLUTION OF STATE ENTERPRISES

Even before the first world war, it was understood that state control was incompatible with industrial management. The need was seen to separate the budget of industrial establishments from the general budget, to make their receipts approximate to their expenditure, to distinguish between investment expenditure and current expenditure, and to establish a depreciation account and a stock account. These ideas had been combined in a theory called the theory of industrial budgets, which proposed making public production or transport firms into autonomous bodies each run by a board of management. This theory was applied even before the first world war, and still more widely after it; it took, in practice, yet more comprehensive form, with administrative as well as financial autonomy—the so-called 'office' system.

AUTONOMY OF ENTERPRISES
IN THE UNION OF SOVIET SOCIALIST REPUBLICS

Similar developments occurred in the first collectivist state, the Union of Soviet Socialist Republics. It soon became clear that enterprises, factories or groups of factories—called trusts or combines—must be given a minimum of autonomy. Round about 1931, this trend was accentuated. Today a Soviet enterprise is a comparatively independent administrative unit, which purchases its own raw materials, pays its workmen wages, and sells its products to consumers, commercial organizations or other enterprises. The difference between its selling prices and its cost prices represents a profit, a proportion of which goes to the manager and the staff.

EVOLUTION OF THE YUGOSLAV ECONOMIC SYSTEM

The same thing happened more quickly, in Yugoslavia. Until 1950, the management of firms was concentrated largely in the hands of the central authority. By the law of 1946, the state laid down the production programmes of enterprises; fixed selling prices, distributed raw materials and power, etc. The disadvantages of such a highly centralized system, excessive rigidity and lack of initiative, were observed. There was no incentive to enterprises to seek the optimum exploitation of the means of production.

That is why Yugoslavia has, since 1950, adopted a different system, designed to give enterprises more freedom of action. They are now managed by directors with the assistance of councils elected by the workers. [1] Government planning still continues; it consists of fixing a certain figure for compulsory investment in certain branches of activity and levying, from each enterprise's production, a certain percentage to cover public expenditure and essential investment. Each enterprise is however free to decide on the quantity and quality of its production and, as a general rule, to fix its selling prices. The receipts of the enterprise cover the wages of the staff, social welfare costs, and the investments of the enterprise in the strict sense. [2]

PRINCIPLES FOR REFORM OF NATIONALIZED ENTERPRISES

The same principles apply to the nationalized sectors of 'capitalist' states. Two developments need emphasizing. Firstly, it has become more and more clear that enterprises which have already been under state control for a long time must be freed from the machinery of the traditional public accountancy system. On the other hand, enterprises recently nationalized have in most cases retained the same form of organization as they had when privately owned. Even so, and this does not appear to have been sufficiently realized, steps must be taken

---

1. The law of 26 June 1950 is entitled Law on the Management of Enterprises by the Workers. The workers of every state enterprise elect a workers' council which appoints its own management committee. The management committee supervises the running of the business, drafts plans, and takes all measures regarding production, output, standards of work, and promotion. But the director in charge of production is appointed by the government; and he may disregard the advice of the management committee if he has the approval of the competent state body. He has the right to dismiss staff.
2. cf. in *Politique Etrangère* of 22 November 1952, the article by Radivoje Uvalic entitled 'Economic Organization of Yugoslavia'. For the sake of simplicity, we do not mention the agricultural system which is more complex, in the case of either the Union of Soviet Socialist Republics or Yugoslavia

to ensure that the financial accounts of these enterprises reflect the degree of efficiency of their management as closely as possible. Otherwise it would be impossible to apply any system of rewards and penalties to the managers of enterprises. It is difficult, if not impossible, simply to make them subject to bankruptcy; some equivalent has to be found in the form of penalties, dismissal and other such measures as would be applied to inefficiency in managers in charge of private firms. But this again requires figures giving a clear picture of the management of public enterprises. In this connexion three conditions must be fulfilled.

The first is that no enterprise must be granted advantages free of charge, but must always pay the interest and depreciation on capital borrowed from the state. Conversely, the state must not require an enterprise to provide services free of charge. If it does, it has a tendency to require comparatively unessential services, which leads to wastage. Moreover, procedures such as these falsify the firm's balance sheets and profit and loss accounts. Thirdly, when public enterprises possess a monopoly or a privilege (production monopoly such as the tobacco monopoly or the privilege of printing banknotes, etc.) they should be liable to a tax or a royalty equivalent to the presumed profit accruing from the said monopoly or privilege, so that the profit made shall actually depend solely on the quality of administration. These principles are by no means all recognized. In France, the central committee of enquiry into the cost and output of the public services has had occasion to note the drawbacks of contrary procedures. These principles, in our view, needed stating.

RE-ESTABLISHMENT OF COMPETITION

It is not impossible, paradoxical though it may appear, to restore competition, or at least the equivalent of competition, within a public enterprise. Any enterprise of a certain size, public or private, may be regarded as the sum of a number of units—transport lines, factories, workshops, warehouses or stores. The cost price of the products manufactured or services rendered by each of these units can be calculated. The combination of these prices constitutes a kind of table, showing that one set of prices is higher than another. This leads to a number of conclusions. The factory with the highest cost prices may be in that position because its manager is inefficient. He must be replaced. This is the penalty which would be imposed by the mechanism of the market, the natural mechanism; it can be applied instead by the director-in-chief of the enterprise, or the authority over him. Another possible explanation for cost prices being so high is that the factory is too small. The obvious solution in this case seems to be to combine it with another. Again, the fault may lie in unsatisfactory material or methods, in which case a general reorganization of the factory is indicated. All these are measures which the competitive system would apply if the factory were an autonomous, privately run enterprise. It is for the central authority to imitate these methods and, through considered decisions, to introduce what may be called 'competition on paper'. [1]

There is nothing Utopian about these ideas. Methods of the kind are already commonly used in some large private enterprises. They appear to be less common in public enterprises. They involve, it must be admitted, calculating the cost prices of each separate unit, which inevitably raises fairly complicated accountancy problems, in particular that of apportioning the overhead expenses. But these problems are by no means insoluble. All specialists in industrial accountancy are familiar with them. There is moreover a French example, that of the state monopoly of tobacco and matches, which, through methods of this kind, has been able to work out the cost price of each product fairly accurately. It has by this means been able to save substantial amounts both on raw materials and on staff.

Even so, methods of this kind need to be more widely applied, and extended to all public enterprises. A clear statement of the theoretical principle behind them may be useful.

PRINCIPLES OF RATIONAL PRICE CONTROL

The analysis of the conditions of optimum choice reveals the principles of rational price control. The mechanism of the market, when operating perfectly, brings selling prices down roughly to the level of cost prices. The result is that the community adopts the most economic methods. But there are many cases when public enter-

---

1. Paper competition between factories of course becomes unnecessary when, as appears to be the case in certain collectivist countries, each factory enjoys financial and administrative autonomy. It remains to be decided whether, in such cases, some kind of competition between workshops should be organized.

prises administer a monopoly; which in itself means that they are not automatically forced to level the selling prices down to cost prices. On the other hand those who stress the public aspect of such enterprises urge that cost prices should be disregarded, and certain products or services sold at less than cost price, the loss being covered by raising prices or tariffs on other commodities. This kind of situation may arise for lack of a sufficiently detailed accountancy system for working out cost prices complete with details for every category of product manufactured or services rendered.

This kind of situation is detrimental to the output of the economy. When a certain product is sold above cost price, users are discouraged from buying it, and tend to buy another commodity which is, by definition, more expensive to the community but cheaper for them. When, on the other hand, the selling price of a commodity is below its cost price, the reverse occurs: users are induced to buy products which are cheaper for them, but which cost the community more than others, the sale of which is thus artificially restricted.

There are, of course, cases when this departure from the natural tariffs based on cost prices may be said to be in the general interest, and it is understandable that it should be made. But such a course must be adopted deliberately and consciously, and must not result merely from ignorance, intentional or unintentional, of the cost prices.

Here again therefore, cost prices must be minutely calculated with a view to imitating the natural mechanism, which tends to equate selling prices with cost prices. Care must be taken to avoid arbitrary public decisions.

It is thus understandable that the Soviet economy should have been based roughly on this conception. Until about 1935, prices were used as the means of controlling the economy. The rulers then realized that it had become impossible, with this method, to decide what means of production were most advantageous. The process which was least costly for a factory manager or his superior was not necessarily the least costly for the community as a whole. In the absence of a system of rational calculation, the best choice was not always made. That is why, from about 1935 onwards, it was decided to base the wholesale prices of products on their cost prices. At the same time the subsidies designed to cover the deficit of certain industries were abolished. This is an application of the principle of 'price neutrality', comparable even in name to the principle of fiscal neutrality, which as we have seen, is so important, both theoretically and practically, in a capitalist economy.

In France, research into the output of public enterprises has emphasized the same principle. We have laid particular stress not only on the principle, but also on the practical condition for its application, i.e. the existence of a sufficiently accurate budget of cost prices.

CONCLUSION

To sum up, it is found that, in order to make the management of state enterprises more efficient, we have to re-establish an equivalent, a transposition or an imitation of the natural mechanisms, with the same kind of incentives, penalties and price-fixing system as under a competitive régime. In this sense, we appear to be justified in speaking of considered mechanisms.

The developments which have already occurred may be attributed to the more or less conscious recognition of the need for solving the problem of choice, or, in other words, the problem of value.

It is significant that economic development has been accompanied, both in Yugoslavia and in the Union of Soviet Socialist Republics, by the recognition—we might almost say the rediscovery—of economic laws. Stalin, in 1952, in a study entitled *The Economic Problems of Socialism* criticizes communists who deny 'the objective nature of the laws of science and in particular of the laws of political economy in a socialist régime'. A little further on, he replies to those who query whether value exists and operates in a socialist régime: 'Yes, it exists and it operates.' It applies both to the distribution of goods and to production. He adds: 'This is not a bad thing, since it is teaching our economists systematically to improve methods of production, reduce cost prices, practise financial autonomy and make enterprises profitable.'

He emphasizes: 'The trouble is not that the law of value operates in our production system. The trouble is that our economists and planners, with few exceptions, are ill-acquainted with the effects of the law of value, do not study it, and do not know how to allow for it in their calculations.'

In 1952 also, a Yugoslav writer, Boris Kidritch, in an article entitled 'Where is the Yugoslav Economy Going?' makes the following remarks:

'The administrative struggle against objective economic laws is, in the last analysis, sterile and irrational; objective economic laws—whether we like it or not—have in fact an objective existence, so that they will always turn relentlessly, and often disastrously, against administrative and bureaucratic measures running counter to them. The bureaucratic conflict with objective economic laws must inevitably end in economic stagnation and retrogression. Nor is this all. Any long-term administrative plan calling for a struggle against objective economic laws inevitably engenders forces which range themselves above society in order to wage this fight, and which invariably develop into a bureaucratic caste which enslaves and exploits producers and the whole of society alike.' [1]

---

1. In the review *Contemporary Problems of Socialism,* December 1952, p. 194.

ECONOMIC ANALYSIS
AND BUDGET TECHNIQUE

The methods of investigating the output of the public services are similar to those used for investigating methods of improving the economic efficiency of public enterprises. The term public services in the strict sense applies to administrations which do not sell their products or their services. This means that their balance cannot be calculated like that of a public enterprise; and that one of the automatic controls, that exercised by the purchaser, is lacking. How can we tell whether services which are free are really useful? Being free, they may be used even if they are comparatively unnecessary. The very fact of a bridge being built will shorten the route of a certain number of persons, be it by ever so little. With the disappearance of tolls, there is no means of assessing their usefulness. The problem of choice is thus thrown into full relief.

Analysis of the problem indicates, however, that it can be at least partially solved, on the basis of the economic law according to which the greatest satisfaction of man is a function of the equalization of the marginal utilities of the various commodities he can procure, and of the equalization of marginal utilities and marginal costs.

What applies to the individual applies also to the community, which must equalize the marginal utility of its various expenditures. This was noted as early as 1883 by Pantaleoni, who said that the parliaments of democratic states should attempt to spread public expenditure over the various items of their budgets, in such a way as to equalize their marginal utilities. Moreover, we have already pointed out that the precursor of marginalism was a chief engineer of the highways department, Dupuit, who in 1844, in an article entitled 'Assessment of the Utility of Public Works', adopted the method of splitting up each commodity into instalments of decreasing utility, which forms the starting point of marginal analysis.

It is probably true to say that, until recent years, no real effort had been made to apply the conclusions of this analysis in practice. Nevertheless, they are based on simple common sense. The point is to eliminate the least useful items of expenditure, to sacrifice superfluity to usefulness, usefulness to necessity as methodically and accurately as possible.

A case in point—that of France—shows that it is possible, on the basis of various investigations and experiments, to determine the technical conditions essential for enabling public expenditure to be planned more efficiently.

The first step is to compare all items of expenditure so as to pick out the least useful, which can be eliminated if necessary. This kind of comparison is made by means of the budget, whose chief purpose is to give a comparative survey of the various items of expenditure, and indicate which items should be eliminated as least useful.

There is, for historical reasons, a tendency to regard the budget as a political instrument only, a means for checking the power of the legislative over the executive; and to forget its economic function. This attitude has certain drawbacks. It has resulted in under-estimating the importance of certain traditional budgetary principles, and also, therefore, ignoring the disadvantages of abandoning them.

To give one example only, one of the budgetary principles which was worked out in France at about the time of the Restoration is the principle of budgetary universality. It is as follows: the budget must include all expenditures without exception; it must not specify any appropriations of receipts. The main purpose of this principle is to avoid keeping any single detail of expenditure from the knowledge of the representatives of the community—otherwise they may reject an item of expenditure which actually has greater utility than some other item which they have been unable to reject for lack of information on the subject, and lack of opportunity for comparing the various items. [1]

But the traditional budgetary principles alone are not sufficient. Comparison is only useful when applied to services whose cost and utility are both known. There is still much practical progress to be made in this field, on the basis of the application of the economic analysis.

It will readily be conceded that the cost of every service must be known. Even so, the fact remains that this information is or was frequently lacking. In order to make this information available, the expenditures of every service, instead of being scattered over various

1. See the article on 'The Economic and Social Bases of the Budgetary Principles', in *Revue de Science et de Législation Financières*, January 1950.

sections of the budget, as they are or, rather, used to be, will have to be listed separately. We shall thus have to apply the method of the functional budget, which in France, for example, is a direct outcome of the above analysis; and which other countries have also adopted, after different experiences perhaps, but by unconscious application of the same rules. This reorganization of the budget is only the first step. Allowance must also be made for expenditures which do not figure in the accounts because there is no immediate disbursement—depreciation of buildings, for instance, and the interest on the capital corresponding to their value.

But details of cost alone are not sufficient; in order that the less useful items of expenditure can be eliminated, their utility must be assessed. One of the most important results of the work of the Central Committee of Investigation into the Cost and Output of the Public Services (Comité Central d'Enquête sur le Coût et le Rendement des Services Publics) has been to make it possible to assess the utility of those services; experience shows that this can lead to very important practical results.

Some of the work of every administration can always be expressed in figures. The number of pupils attending a school, the number of roads maintained by the highways department and, even more easily, the number of cars using a road can be counted. But these are only preliminary indications. The quality of services must be taken into account; and, paradoxical though it may seem, this quality can in fact be assessed. The quality of teaching is measured first and foremost by the examination results; and also by following the careers of former pupils and noting the percentage of those who succeed in the careers for which they were trained. The efficiency of a penal or penitentiary service can be assessed by the percentage of recidivists, assuming that one of the main purposes of prison is to re-educate prisoners and make them law-abiding when restored to freedom.

We have taken two concrete examples. In both, the use of this method of assessment gives important practical indications regarding technical education and the French penal system, respectively.

The economic analysis reminds us however that the marginal utility and the marginal cost as well as the mean utility must be calculated. This is no mere theoretical premise. All persons familiar with public administration know that the problem of how far services should extend is constantly arising. Should new roads be built? Or new canals? Should some be abandoned? Should new schools be built? New post offices? It is with regard to this marginal activity that the question arises.

The cost and utility of expenditure on marginal establishments can be calculated, simply by calculating the cost of all establishments, all services, or all roads, and setting the figures out in a table which shows automatically which of them cost the most. We can then compare the cost price of the marginal school with the cost price of the marginal kilometre of road.

Tables of this kind have been drawn up in France: a table of the cost price of canals, which showed that the marginal canals cost 20 times more than others; a table of the cost price of law courts and prisons, which showed that the cost of some *arrondissement* courts and prisons was too high; a table of the cost price of schools, of various administrative services, etc. Conclusions followed almost automatically: certain roads should be abandoned; the distribution of schools needed revising; some *arrondissement* services which were too expensive needed abolishing; certain services of the *département* needed reorganizing on a regional basis.

These conclusions do not of course emerge entirely automatically; a certain amount of judgment has to be exercised by the representatives of the community. But, aided by tables of this kind, they are able to take their decisions on the basis of facts, as individuals do when giving one item of expenditure priority over another.

The use of a budget of cost prices instead of the classical budget, the principle of which France recently decided to adopt, will enable the problem of choice in the domain of public expenditure to be solved. It is probably true to say that this reform, when generally applied in practice, will be the result of a dual process—of the advance of economic theory as represented by the marginalist analysis, and of experiments in administration, which have shown, firstly, that costs can be calculated, and secondly that important conclusions may be drawn from such calculations.

CONCLUSION

The budget is not the only example of the principle of equalizing marginal utilities, or rather of the techniques for putting this principle into practice—the comparison and measurement of value. Whenever a state, faced with a shortage of foreign currency, decides to curtail imports, it has to draw up a general plan, an imports programme. This is the only way of establishing comparisons, and selecting the demands considered most essential.

Investment plans obey the same rules. They must be complete, the principle of budgetary universality must be applied. They must be based on the most accurate assessment possible of the utility as well as the cost of every investment. Assessment of the cost must take into consideration the interest on sums spent. It is significant that collectivist countries should have admitted that this rate of interest, sometimes called the time factor, has to be taken into account in order to ensure that priority is given to the most useful investments.

Even so, utility has, in this case also, to be assessed. It appears that much still remains to be done in this field.

Experiments made to date indicate that the investigation of considered mechanisms and the application of methods based thereon are among the most promising fields of research. They are a highly significant example of the current application of progress made in economics; and it is to be hoped that the future will bring more such developments.

FINAL CONCLUSIONS

Brief and incomplete as is this review of recent economic theories and trends, a certain number of conclusions nevertheless emerge.

The first concerns the progress made by the science of economics in the past thirty years or so, and the nature of that progress. Born of the contrast between the first insights of theorists and the facts themselves, of the vision of one crisis after another occurring to refute the classical tenets or of the realities of a monopoly market shattering the illusion of a world based on perfect competition, this progress has consisted of challenging and re-examining the over-simplified theories of the past. Economists have sought, by closer observation of facts and more detailed analysis of human behaviour, to acquire a more exact knowledge of economic phenomena. The contribution of psychology to the work of contemporary economists is significant: the psychology of the saver, the psychology of the entrepreneur, and the psychology of the speculator form the basis of the new economic theories. And even so, there are grounds for thinking that we have still not gone far enough in this direction, and that the remaining obscurities are due in large measure to taking too simple a view of fundamental human tendencies. A study has also been made of institutions and customs, and of the effects of social organization on the functioning of the economy.

It is logical to suppose that a branch of science based on concrete facts is better placed than other sciences to propose practical, concrete, positive measures. It is true that difficulties still linger in the spheres of partial equilibrium and considered choice; but we are beginning to discern methods of surmounting them.

These are the conclusions we reach working on the basis not of economic science but of economic technique and policy. The importance of more scientific exactitude is becoming increasingly evident. No technique is comprehensible except in conjunction with the theory on which it is based. We have discovered that the key to budgetary principles, to the functioning of banks of issue or deposit banks, to the legislation of joint stock companies and the fiscal system alike

221

lies in a certain view of economic facts. In certain recent techniques, the connexion between theory and practice is particularly evident: compulsory saving, national accountancy systems and budgets of cost prices, all of which are based on precise scientific theories, are typical examples.

This connexion becomes even more obvious when we consider economic policy as a whole. One of the main problems of the modern world is unemployment. No stability is possible in a world where the workers feel themselves insecure and under constant threat. There is a danger of economic progress too being compromised. Production policies meet with resistance from farmers or industrialists who, because they fear having to sell at a loss or fear a slump in prices, tend to espouse protectionist policies and to restrict production. The only way of countering this retrograde influence is by a policy of full employment, as outlined above. On this too hangs the problem of peace or war; the experiences of the recent past must always be kept in mind. The question is whether man will be able to mobilize for peaceful work the same resources that he can mobilize for war or preparation for war. The problem cannot be solved except with the aid of a science and a technique, which we know are not perfect, but which nevertheless represent a considerable advance on earlier ideas and policies.

It is true, of course, that human progress does not depend on rational conceptions alone; it depends also on the enthusiasm evoked by the search for progress. But how are we to explain the discouragement of certain countries? To what is this due but to the belief that science has proved bankrupt—whereas it is only false applications of science, and empiricism, which have proved to be the real bankrupts. The science of economics shows the possibility of ordered progress.

Conversely, certain experiments have shown convincingly that high ideals, goodwill and the desire to build a better world are not in themselves enough, unless they are accompanied by scientific technique, without which the best of intentions founder.

It is, of course, the rulers who must be imbued with these ideas. But it is impossible, in a democratic world, to convince the rulers without first winning over those to whom they owe their power.

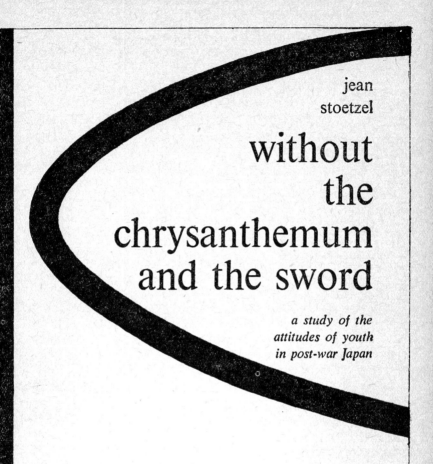

jean
stoetzel

without
the
chrysanthemum
and the sword

*a study of the
attitudes of youth
in post-war Japan*

What is the youth of Japan thinking today, how is it facing the new problems brought by war and occupation?

The study, based on a recent questionnaire, gives full details—social, economic and political—of present-day Japan

Published jointly by Columbia University Press and Unesco

334 pages/Illustrations   Cloth bound: $4.00

UNESCO PUBLICATIONS: NATIONAL DISTRIBUTORS

ALGERIA
Noël Schuman,
Editions de l'Empire,
28 rue Michelet,
ALGIERS.

ARGENTINA
Editorial Sudamericana, S.A.,
Alsina 500,
BUENOS AIRES.

ASSOCIATED STATES OF CAMBODIA, LAOS AND VIETNAM
Librairie Nouvelle
Albert Portail,
Boîte Postale 283,
SAIGON.
Sub-depot:
Librairie Albert Portail,
14 avenue Boulloche,
PHNOM-PENH.

AUSTRALIA
Oxford University Press,
346 Little Collins St.,
MELBOURNE.

AUSTRIA
Wilhelm Frick Verlag,
27 Graben,
VIENNA I.

BELGIUM
Librairie Encyclopédique,
7, rue du Luxembourg,
BRUSSELS IV.

BOLIVIA
Librería Selecciones,
Avenida Camacho 369,
Casilla 972,
LA PAZ.

BRAZIL
Livraría Agir Editora,
rua México 98-B,
Caixa postal 3291,
RIO DE JANEIRO.

CANADA
University of Toronto
Press,
TORONTO.
Periodica Inc.,
5112 avenue Papineau,
MONTREAL 34.

CEYLON
Lake House Bookshop,
The Associated Newspapers of
Ceylon Ltd., P.O. Box 244,
COLOMBO I.

CHILE
Librería Lope de Vega,
Calle Estado 54,
SANTIAGO DE CHILE.

COLOMBIA
Emilio Royo Martin,
Carrera 9a, No. 1791,
BOGOTA.

COSTA RICA
Trejos Hermanos,
Apartado 1313,
SAN JOSE.

CUBA
Unesco Centro Regional
en el Hemisfero
Occidental,
Calle 5 No. 306 Vedado,
Apartado 1358,
HAVANA.

CYPRUS
M. E. Constantinides,
P.O. Box 473,
NICOSIA.

CZECHOSLOVAKIA
Artia Ltd.,
30 Ve smečkách,
PRAGUE 2.

DENMARK
Ejnar Munksgaard Ltd.,
6 Norregade,
COPENHAGEN K.

ECUADOR
Libreria Cientifica,
Luque 233,
Casilla 362,
GUAYAQUIL.

EGYPT
La Renaissance d'Égypte,
9 Adly Pasha Street,
CAIRO.

ETHIOPIA
International Press Agency,
P.O. Box 120,
ADDIS ABABA.

FINLAND
Akateeminen Kirjakauppa.
2 Keskuskatu,
HELSINKI.

FORMOSA
The World
Book Co. Ltd.,
99 Chung King Rd.,
Section I,
TAIPEH.

FRANCE
Unesco Bookshop,
19 avenue Kléber,
PARIS-16e.

FRENCH WEST INDIES
J. Bocage,
Librairie,
rue Lavoir,
Fort-de-France,
MARTINIQUE.

GERMANY
Unesco Vertrieb für Deutschland,
R. Oldenbourg,
MUNICH.

GREECE
Librairie H. Kauffmann,
28 rue du Stade,
ATHENS.

HAITI
Librairie 'A la Caravelle',
36 rue Roux,
Boîte postale III-B,
PORT-AU-PRINCE.

HONG KONG
Swindon Book Co.,
25 Nathan Road,
KOWLOON.

HUNGARY
Kultura, P.O.B. 149.
BUDAPEST 62.

INDIA
Orient Longmans Ltd.,
Indian Mercantile Chamber,
Nicol Road,
BOMBAY.
17 Chittaranjan Ave.,
CALCUTTA.
36-A Mount Road,
MADRAS.
Sub-depots:
Oxford Book and
Stationery Co.,
Scindia House,
NEW DELHI.
Rajkamal Publications Ltd.,
Himalaya House,
Hornby Road,
BOMBAY I.

INDONESIA
G.C.T. van Dorp and Co.,
Djalan Nusantara 22,
JAKARTA.

IRAQ
McKenzie's Bookshop,
BAGHDAD.

ISRAEL
Blumstein's Bookstores, Ltd.,
35 Allenby Road,
P.O.B. 5154,
TEL AVIV.

ITALY
Libreria Commissionaria G.C.
Sansoni,
via Gino Capponi 26,
Casella postale 552,
FLORENCE.

JAMAICA
Sangster's Book Room,
99 Harbour Street,
KINGSTON.
Knox Educational Services,
SPALDINGS.

JAPAN
Maruzen Co. Inc.,
6 Tori-Nichome,
Nihonbashi,
TOKYO.

JORDAN
Joseph I. Bahous and Co.,
Dar-ul-Kutub,
Salt Road,
AMMAN.

KOREA
Korean National
Commission for Unesco,
Ministry of Education,
SEOUL.

LEBANON
Librairie Universelle,
Avenue des Français,
BEIRUT.

LIBERIA
J. Momolu Kamara,
69 Front and Gurley Streets,
MONROVIA.

LUXEMBOURG
Librairie Paul Bruck,
33 Grand-Rue.

MADAGASCAR
La Librairie de Madagascar,
TANANARIVE.

MALAYAN FEDERATION
AND SINGAPORE
Peter Chong and Co.,
P.O. Box 135,
SINGAPORE.

MALTA
Sapienza's Library,
26 Kingsway,
VALLETTA.

MEXICO
Difusora de las publicaciones
de la Unesco,
Artes 31, int. bajos,
MEXICO, D.F.

NETHERLANDS
N.V. Martinus Nijhoff,
Lange Voorhout 9,
THE HAGUE.

NEW ZEALAND
Unesco Publications Centre,
100 Hackthorne Rd.,
CHRISTCHURCH.

NIGERIA
C.M.S. Bookshop,
P.O. Box 174,
LAGOS.

NORWAY
A/S Bokhjornet,
Stortingsplass 7,
OSLO.

PAKISTAN
Ferozsons,
60 The Mall,
LAHORE.
Bunder Road,
KARACHI.
35 The Mall,
PESHAWAR.

PANAMA
Agencia Internacional
de Publicaciones,
Apartado 2052.
Plaza de Arango No. 3,
PANAMA, R.P.

PERU
Librería Mejia Baca,
Azangaro 722,
LIMA.

PHILIPPINES
Philippine Education Co.,
1104 Castillejos,
Quiapo,
MANILA.

PORTUGAL
Publicaçoes Eurôpa-América,
Ltda.,
Rua das Flores 45, 1o,
LISBON.

PUERTO RICO
Pan-American Book Co.,
SAN JUAN 12.

SENEGAL
Librairie
'Tous les Livres',
30 rue de Thiong,
DAKAR.

SPAIN
Aguilar, S.A. de Ediciones,
Juan Bravo 38,
MADRID.

SURINAM
Radhakishun and Co. Ltd.,
(Book Dept.),
Watermolenstraat 36,
PARAMARIBO.

SWEDEN
A/B C.E. Fritzes Kungl.,
Hovbokhandel,
Fredsgatan 2,
STOCKHOLM 16.

SWITZERLAND
Librairie Antoine Dousse,
Ancienne Librairie de l'Uni-
versité,
Case postale 72,
FRIBOURG.
Europa Verlag,
5 Rämistrasse,
ZÜRICH.
Sub-depot:
Librairie Payot,
Place Molard,
GENEVA.

SYRIA
Librairie Universelle,
DAMASCUS.

TANGIER
Centre International,
(Marcel Teisseire),
20 rue Molière.

THAILAND
Suksapan Panit,
Arkarn 9,
Rajdamnern Ave.,
BANGKOK.

TUNISIA
Victor Boukhors,
4 rue Nocard,
TUNIS.

TURKEY
Librairie Hachette,
469 Istiklal Caddesi,
Beyoglu,
ISTANBUL.

UNION OF BURMA
Burma Educational
Bookshop,
551-3 Merchant Street,
P.O. Box 222,
RANGOON.

UNION OF SOUTH AFRICA
Van Schaik's Bookstore (Pty)
Ltd.,
P.O. Box 724,
PRETORIA.

UNITED KINGDOM AND
N. IRELAND
H.M. Stationery Office,
P.O. Box 569.
LONDON, S.E.1.

UNITED STATES OF
AMERICA
Columbia University Press,
2960 Broadway,
NEW YORK 27, N.Y.

URUGUAY
Unesco,
Centro de Cooperación
Cientifica para América Latina,
Bulevar Artigas 1320,
MONTEVIDEO.

VENEZUELA
Librería Villegas Venezolana,
Madrices a Marrón N. 35,
Pasaje Urdaneta,
Local B,
CARACAS.

YUGOSLAVIA
Jugoslovenska Knjiga,
Terazijc 27/II,
BELGRADE.

UNESCO BOOK COUPONS

Unesco Book Coupons can be used to purchase all books and periodicals of an
educational, scientific or cultural character. For full information please write to:
Unesco Coupon Office, 19 avenue Kléber, Paris-16e, France